SMART
SPENDING

SMART SPENDING

THE GAY AND LESBIAN GUIDE TO SOCIALLY RESPONSIBLE SHOPPING AND INVESTING

By Grant Lukenbill

alyson books
los angeles | new york

© 1999 BY GRANT LUKENBILL. ALL RIGHTS RESERVED.

MANUFACTURED IN THE UNITED STATES OF AMERICA.

THIS TRADE PAPERBACK ORIGINAL IS PUBLISHED BY ALYSON PUBLICATIONS,
P.O. BOX 4371, LOS ANGELES, CALIFORNIA 90078-4371.
DISTRIBUTION IN THE UNITED KINGDOM BY
TURNAROUND PUBLISHER SERVICES LTD.,
UNIT 3 OLYMPIA TRADING ESTATE, COBURG ROAD, WOOD GREEN,
LONDON N22 6TZ ENGLAND.

FIRST EDITION: DECEMBER 1999

00 01 02 03 04 a 10 9 8 7 6 5 4 3 2 1

ISBN 1-55583-414-0

LIBRARY OF CONGRESS CATALOGING-IN-PUBLICATION DATA
    APPLICATION IN PROCESS

COVER PHOTOGRAPHY BY PHOTODISC.

Contents

Acknowledgments xv
Introduction xvii
Part One: Shopping for a More Gay- and Lesbian-Inclusive World
    The Consumer You Are 1
    Our Consumer Behavior as a Group 3
    Virtual Visibility 5
    Progressive Organizations 5
    Organizations to Watch Out For 6
    Big Names and Big Budgets 7
    Tuning Your Queer Consumer Antennae 8
    Sort Out the Hype, Focus on Issues 10
    Sexual Orientation and Domestic-Partnership Benefits 10
Part Two: The Most Influential Companies, Their Policies and Products
    A Note About Company Profiles 12
    Advertising, Marketing, and Public Relations 19
        NW Ayer & Co. 20
        Foote, Cone, & Belding 21
        Hill, Holiday, Connors, Cosmopulos 22
        Hill & Knowlton Inc. 23
    Banking and Investment 24
        American Express 25
        Bank of America 27
        BankBoston 29
        Charles Schwab and Co. 30
        Chase Manhattan 31
        Chubb Corp. 32
        Citicorp Citibank 33
        H&R Block 34
        J.P. Morgan & Co. 35
        Kinder, Lydenberg, Domini, & Co. 36
        Lincoln Financial Group 37
        Merrill Lynch 38
        Meyers Capital Management LLC 39
        Principal Financial Group 41

Provident Financial Group Inc. 42
St. Paul Cos. 43
Trillium Asset Management 44
U.S. Bancorp Piper Jaffray 45
Wainwright Bank and Trust 46
Wells Fargo 47
Working Assets 48
Clothing and Sportswear 49
Abercrombie & Fitch 50
Adidas-Salomon AG 51
Dayton Hudson 52
Donna Karan Inc. 53
Federated Department Stores Inc. 54
Gap Inc. 55
Tommy Hilfiger Corp. 56
JC Penney 57
Kenneth Cole 58
Lands' End 59
Levi Strauss & Co. 60
Lillian Vernon 62
The Limited 63
Liz Claiborne 64
Nike Inc. 65
Nordstrom 66
Reebok 67
Sears 68
The Warnaco Group Inc. 69
Communications and Technology 70
Adobe Systems 72
Advanced Micro Devices 73
America Online 74
Ameritech 76
Apple Computer 77
AT&T 79
Autodesk 81
Banyan Worldwide 82
Bell Atlantic 83
Bell South 85

Cadence Design Systems Inc. 86
Cambridge Technology Partners 87
Cisco Systems Inc. 88
Digital Origin 89
Egghead Software 90
Hewlett-Packard Co. 91
Honeywell 92
IBM 93
Informix Software 95
Inprise Corp. 96
Intel Inc. 97
Interleaf 99
International Data Group 100
Lucent Technologies 101
MCI Worldcom 102
Microsoft 103
NCR 105
Nortel Networks Corp. 106
Novell 107
Oracle 108
Pacific Bell 109
Paradigm 111
PeopleSoft Inc. 112
Pitney Bowes 113
Platinum Technology 114
Qualcomm 115
Quark... 116
Silicon Graphics Inc. 117
Sprint 118
Sun Microsystems 119
Sybase 120
U.S. West Inc. 121
Visioneer 122
Xerox 123
Consumer Products and Home Furnishings 124
Alberto Culver 125
Black & Decker Corp. 126
Body Shop 127

    Clorox Co. 128
    Colgate-Palmolive 129
    Deluxe Corp. 130
    Dial Corp. 131
    Eastman Kodak 132
    The Estée Lauder Cos. Inc. 134
    Gillette 135
    Herman Miller 136
    Home Depot 137
    IKEA 138
    Johnson & Johnson 139
    Kimberly-Clark 140
    Kmart Corp. 141
    Maytag 142
    Newell Rubbermaid 143
    Polaroid 144
    Procter & Gamble 145
    Revlon Inc. 147
    Rite Aid Corp. 148
    Toys "R" Us 149
    Unilever N.V. 150
    Wal-Mart Stores Inc. 151
    Whirlpool 152
Entertainment, Media, and Publishing 153
    Barnes and Noble 154
    Bureau of National Affairs 155
    Gannett Co. 156
    MCA/Universal 158
    McGraw-Hill 159
    New York Times Co. 160
    Scholastic 161
    Sony Corp. 162
    Time Warner 163
    Viacom 164
    Village Voice (Stern Publishing) 165
    Walt Disney/ABC 166
    Ziff-Davis Publishing 168
Food and Beverage Service 169

Adolph Coors Co.	170
Anheuser-Busch	171
Archer Daniels Midland Co.	172
Ben & Jerry's Homemade	173
Burger King (Diageo PLC)	174
Campbell Soup Co.	175
Celestial Seasonings	176
Cracker Barrel Old Country Store	177
Darden Restaurants Inc.	178
Denny's Restaurants	179
Domino's Pizza	180
General Mills	181
Hershey Foods Corp.	182
Hormel Foods Corp.	183
Kellogg Co.	184
McDonald's	185
Nabisco Group Holdings Corp.	186
Naya Inc.	187
Nestlé S.A.	188
PepsiCo Inc.	189
Philip Morris Cos. Inc.	190
Quaker Oats	192
Ralston Purina	193
Safeway Inc.	194
Sara Lee	195
The Seagram Co. Ltd.	197
7-Eleven Inc.	199
Starbucks Coffee Co.	200
Tyson	201
Wendy's International Inc.	202
Insurance and Health Care	**203**
Aetna	204
Allstate	205
American Home Products	206
Bayer Corp.	207
Blue Cross/Blue Shield of Massachusetts	208
Bristol-Myers Squibb	209
Chiron	210

    Cigna 211
    Glaxo Wellcome Inc. 212
    The Hartford 213
    Hoffman-LaRoche 214
    Merck... 215
    Mylan Laboratories 216
    Pfizer 217
    Schering-Plough 218
    Smith Kline Beecham 219
Transportation and Travel 220
    American Airlines 222
    American President Lines 224
    Avis 225
    DaimlerChrysler... 226
    Ford Motor Co. 227
    General Motors 228
    Genuine Parts.. 229
    Harley-Davidson 230
    Hilton.. 231
    Marriott 232
    Mirage Resorts... 233
    National Car Rental 234
    Ryder System 235
    Subaru (Fuji Heavy Industries Ltd.) 236
    United Airlines.. 237
    Virgin Atlantic Airlines 239
    Volkswagen 240
Utilities, Chemicals, Materials, and Engineering 241
    3M 242
    Boeing 243
    Chevron 244
    Dow Chemical Co. 245
    DuPont.. 246
    Edison International 247
    Exxon... 248
    General Electric 249
    Illinois Tool Works 250
    Lockheed Martin 251

Mobil 252
Monsanto 253
Owens-Corning 254
Pacific Gas and Electric 255
Shell Oil 256

Part Three: Resources and Stock Options for Gay and Lesbian Investors
Socially Responsible Investing 257
Socially Responsible Case Studies 265

Part Four: Gay and Lesbian Desk Reference
Key Employers with No Written Sexual Orientation
   Nondiscrimination Policy 272
Employers With Domestic-Partnership Health Care Plans .. 272
Gay and Lesbian Corporate Employee Groups 282
Gay and Lesbian Organizations and Affiliations 292
Credit Cards, Charge Cards, and Credit Reports 293
Leading Consumer Advocacy Organizations 294
Ongoing Nongay Consumer Boycotts and Their Sponsors .. 297
Socially Responsible Mutual Funds 302
Gay and Lesbian Consumer Dos and Don'ts 307
Suggested Additional Reading 308

Part Five: Appendices
Domini Social Index (DSI 400) 310
GLV 100 Index 314
Glossary of Terms 316
Bibliography 319
Master Finder Index 323

Acknowledgments

My thanks to James Franklin, Sam Watters, Greg Constante, Scott Brassart, and Gerry Kroll for believing in this work, and to Jeff Yarbrough and David Groff for their early votes of confidence.

I owe a great debt of gratitude to Kevin Bentley and Jane Loeb, whose organizational insights, patience, and superb editing skills have helped bring about a text far more concise and usable than I ever could have delivered on my own.

For helping me compile lists, conduct surveys, track down hard to find corporate data, and for standing by me during database crashes, temper tantrums, and sugar hangovers, I'm most grateful to editorial assistants and trusted friends Josie Marode, Lisa Miller, and Patrick Arena.

Although they are too numerous to mention, it is important that I acknowledge how much I was helped by members of corporate gay and lesbian employee groups—especially those working diligently at companies slow to change. I found their competitive spirits and determined constitutions inspiring—particularly when my own patience was being tested by corporate indifference.

I thank my trusted friends Adrian Milton, Bob Riner, Sidney Silver, Jimmy Wilmore, and David Winters for their personal insights and the quiet counsel when the going got rough.

Many thanks are due to my brother, Ralph Lukenbill, for his helpful political observations and steady stream of newspaper clippings. I am also most grateful for the phenomenal online research work of Aleta Fenceroy and Jean Mayberry and the contributions made by bibliographer Janet Kvamme.

Numerous organizations and individuals made special contributions:

ACT UP New York	Elizabeth Birch
The Advocate magazine	Stephanie Blackwood
Shelley Alpern	Diane Bratcher
Apple Computer	Tad Clarke
Patrick Arena	Colleagues Workplace Organization
Bob Baublitz	*Curve* magazine
Bell Atlantic Advisory Board	Stuart Elliot

The Equality Project
Tess Factor
Joan Garry
Gay and Lesbian Alliance Against Defamation
Gay, Lesbian, and Straight Education Network
Human Rights Campaign
Alan Klein
Sally Kohn
Lesbian Herstory Archives
LGNY
Steve Levenberg
Kerry Lobel
Dave and Paula Lukenbill
Steve Lydenberg
Troy Masters
Shelly Meyers
Ed Mickens
Lisa Miller
Kim Mills
National Gay and Lesbian Task Force
National Lesbian and Gay Journalists Association
New York Lesbian and Gay Community Center
Out magazine
Planet Out
Progress Workplace Organization
Rivendell Marketing
Scott Seitz
Sex Panic!
David Smith
Mike Stauffer
Mark Sullivan
Howard Tharsing
Urvashi Vaid
The Washington Blade
The Family of Bill and Lois Wilson
Liz Winfeld

Introduction

Smart Spending is not a book about the best companies in America for gays and lesbians. The best companies for us tend to be small, gay-owned businesses in our own neighborhoods where economic ties and community relations can be individually strengthened. Instead, this is a book about reinforcing our pursuit of equality by building strategic consumer and investor relationships with the world's most influential corporate powers.

We can build these alliances by letting as many companies as possible know who we are, where we are, and what each of us really wants.

What do you want? Do you want to be targeted as a gay or lesbian consumer? Are you willing to buy from companies that advertise for your dollars? What about the companies that don't acknowledge you? How do you feel about companies that constantly target you in advertising but have less-than-progressive workplace policies?

In recent years, selected portions of gay and lesbian culture have become prominently examined and exploited through national media. And with each new season, more film, television, and entertainment companies pursue us as either a targetable market or a salable commodity.

This recent trend has helped gays and lesbians gain group visibility in business and popular culture. But our notoriety has come at a price. Much of the attention is motivated by profit and driven by hypercompetitive media and sound-bite journalism, a situation exacerbated by the fact that our income and spending power have been wildly exaggerated. Media leaders and advertising pundits portray us as more mainstream and affluent than we really are.

As our culture is packaged into entertainment product while our income is overstated, a powerful impression with a dangerous subtext is created: gay people are not only chic, they're financially well-off and socially advantaged. This notion, of course, is patently false. And it has been used by our detractors to manipulate the public into believing we are secure—that we have the same protections under the constitution as heterosexuals. We do not. We don't have them in the workplace, we don't have them in the military, and we don't have them in the tax code.

We simply have not come as far as our media-created post-*Ellen* image would have everyone believe. We are exploited both as gay consumers and as consumer product for the consumption of heterosexuals.

This leaves us with a disturbing problem: We now find ourselves more catered to and in some cases more protected by businesses than by our democratic government. Such a situation has not historically proven to be a secure position for any minority group. Indeed, we need only look at history and the rapidly increasing number of hate crimes against us to be alarmed by what may lie in our future.

The fact is, we are still a vulnerable people—perhaps, in legal terms, the most vulnerable in contemporary democratic America. We are supported as citizens in some areas of the country, yet our rights are minimized or ignored in others. Our vulnerability was especially apparent following the murder of Matthew Shepard in Wyoming when radical right-wing groups labeled our community's call for stronger hate-crimes legislation as an exploitative attempt to further a "gay agenda." What happened, of course, is the radical right advanced *its* agenda by spinning the idea that "radical homosexual groups" were using Shepard's death to grab "special rights."

And just days after Shepard's murder, during the 1998 election, legal protections for gays and lesbians were widely rejected in referendums across the country. Even residents in the Colorado county that is home to the hospital were Matthew Shepard died voted *against* a ban on discrimination based on sexual orientation. And there wasn't much comfort in the lightweight 30-minute MTV documentary about Shepard's death three weeks later—especially when it was aired with commercials for the PlayStation video game "Dukem Nukem: Time To Kill" and commercials for Ford, a company that does not offer domestic-partner benefits to its lesbian and gay employees.

The insidious nature of allowing our moral and political merit to be continually packaged, dissected, and devalued while our economic worth is simultaneously targeted and overstated adds to our vulnerability and dilutes our need for protection in the eyes of the average citizen—not to mention a great number of CEOs.

This phenomenon extends to our consumer experience as well as our status as employees. Many companies have neither nondiscrimination statements that include sexual orientation nor domestic-partner health insurance for gay and lesbian employees. And even companies with nondiscrimination policy statements that include sexual orientation sometimes discriminate by not offering domestic-partner health care coverage to lesbian and gay employees. This means that some allegedly progressive companies are, in effect, violating their own policies. And in most states this predicament cannot be legally challenged because there are no existing statutes to protect people against discrimination based on sexual orientation.

Should we buy products from these companies? Is it ethical for us to own stock in such businesses? Should gay and lesbian organizations be accepting these companies' questionable corporate contributions?

It's time for gay people to reengineer their talents for sophistication, thrift, and accountability. It's time to make the real facts more readily apparent in labor statistics, election returns, and marketing reports. Our visibility is just as important in these venues as it on Gay Pride Day. We must become the people whose story is always (not rarely) told in corporate diversity reports alongside racial, religious, and other groups. We must demand that news and entertainment conglomerates regularly report exit-polling results of gay and lesbian votes in elections, just as they provide the political analysis of the voting patterns of African-Americans, baby boomers, blue-collar workers, and Christian conservatives.

We must also take a strong inventory of ourselves. We need to look more closely at what our money is really buying. We must not allow our current *virtual visibility* to be become what veteran activist Urvashi Vaid has warned us about: *virtual equality*.

Despite ongoing persecution, we are surrounded by good news. Strategically important companies are beginning to recognize their competitive and moral obligation to administer policies that are equality-based across the board, from the screening and interviewing process to health and retirement benefits. And some companies are signaling their willingness to join us in our battle for equal protection under the law.

But we need to recognize that getting companies to pay attention to us, to provide inclusive workplace environments and civic support, did not occur because heterosexual businesspeople took it upon themselves to make changes on our behalf. The most important changes in big businesses' attitudes toward us came about, in nearly every case, because gay and lesbian employees and consumers made their presence known to corporate leaders.

Companies do change—once they hear us. And therein lies good news: Business history has shown that no company can afford to be perceived as antigay, and plenty of companies will go out of their way to make sure that they are not.

At the moment, however, there are far too many companies that have yet to realize our potential relationship to their long-term strength and vitality. This is where our sophisticated influence can come in and why I wrote this book. Only informed consumers can know which companies to buy from and invest in and which to reject.

Once you're armed with the facts, you can use them when you go to the grocery store, the mall, an insurance broker, an auto dealer, or your stockbroker.

Use the information in this book to help yourself, your friends, and your family begin finding and supporting gay-friendly companies. Even companies with less-than-admirable policies are included in this book so you can know who to write to and what to say if you like their products but not their policies.

Bear in mind, though, that gender and gender politics cannot be disassociated from marketplace dynamics or the workplace environment. Nor can race, class, income, or parental status. And in researching the material presented herein, I made it a point to consider social concerns beyond sexual orientation, such as gay and lesbian parenting; the rights of women, people of color, and those living with HIV; and, where appropriate, animal and environmental concerns.

For the record, though, it should be noted that hundreds of American companies with spectacular records on sexual orientation are not profiled because I didn't believe them to be influential enough or competitive enough to warrant inclusion.

Use this book as a general guide, a starting point from which to begin making more informed decisions when shopping and investing. But remember, no company is perfect, and even though some are better than others, *you* are ultimately the one who has to be comfortable with a product, a company, or a stock. Because in the final analysis there is no such thing as a bad purchase—only an uninformed one.

How to Use This Book

Smart Spending is designed to put fast facts about companies and their products at your fingertips. The book will help you make informed decisions and will provide you with the information you need to write letters, send faxes, or transmit E-mails expressing your opinions on both products and policies.

This text is arranged in five basic parts: a general consumer discussion;

profiles of the most influential businesses; an investors' guide; a comprehensive desk reference; and an appendix and master index. To get the most out of the master index, be sure to search for product category terms like "Soap" as well brand names like "Dove" or "Dial."

With literally millions of brand-name products on the market, it is impossible to list all of them in the index. However, as much information as was feasible has been incorporated. If a product or company you are looking for is not listed, it may simply not have met the company inclusion criteria outlined below.

Company Inclusion Criteria

The businesses profiled in Part II of this book were chosen for inclusion based on one or more of the following:

- The company has set an exceptional historical precedent (good or bad) regarding sexual orientation;
- The company employs a disproportionately large number of people or is a sales leader in its industry;
- The company plays an important strategic, political, or otherwise influential role in the health and integrity of the nation's workforce and economy;
- The company is particularly visible, or the names of many of its products are likely to be well-known among the majority of consumers in any moderately populated region of the country.

Every attempt has been made to provide accurate and comprehensively verified information on companies, their current policies, and the products they make. Because business is constantly changing, however, no publisher or author can guarantee how long a given portion of text will remain timely and accurate. Any misprints or mischaracterizations of companies, their policies, or the products they make are unintentional, and the publisher and author cannot be held responsible for their occurrences.

Confirmation of Sexual Orientation Policies

Because a considerable amount of conflicting information exists on Web sites regarding companies and their policies on sexual orientation, it is important that I clarify how I verified actual records on policies.

For each company profile, one or more of the following methods was used to obtain or verify sexual orientation policy information:

- A survey of the company was attempted at least twice via mail, fax, Internet, or telephone by me or one of my assistants. This survey included questions about written workplace policies, diversity training, employee groups, and charitable giving. In instances where the company declined to officially participate in the survey or to answer certain questions, attempts were made to locate confidential sources.
- The company recently participated in a Gay/Lesbian Values (GLV) 100 Index survey.
- The company's written employee nondiscrimination policy statement on sexual orientation was verified by the Meyers Pride Value Fund, Howard Tharsing of V-Management, or Shelly Alpern at Trillium Asset Management.
- The company's domestic-partner health care benefits plan was verified by me directly, the Human Rights Campaign, or Common Ground consultant Liz Winfeld.

If a company did not officially participate in a survey, that failure is indicated in its profile. Information on sources for general corporate data beyond sexual orientation policy is outlined in the appendix.

Part One

*Shopping for a More Gay- and
Lesbian-Inclusive World*

The Consumer You Are

If you identify as gay or lesbian, your view of the world is probably different from that of most heterosexuals. You've got a worldly awareness that comes naturally when you're queer and living on a hetero-dominated planet. You're more sensitive, more intuitive, more aware of and involved with urgent cultural and human rights issues. You notice everything. You think about everything. Chances are, you've asked yourself numerous questions about the future: What happens after the Employment Non-Discrimination Act (ENDA) passes? Could it ever be repealed? How will it affect state sodomy laws or the Hawaii same sex marriage decision? Should Ellen DeGeneres run for Congress? Will *Will & Grace* be as good as it gets on prime-time television? Perhaps you even paid attention when CNN did a feature on *Teletubbies*, Britain's animated children's show, because you wondered if they'd say anything about the character Tinky Winky, branded by a London-based pundit as "the first gay icon for preschool children, because of the way he cavorts with his handbag." Perhaps you were enraged when you learned that the handbag was later omitted in worldwide licensing deals with restaurants and toy companies.

What about more serious matters such as the Centers for Disease Control's call for HIV contact tracing? How about our nation's ongoing debate on race relations and affirmative action, but its almost complete denial of the existence of equally important social issues like lesbian and gay teen suicide, queer hate crimes, and job discrimination?

You're probably aware of all of these challenges and their nuances. If you're the spirited type, maybe you're involved in activism on the issues. But if you're like a lot of gay and lesbian Americans, you were tired of fighting everything and everybody long before you ever came out. And since that time, you've come to accept that a certain amount of injustice is part of the territory of being gay or lesbian.

This awareness of injustice makes us more cautious, more insightful, more cognizant of our surroundings. We learned how to be this way early on as part of our survival instinct. As we mature, we develop a shrewd awareness mechanism—something many of us affectionately refer to as "gaydar."

This book is about developing and putting to work a kind of "consumer gaydar" in our fight for equality and protection under the law. It's about developing a second nature response when we hear certain words or come in contact with certain product brand names. Once you've developed your consumer gaydar, you'll think differently when you hear names such as Calvin Klein, Ralston Purina, Celestial Seasonings, Donna Karan, Sara Lee, Cracker Barrel, and Nike.

Being gay or lesbian can determine where you live and where you're employed. It may determine what kind of gym you belong to and in what neighborhood. It influences what supermarket locations you frequent, what route you'll take to get home after dark, what bank machines you feel most comfortable using, even the clothes, food, and health insurance you purchase.

Our individual life experiences determine to what degree our sexual orientation takes priority in our lives, but whether we are aware of it or not, many of those experiences and our responses to them have roots in consumer motivations. Plenty of companies have clocked your address and preferences, cataloged them, and stored them in their databases. In fact, that may be how you got your most recent department store catalog.

Being gay or lesbian affects how you use your credit card, to whom you'll show your driver's license, and whether or not you put your home address on a contest entry form. It affects the way you behave in the community you live in and perhaps the one you grew up in.

Like other consumers, gays and lesbians behave differently as consumers in different parts of the country. For instance, we like certain beers better on the West Coast than the East. We actually have dozens of differing brand and service preferences based on regional culture, product distribution methods, and more. But not all companies recognize this. Few businesses understand us as consumers, and plenty don't acknowledge us as workers. This should give us pause when we make choices about buying certain products or investing in certain companies.

If you're like a lot of gay consumers, you consider life too short and stressful to track down all the details associated with buying and working in a predominantly heterosexually-oriented economy. Still, even the most jaded consumer is often surprised to learn how basic and easy to understand many of the issues really are. And once armed with facts, most of us are more than willing to change the way we spend our hard-earned lesbigay bucks.

Our Consumer Behavior as a Group

As a general rule, lesbians and gay men are more protective of themselves and the environment than are heterosexuals. This personality trait has repeatedly been observed in the better marketing studies of gays and lesbians as consumers in various communities.[1] In specialized focus groups about products and policies, we are often more outspoken about environmental and labor practices as well as issues regarding human rights and business ethics.

In conjunction with being more protective, gay and lesbian consumers are also more skeptical. We are less trusting of big institutions and more quick to see through marketing smoke and promotional mirrors. We are actually not that easy to sell to (although there is research that suggests we are more loyal). So it should be no surprise that recently, more of us have become less willing to buy into the contemporary stereotype of lesbian and gay people leading charmed, affluent lives free from the bondage of heterosexual domesticity. We know from simply looking around that plenty of us are not part of some stereotypical dream market; we don't all take whirlwind vacations and sip premium liquor. Some of us even admit to having less than expensive taste. Still, we may be justifiably confused by media hype about our alleged wealth as gay consumers.

A lot of investors, business managers, and corporate marketing representatives have begun looking a little closer at gay and lesbian consumers. And plenty of others have learned the hard way—some losing millions—by buying into the hype about what gay people are supposed to be like, as opposed to more solidly researching the way we really are and the common values that we hold.

The following chart, supplied by Yankelovich Partners for a previous busi-

4 / Smart Spending

ness book I wrote on marketing to gays and lesbians, published in 1995 and republished in 1999, breaks down the statistical relevance of our income. The details of this income story often get censored in national news broadcasts.

	Gay/Lesbian %	Heterosexual %
PERSONAL INCOME:		
Under $25K	85	78
$25K–$49,999	12	19
$50K–$99,999	2	3
$100K+	1	*
HOUSEHOLD INCOME:		
Under $25K	44	38
$25K–$49,999	39	39
$50K–$99,999	14	20
$100K+	3	3
MEAN PERSONAL INCOME (000)	$16.9	$17.6
MEAN HOUSEHOLD INCOME (000)	$35.8	$36.7
MEAN HOUSEHOLD SIZE	2.89	3.01

*Less than .5%

Income Between the Sexes (Gay/Lesbian and Heterosexual)

	Gay Male %	Heterosexual Male %	Lesbian %	Heterosexual Female %
PERSONAL INCOME:				
Under $25K	81	65	87	88
$25K–$49,999	13	29	11	11
$50K–$99,999	3	5	1	1
$100K+	3	1	*	*
HOUSEHOLD INCOME:				
Under $25K	37	32	47	43
$25K–$49,999	49	42	33	37
$50K–$99,999	9	23	18	17
$100K+	5	3	2	3
MEAN PERSONAL INCOME (000)	$21.5	$22.5	$13.3	$13.2
MEAN HOUSEHOLD INCOME (000)	$37.4	$39.3	$34.8	$34.4
MEAN HOUSEHOLD SIZE	3.03	3.05	2.78	2.97

*Less than 0.5%
SOURCE: Yankelovich MONITOR Gay/Lesbian Perspective

As you can see, lesbians and straight women earn about the same when you look at them as individuals. So do gay men and straight men, as individuals. But if you put two gay men in a household, they likely have a higher household (combined) income than a heterosexual couple because women tend to earn less than men. Two women in a household will usually have a lower combined income than an all-male or a heterosexual couple. Our sound-bite media culture always leaves these details out of their stories.

Virtual Visibility

Awareness of gay and lesbian people in commercial media has soared in recent years, but hard facts and statistics about who we really are, are scarce—particularly when it comes to how much we earn, spend, and invest. Even less is known about what brands we buy and why. This is because too many business leaders still have unrealistic impressions of who we actually are as part of the American consumer populace.

While the film and television industry is an area where we are actually overrepresented, other, perhaps more critical industries, such as advertising, manufacturing, and education, leave us much less represented and visible. This imbalance of visibility has resulted in a lack of influence in certain industries and in thousands of products and services never being specifically marketed to lesbians and gay men.

If you don't mind buying products from companies that don't acknowledge you as one of their customers, then perhaps this is not a problem for you, but what if a company whose product you enjoy doesn't have a sexual orientation nondiscrimination policy? Would such knowledge influence your perception of the company?

Progressive Organizations

There are a number of names that came up continually in my research. Many arose not only in terms of visibility and ease to work with but because there was a sense of genuine corporate commitment to working closely with gays and lesbians beyond routine marketing opportunities. Interestingly, some of these companies are not considered leading-edge when it comes to workplace issues. But the general impression is that there are individuals within these companies working to move things in the right direction regarding gay and lesbian issues.

These companies are:

ABC News	The Limited
Adolph Coors	Liz Claiborne
America Online	Lucent Technologies
American Airlines	Meyers Capital Management
American Express	Miramax Films
AT&T	MTV
Bank of America	Naya Inc.
BankBoston	Norman Foundation
Bell Atlantic	Paul Rapaport Foundation
Charles Schwab	Quark
Chase Manhattan	Scudder Funds
CNN	Seagram
Donna Karan	Showtime Networks
The Hartford	Starbucks
HBO	Time Warner
Hormel	Trillium Asset Management
IBM	Viacom
Joyce Mertz-Gilmore Foundation	Virgin Atlantic
Kodak	Walt Disney
Kresge Foundation	Xerox
Levi Strauss	

Organizations to Watch Out For

The following names are associated with ongoing consumer and human rights problems—the majority of which deal with nongay issues such as women's advancement, international labor abuse, environmental abuse, and cruelty to animals. As you can see, some paradoxically also appear in the previous list.

These companies are:

A&P	A.E. Staley
Adidas	Alaska Airlines
Adolph Coors	American Express

American Home Products
Baskin Robbins
Bordens
BP Amoco
Carl's Jr.
Chevron
Cracker Barrel Old Country Store
Domino's Pizza
Dannon
Exxon
Federal Express
Ford Motor
General Electric
Georgia-Pacific
Gillette
Häagen-Dazs
Hormel
Mitsubishi
Monsanto
Nike
Philip Morris
Procter & Gamble
Seagram
Texaco
United Airlines
Wendy's

If you buy products from any of these companies, be sure to check its profile in Part Two. In addition, you may wish to check the "Boycotts and Their Sponsors" section in Part Four.

Big Names and Big Budgets

Having major corporate names associated with the promotion of gay and lesbian pride events and equal rights is important, but changing laws and workplace policies and establishing safe communities for gays and lesbians ultimately depend on the work of political activists and those working within a comparatively small number of important organizations.

Following is a composite list of popular gay and nongay organizations and their budgets.[2] The dollar amounts represent, as of press time, the most recent budget information available. As you can see, gay organizations are modestly funded in comparison with nongay organizations.

From my perspective, most gay and lesbian organizations are more efficient in their administration and generally more successful in terms what they accomplish than nongay organizations—especially when you consider how little most gay groups have to work with in the way of funds. In addition, if you want your contributions to go toward helping people instead of toward paying administrative costs, you can count on gay-identified charitable giving to generally go much further.

8 / Smart Spending

AIDS Project Los Angeles	$20.9 million
American Cancer Society	$359.1 million
American Heart Association	$239.9 million
American Red Cross	$535.7 million
Astraea Foundation	$0.78 million
Boys and Girls Clubs of America	$302 million
CARE	$446 million
Catholic Charities USA	$344.1 million
Corporation for Public Broadcasting	$229.9 million
Empire State Pride Agenda	$1.3 million
Gay and Lesbian Alliance Against Defamation	$1.9 million
Gay Men's Health Crisis	$27.0 million
God's Love We Deliver	$7.6 million
Hetrick Martin Institute	$3.3 million
Horizons, Chicago	$1.2 million
Human Rights Campaign	$9.0 million
Lesbian Herstory Archives	$0.042 million
Los Angeles Gay and Lesbian Community Center	$19.0 million
National Gay and Lesbian Task Force	$2.5 million
New York Lesbian and Gay Community Center	$3.8 million
PrideFest, Philadelphia	$0.12 million
Salvation Army	$682.9 million
Second Harvest	$430.6 million
United Jewish Appeal Federation	$408.2 million
YMCA	$361.2 million

For more information on the details of charitable giving, consult a library copy of *The Chronicle of Philanthropy,* which can be reached at (202) 466-1200; the *National Directory of Corporate Giving,* (212) 620-4230), or *The NonProfit Times,* (609) 921-1251.

Tuning Your Queer Consumer Antennae

Gay and lesbian consumers should determine for themselves if a product or company is worthy of their patronage or investment dollar by examining the company's overall record on a range of social matters relating to policies in addition to gay and lesbian issues, along with company or product performance. Policy and performance, however, do not always mirror one another. Consequently, individuals must sometimes balance one against the other to make an individually acceptable purchasing or investing decision.

The first and perhaps most critical litmus test for gay and lesbian consumers regarding policy issues is written corporate policy on sexual orientation. A strong, written nondiscrimination policy not only protects gay and lesbian employees from workplace harassment but also provides legal grounding in areas of the country where workplace discrimination is not yet outlawed.

Other policies may be of concern to you as well, such as a company's track record on international labor issues, tobacco or alcohol production, the environment, animal testing, and promoting women and minorities to senior management positions. Whether or not you would stop buying one of your favorite products based on workplace or environmental policies is, of course, for you to decide.

There is also the issue of domestic-partner health care coverage. Would you alter your relationship with a business if you suddenly became aware that it didn't offer domestic-partner health care benefits to its gay and lesbian employees? Would you lobby for the company you work for to stop conducting business with a certain company based on knowledge of that fact?

The visibility of products we see being advertised in gay or lesbian publications is not always a thorough indicator of corporate merit—which is why *Smart Spending* includes information on a range of issues, including policies regarding sexual orientation, domestic-partner health care coverage, the environment, animal rights, and parental support in the workplace. I have also indicated whether companies are listed on the Domini Social Index, which reports on whether the company is deriving a majority of its profits from alcohol, tobacco, or military weapons sales.

In addition to policy issues, reasonable consumers place a major emphasis on a product or stock's performance. And performance inevitably boils down to one question: How well does the product or stock perform for you?

Knowing what is most important to you in different situations is the key to making smart spending decisions. And the personal emphasis you place on product value and performance versus the company's record as a corporate citizen is going to vary based on the issues and the product you are analyzing.

Perhaps buying an appliance you really want isn't so bad even if you don't agree with all the company's policies. But consider sending a copy of the receipt to the company CEO with an explanation of why you liked the product and what you wish he or she would do about changing a given policy that concerns you.

Writing letters matters; companies respond to letters—especially those involving controversial matters like sexual orientation. The more letters they get, the more likely they are to respond.

Sort Out the Hype, Focus on Issues

Making decisions about products based on issues important to you takes practice, especially if you are truly concerned about being a more responsible gay or lesbian consumer. Plenty of companies may be reaching out to you as a queer consumer, but that doesn't necessarily mean they are great companies on all counts.

During the '80s, seeing a company or its products advertised in gay and lesbian newspapers and magazines usually indicated it was a savvy company that understood and approved of treating us as equals. But did you know that Benetton doesn't have domestic-partner benefits for its gay and lesbian employees? Neither did Carillon Importers while it was handling the Absolut vodka brand. But Benetton, a relatively small company, did raise public awareness about diversity, racism, and war. And Absolut's importers did support the gay press long before Johnnie Walker, Budweiser, and Coors. In fact, Budweiser is still running the same old tired gay male-focused ads. Where are the lesbians? Where is the company's domestic partner healthcare benefits plan?

Sexual Orientation and Domestic-Partnership Benefits

Fringe benefits such as health and life insurance, a pension, profit sharing, or a percentage of profits have long been a way for employers to compensate workers, and for one company to gain a competitive advantage over another. Benefits generally constitute about 40% of a worker's total compensation and are no longer considered extras, according to the Society for Human Resource Management.

Such benefits, however, are a privilege, not a right. Of the 11 states prohibiting workplace discrimination based on sexual orientation, none mandates workplace benefits for nontraditional families. Neither do any state executive orders or local ordinances. And the Employment Non-Discrimination

Act, which is pending in Congress, would not require such benefits either.

While most employers that offer benefits such as health insurance and dental care also make those benefits available to their employees' legal dependents, the idea of extending such benefits to the domestic partners of lesbian and gay employees is relatively new.

In 1982 *The Village Voice,* a New York City weekly, became the first employer to offer domestic-partner benefits to its lesbian and gay employees. By 1990 there were still fewer than a half-dozen U.S. employers offering "spousal equivalent" benefits to their gay employees' families.[3]

Today, although it is believed that thousands of American companies provide some form of domestic partner benefits to their gay employees, there are only about 100 Fortune 500 companies offering full domestic-partner health care coverage.

The Employment Non-Discrimination Act would basically prohibit employers, employment agencies, and labor unions from discriminating on the basis of sexual orientation, but ENDA does not require that benefits be extended to same-sex partners of employees, since companies are not currently required to extend such benefits to legally married heterosexual spouses. ENDA also does not cover businesses with fewer than 15 employees or religious organizations. (A detailed analysis of ENDA is in the appendix). HRC, GLAAD, and NGLTF all provide excellent resources on domestic-partner health care plans.

---

1 The most verifiable confirmation of this trend at the national level was detailed in the groundbreaking 1994 Yankelovich *Monitor* Gay and Lesbian Perspective, the first nationally generalizable study of self-identifying gays and lesbians based on random sampling and weighted against the 1990 Census data.

2 Obtained from annual reports or direct conversations with executive directors or development campaign staff members.

3 According to the Human Rights Campaign Web site, Washington, D.C., Elizabeth Birch, executive director, March 1998.

Part Two

The Most Influential Companies, Their Policies and Products

A Note About Company Profiles

This company and product reference section includes individual company profiles listed alphabetically under the following ten industry categories:

1) Advertising, Marketing, and Public Relations Agencies
2) Banking and Investment Firms
3) Clothing and Sportswear Manufacturers
4) Communications and Technology Companies
5) Consumer Products and Home Furnishings Companies
6) Entertainment, Media, and Publishing Companies
7) Food and Beverage Service Companies
8) Insurance and Health Care Providers
9) Transportation and Travel Firms
10) Utilities, Chemicals, Materials, and Engineering Companies

Each company profile contains, whenever possible, address, telephone, fax, and Internet contact information followed by an overall appraisal, general checklists of consumer cautions, important considerations that reflect well on the company, and a summary of the company's record on sexual orientation issues. In addition, most of the profiles contain a brief overview of the company's history with gays and lesbians, both positive and negative, as well as employee comments and general sales information. Some profiles contain a checklist of cautions and considerations without a discussion overview because no significant gay-specific history could be verified beyond workplace policies. In as many cases as possible, a listing of each company's major brand-name products has also been included.

In general, the company overview discussion in each profile is intended to draw your attention to what is most noteworthy or most problematic within its corporate culture.

Overall appraisals are characterized as follows:

> **Very progressive:** A business characterized as "very progressive" has a long history of being a leader on sexual orientation issues. A near-perfect score.
>
> **Progressive:** A business characterized as "progressive" has a better-than-average record on sexual orientation issues.
>
> **Progressing:** A business characterized as "progressing" has a recent history of incorporating some progressive policies on sexual orientation into its business practices.
>
> **Progressing somewhat:** A business characterized as "progressing somewhat" has shown a willingness to discuss issues related to gays and lesbians, but may have not yet made substantive changes affecting policy.
>
> **Progressing too slowly:** A business characterized as "progressing too slowly" has refused to meet with gay and lesbian employees or has given little serious consideration to their concerns.
>
> Less than progressive: A business characterized as "less than progressive" has a poor overall record on sexual orientation issues.
>
> **Not progressive:** A business characterized as "not progressive" appears to want to distance itself from any association with gay or lesbian consumers or employees.

The Domini Social Index

Companies that have appeared on the Domini Social Index at any time in the past three years have that fact listed under "Important Considerations" in the company profile.

The Domini Social Index is a listing of 400 different companies that meet Kinder, Lydenberg, Domini's financial and social screening criteria. Companies on the DSI are not affiliated with nuclear technology, military development, or alcohol or tobacco production and are businesses where labor abuses have not been recently documented. As of January 1999, DSI companies were fully screened for sexual orientation policy guidelines. Companies appearing on the DSI during 1999 may not yet provide domestic-partner health care benefits but can generally be assumed to have a written nondiscrimination policy on sexual orientation.

The Meyers Pride Value Fund

Companies that have been held by the Meyers Pride Value Fund within the past three years are so designated in the "Important Considerations" section of the company's profile. If a company is held by the Meyers Pride Value Fund, then Meyers Capital Management of Beverly Hills has verified that the company's written nondiscrimination policy is up-to-date and being enforced.

The Meyers Pride Value Fund is the first investment vehicle of its kind. It is currently the only mutual fund that exclusively prescreens stocks for progressive workplace policy in relation to sexual orientation.

The GLV 100 Index

Each year, during gay pride season, I release the GLV (Gay/Lesbian Values) 100 Index of the best companies for gays and lesbians. The rating system is explained in Part Three of this book, and the most recent GLV 100 listing appears in the appendix. If a company has been listed on the GLV 100 Index during the past three years, that information will appear in the "Important Considerations" section of the company's profile.

The GLV 100 Index was originally formulated as part of a research consulting partnership I shared with financial adviser Howard Tharsing of V-Management in San Francisco.

Women and the Workplace

Below is a brief list of companies I believe, based on my research and impressions of company management, to be more progressive on women's issues, followed by a list of those I believe to be less progressive.

More Progressive Companies For Women:

Alberto Culver	General Mills
American Home Products	Hershey Foods
Apple	IBM
Ben & Jerry's Homemade	Monsanto
Bell Atlantic	Newman's Own
Campbell Soup	PepsiCo

Pet
Procter & Gamble
Quaker Oats

Sara Lee
Warner Lambert
William Wrigley Jr.

Less Progressive Companies For Women:

Archer Daniels Midland
ConAgra
Dial
Hormel
Mars
Nestlé

Smithfield Foods
Tyson Foods
Unilever
United Biscuit Holdings
Universal Foods
Welch Food

Parents and the Workplace

Because many gay men and lesbians are parents, I've noted in the "Important Considerations" section of company profiles if employees reported better than average support by management for them as working parents, or if *Working Mother* magazine cited the company within the past three years on its annual Best 100 List for Working Mothers.

The Ethical Treatment of Animals

Entire books have been written on animal treatment ethics in relation to commerce. I have an opinion as to what is and is not ethical, but as an author I have no interest in refereeing this debate. I will, however, draw your attention to the following companies that test some of their products on animals, so that readers who consider such information relevant can make informed decisions:[1]

Alberto Culver
Allergan
Arm & Hammer
Bausch & Lomb
Beecham
Bic Corp.
Bristol-Myers
Carter Wallace
Chesebrough Ponds

Colgate-Palmolive
Dow Chemical
Eli Lilly & Company
Gillette
Helene Curtis
Johnson & Johnson
Kimberly Clark
Kroger
Mead

Pfizer   Unilever
SmithKline   Warner Lambert
3M

Potential Labor Abuses of Women and Children

Any company conducting operations overseas in countries where women or children are likely to be employed under questionable conditions has been noted as a company with "possible overseas labor problems." This by no means indicates that the company is currently or has ever been guilty of abuse—merely that the conditions make such abuse possible, and that further investigation was beyond the scope of this book.

Nuclear Technology, Weapons, Tobacco, and Alcohol

For those concerned, as I am, about nuclear technology and the manufacture of weapons, alcohol, and tobacco products, I've included relevant information in the company profiles. If a company is listed as being "affiliated with nuclear weapons technology," then that company derives in excess of 2% of its annual profits from sales or service connected to nuclear technology.

Chemicals

Anyone who doubts the extent to which chemicals affect our health might want to read Marc Lappé's *Chemical Deception*.[2] The most worrisome issue covered in Lappé's book is the impact our increasingly chemically infused environment is having on future generations. Of over 70,000 known chemicals currently used in commerce, only 1,600 have been sufficiently researched for us to know about their potentially hazardous effects on developing fetuses.

With breast cancer increasing and the HIV pandemic continuing, the last thing any of us needs is the introduction of more potentially damaging substances into our bodies. It should also be noted that many of the major chemical companies have a less than admirable record regarding sexual orientation issues.

For easy reference, I have provided lists of some of the best and worst household products, chemically speaking.

The Most Influential Companies / 17

Fifty of the Healthiest, Most Environmentally Safe Name-Brand Household Products:[3]

Abracadabra Bath Soaps
AFM Safety Cleaner
Agree Shampoo and Conditioners
Airwick Carpet Fresh & Stickups
Ajax All Purpose Liquid Cleaner
Alexander Oil Colors
All Free and Clear Liquid
Almay Antiperspirants
Amor All Leather Care
Arm & Hammer Fabric Softener
Arm and Hammer Baking Soda
Bare Essentials Brand Cosmetics
Barth Aloe Soaps and Stick Deodorant
Bissell Wall to Wall
Bon Ami
Bounce Fabric Softener
Brite Floor Cleaner
Caress Soaps
Cheer Free
Cinch
Clorox II
Comet
Dermassage
Descale-It Bathroom Cleaner
Desert Essence Products
Dove Soaps
Dove Dishwashing Liquid
Dr. Bronner's Soaps
Easy Off (fume free)
Eco Bella Products
Ecover Cream Cleanser
Enforcer Pet Flea Powder
Faberge Antiperspirants
Faith In Nature Shampoos
Fantastic Swipes
Finesse Shampoos
Future Wax
Giovanni Shampoos
Glade Potpourri
Glamourene
Glass & Surface
Glidden Spread 2000
Glo-Coat Wax
Harvey's All Purpose Clean
Home Health Roll-On Deodorants
Hope's Brass & Silver Polishes
Kmart Bathroom Cleanser
Keri Lotions
Kiss My Face Lotions and Creams
3M Safest Stripper

50 of the Least Healthy, Most Environmentally Toxic Name-Brand Household Products:[4]

Arm & Hammer Heavy Duty Brand Detergent
Auri Car Polish
Bag a Bug Pesticide
Bissell One Step Floor Care
Black Flag Professional Ant & Roach Killer

18 / Smart Spending

Bruce One Step Floor Cleaner
Clorox
Combat Room Fogger
Cover Girl
Drano Crystal (nonbiological brand)
Dutch Boy Paint
Endurance Oil Stains
Energine Cleaners and Spot Removers
Enforcer Ant and Roach
Forby's Furniture Polish
Formby Paint Removers and Strippers
Formula 1 Car Products
Grecian Formula
Gillette Foaming Skin Conditioner
K & W Leather and Vinyl Spray
K2r Spot Lifter
Kelly Moore Paints
Kiwi Liquid Leather Dyes and Wax
Kiwi Scuff Magic
Liquid Paper
Liquid-Plumr drain opener
Long Life Flea Collars
Lucas Wood Stains
Lysol Disinfectant
Marble Shine
Minwax Floor Cleaners and Wax
Old English Lemon Furniture Wax
Ortho Weed Be Gone
Parks Paint Removers and Strippers
Pet Agree Flea Collars
Plunge Drain Opener
Prevail Bathroom Cleaner
Radiator Specialty All Purpose Cleaner
Raid Bug Sprays and Killers
Rid-a-bug flea fogger
Scott's Liquid Gold Cleaner
Scratchex Flea & Tick Collars
Sergeant's Flea & Tick Collars
Sergeant's Flea & Tick Powders
Shoe Goo 144 Spot Remover
Shout Aerosol Cleaner
Spray 'n Wash Stain Remover
Sunny Side Paint Removers
Tilex Cleaners
3M Brand Carpet Spray

1 According to *Animals*, PETA (People for the Ethical Treatment of Animals) as of February, 1997.
2 Lappé, Marc, *Chemical Deception: The Toxic Threat to Health and Environment*, Sierra Club Books, 1991.
3 Selected from *Safe Shopper's Bible* by David Steinman and Samuel S. Epstein. Excerpted with permission of Macmillan General Reference USA, a Simon & Schuster Macmillan Company. Copyright 1995 by David Steinman and Samuel S. Epstein.
4 Selected from *Safe Shopper's Bible* by David Steinman and Samuel S. Epstein. Excerpted with permission of Macmillan General Reference USA, a Simon & Schuster Macmillan Company. Copyright 1995 by David Steinman and Samuel S. Epstein.

Advertising, Marketing, and Public Relations

The majority of advertising, marketing, and public relations agencies are less than progressive on issues relating to sexual orientation. Most do not offer domestic-partner health care insurance for their gay and lesbian employees. Moreover, the large advertising agencies have an exceptionally poor record on advising their clients about how to market to gay and lesbian consumers.

Some of the larger agencies have actually advised major companies to *not* target the gay and lesbian marketplace. The result has been an explosion of small gay- and lesbian-owned agencies, which many major corporations now turn to for marketing counsel and integrated media placement services.

On the bright side, most large firms offer some amount of pro bono service to nonprofit organizations. The industry, generally speaking, has been supportive of breast cancer awareness, AIDS education and fund-raising, and safe-sex education campaigns aimed at young adults.

General Industry Resources:

Advertising Age
   adage.com
The Advertising Council
   www.adcouncil.org
Adweek
   www.adweek.com
Advertising World
   advertising.utexas.edu/world/index.html
American Advertising Federation
   www.aaf.org
American Association of Advertising Agencies
   www.aaaa.org
New York Advertising and Communications Network (GLBT-oriented organization)
   www.nyacn.com

NW Ayer & Co.
825 8th Ave.
New York, NY 10019-7498
(212) 474-5805
(212) 474-5196 (fax)

Author's Overall Appraisal
Progressive

Consumer Cautions
Client work may affiliate company with sales of alcohol or tobacco

Important Considerations
Affiliated with groups supportive of gay and lesbian rights
Diversity training inclusive of people with disabilities
Includes gay- or lesbian-suggestive imagery in mainstream advertising or programming
Listed on GLV 100 Index
Significantly visible supporter of ENDA
Supports AIDS services/men's health groups
Supports breast cancer research/women's health groups

Workplace Record on Sexual Orientation
Diversity training inclusive of sexual orientation
Full domestic-partnership health care benefits
Gay and lesbian employee group officially acknowledged
Written sexual orientation nondiscrimination policy statement

Company Overview
NW Ayer was one of the first American advertising agencies to offer domestic-partnership benefits to its gay and lesbian employees. The company was acquired by the MacManus Group in 1996, and as of this writing, MacManus was considering extending domestic-partnership benefits to all MacManus Group employees.

NW Ayer is the only major advertising agency to report having a management-acknowledged gay and lesbian employee group. It is also the only New York advertising agency to report that it has openly gay management. Its most recent client list was not available at press time.

Foote, Cone, & Belding

150 East 42nd St.
New York, NY 10017
(212) 885-3000
(212) 885-3191 (media fax)

Author's Overall Appraisal

Progressive

Consumer Cautions

Client work may affiliate company with sales of alcohol or tobacco

Important Considerations

Affiliated with groups supportive of gay and lesbian rights

Exceptional workplace record supporting parents

Has included gay- or lesbian-suggestive imagery in mainstream advertising or programming

Listed on GLV 100 Index

Significantly visible supporter of ENDA

Supports AIDS services/men's health groups

Supports breast cancer research/women's health groups

Workplace Record on Sexual Orientation

Full domestic-partnership health care benefits

Gay and lesbian employee group

Written sexual orientation nondiscrimination policy statement

Company Overview

Foote, Cone, & Belding is part of True North Communications. It is a very important, high-profile advertising agency with many dedicated gay and lesbian employees. It is also one of only two major New York advertising agencies to offer domestic partnership benefits to its gay and lesbian employees. (The other is NW Ayer & Co.) FCB clients have included Citicorp, Citibank, Procter & Gamble, and the U.S. Postal Service.

Hill, Holiday, Connors, Cosmopulos

200 Clarendon St.
Boston, MA 02116
(617) 437-1600

Author's Overall Appraisal
Progressive

Consumer Cautions
Client work may affiliate company with sales of alcohol or tobacco

Important Considerations
Affiliated with groups supportive of gay and lesbian rights
Exceptional workplace record supporting parents
Listed on GLV 100 Index
Supports AIDS services/men's health groups
Supports breast cancer research/women's health groups

Workplace Record on Sexual Orientation
Full domestic-partnership health care benefits
Gay and lesbian employee group

Company Overview
Hill, Holiday, Connors, Cosmopulos is one of only three major advertising agencies (and the only agency based outside New York City) known to offer domestic-partnership health care coverage to gay and lesbian employees. As of this writing, HHCC was being acquired by Interpublic Inc. HHCC's policies regarding gay and lesbian workers were not expected to change, but it had not yet been determined whether domestic-partnership benefits would be extended to all Interpublic employees. HHCC clients have included John Hancock, Fidelity Mutual, Marshalls, Mellon Bank, North American Mortgage, NCR, Spaulding Sports, Bay Networks, Harvard Pilgrim Healthcare, and Gillette.

Hill and Knowlton Inc.

466 Lexington Avenue
New York, New York 10017
(212) 885-0300
(212) 885-0570 (fax)
www.hillandknowlton.com

Author's Overall Appraisal
Progressing

Consumer Cautions
Client work may affiliate company with sales of alcohol or tobacco
Client work may affiliate company with military contracts or foreign governments

Important Considerations
Affiliated with gay/lesbian community groups
Listed on GLV 100 Index

Workplace Record on Sexual Orientation
Full domestic-partnership health care benefits
Gay and lesbian employee group

Company Overview
Hill and Knowlton became controversial during the Persian Gulf War because of its affiliation with a group calling itself "Citizens for a Free Kuwait." The group's stated goal was to garner support for victims of the Iraqi invasion of Kuwait. But a teenage girl's tale of seeing Iraqi soldiers pull babies from incubators in a Kuwait hospital—a tale she told Congress in an appearance arranged by Hill and Knowlton—turned out to be fabricated.

What's important for gay and lesbian consumers to know is that Hill and Knowlton clearly drew a line in the sand against bigotry and workplace discrimination based on sexual orientation when it chose, in 1997, to make domestic-partnership benefits available to its gay and lesbian employees. In addition, numerous senior-level managers at the firm are openly gay. Hill and Knowlton's recent clients have included Procter & Gamble, Mazda, Johnson & Johnson, Citibank, Chase, Heinz Foods, Puerto Rico Tourism Company, and Florida Citrus.

Banking and Investment

The majority of large financial institutions have become more progressive on issues relating to sexual orientation in the workplace over the past two years. More than half now offer domestic-partner health care insurance for their gay and lesbian employees. However, smaller savings and loan organizations still have a long way to go.

What is perhaps of more concern at present is the fact that nearly every large banking institution in the country has only a fair record of contributing to gay and lesbian nonprofit organizations.

General Industry Resources:

American Stock Exchange
  www.amex.com
Chicago Board of Trade
  www.cbot.com
NASDAQ
  www.nasdaq.com
New York Cotton Exchange
  www.nyce.com
New York Mercantile Exchange
  www.nymex.com
New York Stock Exchange
  www.nyse.com

American Express
World Financial Center
New York, NY 10285
(800) 528-4800 (toll-free)
(212) 640-2000
www.americanexpress.com

Author's Overall Appraisal
Progressive

Consumer Cautions
None

Important Considerations
Affiliated with groups supportive of gay and lesbian rights
Contributes to gay/lesbian nonprofit group(s)
Diversity training inclusive of people with disabilities
Good workplace record supporting parents
Has advertised in the gay and lesbian press
Has included gay- or lesbian-suggestive imagery in mainstream advertising or programming
Listed as a Fortune 500 Company
Listed on Domini Social Index
Listed on GLV 100 Index
Listed on Standard & Poor's Index
Supports AIDS services/men's health groups
Supports breast cancer research/women's health groups

Workplace Record on Sexual Orientation
Diversity training inclusive of sexual orientation
Full domestic-partnership health care benefits
Gay and lesbian employee group officially acknowledged
Written sexual orientation nondiscrimination policy statement

Company Overview
American Express has approximately 70,000 employees and provides financial and investment services. It is one of the world's largest travel agencies, and it publishes a variety of travel-related magazines, including *Food & Wine, Departures,* and *Travel & Leisure.* The company also offers AMEX Life Assurance in the United States.

The company has begun marketing Travelers Cheques through gay and lesbian magazines. Although there was some initial denial that the ads were gay-focused when they first appeared—the signatures on the checks represented members of the same sex—the company has since become less skittish about its policies regarding gays and lesbians. American Express is now considered a corporate leader on a multitude of sexual orientation–related issues in both the marketplace and the workplace.

Bank of America
100 N. Tryon St.
Charlotte, NC 28255-0001
(704) 386-5000
www.bankofamerica.com

Author's Overall Appraisal
Progressing

Consumer Cautions
May be affiliated with groups less than supportive of gay and lesbian rights
Possible overseas labor problems

Important Considerations
Affiliated with groups supportive of gay and lesbian rights
Diversity training inclusive of people with disabilities
Exceptional workplace record supporting parents
Includes gay- or lesbian-suggestive imagery in local advertising or programming
Listed as a Fortune 500 Company
Listed on Domini Social Index
Listed on GLV 100 Index
Listed on Standard & Poor's Index
Supports AIDS services/men's health groups
Supports breast cancer research/women's health groups

Workplace Record on Sexual Orientation
Diversity training inclusive of sexual orientation
Full domestic-partnership health care benefits
Gay and lesbian employee group
Mixed remarks from vendors or gay and lesbian employees
Written sexual orientation nondiscrimination policy statement

Company Overview
Bank of America is one of the largest banks in the United States, employing 161,300 people and providing financial services nationwide and in 37 other countries. Long based in San Francisco, Bank of America moved its corporate headquarters to Charlotte, N.C., after merging with NationsBank in the late 1990s, but it continues to do a great deal of business in San Francisco and all over California. Bank of America, unlike Levi Strauss, continued to fund the Boy Scouts of America even after the organization publicly declared homosexuality morally wrong.

Despite this insult and a less-than-cozy relationship with many in San Francisco's lesbian, gay, bisexual, and transgendered population, Bank of America has a better scorecard on gay and lesbian issues than most big banks.

BankBoston

100 Federal
Boston, MA 02110
(800) 252-6000 (toll-free)
(617) 434-2200
(617) 434-7547 (fax)
www.bkb.com

Author's Overall Appraisal

Very progressive

Consumer Cautions

Possible overseas labor problems

Important Considerations

Early and significantly visible supporter of ENDA
Listed as a Fortune 500 Company
Listed on GLV 100 Index
Supports AIDS services/men's health groups

Workplace Record on Sexual Orientation

Diversity training inclusive of sexual orientation
Full domestic-partnership health care benefits
Gay and lesbian employee group officially acknowledged
Written sexual orientation nondiscrimination policy statement

Company Overview

With over 2,000 employees, BankBoston is the largest bank in Massachusetts. The company delivers a full range of banking services to its clients, including trust and asset management, insurance and brokerage services, and mortgages. BankBoston has many commercial clients, and provides numerous banking services for Latin and Chinese trade clients. Also, through its subsidiary company BankBoston Development, it has made an equity investment in Meyers Capital Management, with the funds going toward marketing the first gay and lesbian mutual fund, the Meyers Pride Value Fund. Gay and lesbian consumers opposed to companies that have business ties to China may not be impressed with BankBoston, but for those interested only in issues related to sexual orientation, there's nothing to worry about here. In 1999 Fleet Financial Group announced it planned to acquire BankBoston; as of this writing, the transaction was awaiting regulatory approval.

Charles Schwab and Co.

101 Montgomery St.
San Francisco, CA 94104
(800) 435-4000 (toll-free)
(415) 627-7000
(415) 627-7076 (fax)
www.schwab.com

Author's Overall Appraisal
Very progressive

Consumer Cautions
None

Important Considerations
Affiliated with groups supportive of gay and lesbian rights
Early supporter of ENDA
Good workplace record supporting parents
Has advertised in the gay and lesbian press
Listed on Domini Social Index
Listed on GLV 100 Index
Listed on Standard & Poor's Index
Supports AIDS services/men's health groups
Supports breast cancer research/women's health groups

Workplace Record on Sexual Orientation
Diversity training inclusive of people with disabilities
Diversity training inclusive of sexual orientation
Encouraging remarks from vendors or gay and lesbian employees
Full domestic-partnership health care benefits
Gay and lesbian employee group officially acknowledged
Written sexual orientation nondiscrimination policy statement

Company Overview
Charles Schwab is a leader in discount brokerage services. The company has long been known for offering easily accessible financial and stock market information at a lower price than its competitors. As a financial and brokerage services provider, the company continues to grow, maintaining a high level of visibility with approximately 225 customer service outlet locations. Charles Schwab was one of the first brokerage services companies to offer domestic-partnership health care coverage to its gay and lesbian employees. The company owns Street Smart online financial software programs.

Chase Manhattan
270 Park Avenue
New York, NY 10017
(212) 270-6000
(212) 270-7325 (Chase Investor Relations)
www.chase.com
Author's Overall Appraisal
Progressing somewhat
Consumer Cautions
None
Important Considerations
Affiliated with groups supportive of gay and lesbian rights
Diversity training inclusive of people with disabilities
Exceptional workplace record supporting parents
Listed as a Fortune 500 Company
Listed on Standard & Poor's Index
Supports AIDS services/men's health groups
Supports breast cancer research/women's health groups
Workplace Record on Sexual Orientation
Diversity training inclusive of sexual orientation
Domestic-partnership health care benefits delayed until 1999
Gay and lesbian employee group acknowledged
Written sexual orientation nondiscrimination policy statement
Company Overview
In 1996 Chemical Bank and Chase Manhattan Bank merged. The newly formed company became known as Chase Manhattan. It is now the largest bank in the United States, and one with a leading record on supporting AIDS education in local communities. Chase Manhattan provides services to individual and commercial customers in a multitude of areas, including equity underwriting, foreign currency, and business finance. The company just recently got around to extending domestic-partnership health care coverage to its gay and lesbian employees.

Chubb Corp.

15 Mountain View Road
Warren, NJ 07059
(800) 248-2275 (toll-free)
(908) 903-2000
www.chubb.com

Author's Overall Appraisal

Progressive

Consumer Cautions

None

Important Considerations

Affiliated with groups supportive of gay and lesbian rights
Full domestic-partnership health care benefits
Has advertised in the gay and lesbian press
Supports AIDS services/men's health groups
Supports breast cancer research/women's health groups

Workplace Record on Sexual Orientation

Diversity training inclusive of sexual orientation
Encouraging remarks from vendors or gay and lesbian employees
Gay and lesbian employee group officially acknowledged

Company Overview

According to confidential employee reports, the company's management has celebrated Gay Pride Month for the past three years. There have been programs on sexual orientation–related matters, including the film *It's Elementary,* presented by diversity counselor and speaker Brian McNaught. The general atmosphere at Chubb was termed by one employee as "polite." Other employees said there are plenty of individuals within the company who are not accepting of gay people.

Citicorp Citibank

399 Park Avenue
New York, NY 10043
(301) 714-5326 (corporate)
(212) 627-3999 (customer service)
(212) 559-5138 (fax)
www.citibank.com

Author's Overall Appraisal
Progressing too slowly

Consumer Cautions
Affiliated with groups less than supportive of gay and lesbian rights
Possible overseas labor problems
No domestic partner healthcare benefits

Important Considerations
Exceptional workplace record supporting parents
Has included gay- or lesbian-suggestive imagery in mainstream advertising or programming
Stock is held by the Meyers Pride Value Fund
Supports AIDS services/men's health groups
Supports breast cancer research/women's health groups

Workplace Record on Sexual Orientation
Gay and lesbian employee group
Written sexual orientation nondiscrimination policy statement

Company Overview
Some representatives of gay and lesbian organizations, most notably the New York Lesbian and Gay Community Center, have good things to say about Citicorp's willingness to contribute to and sponsor community events. But when you consider the company's size and influence in the American banking industry and the overall world economy, the company can hardly be considered a leader on gay and lesbian issues.

The company has recently formed a gay and lesbian marketing group. Whether this is a signal that things are changing for the better remains unclear.

H&R Block
4410 Main St.
Kansas City, MO 64111
(816) 753-6900
www.handrblock.com

Author's Overall Appraisal
Progressing slowly

Consumer Cautions
No domestic partner healthcare benefits

Important Considerations
Listed on Standard & Poor's Index
Listed on Domini Social Index

Workplace Record on Sexual Orientation
Diversity training inclusive of sexual orientation
Gay and lesbian employee group
Written sexual orientation nondiscrimination policy statement

Company Overview
H&R Block is the parent of H&R Block Tax Service, the most well-known tax preparation company and franchiser of tax service outlets in the United States. Many of these outlets are located in Sears stores. H&R Block also owns Option One Mortgage, Block Financial, and Block Investment. The company no longer holds stock in CompuServe.

J.P. Morgan & Co.
60 Wall St.
New York, NY 10260
(212) 483-2323
(212) 648-5213 (fax)
www.jpmorgan.com

Author's Overall Appraisal
Progressive

Consumer Cautions
Possible overseas labor problems

Important Considerations
Affiliated with groups supportive of gay and lesbian rights
Exceptional workplace record supporting parents
Listed as a Fortune 500 Company
Listed on Domini Social Index
Significantly visible supporter of ENDA
Supports AIDS services/men's health groups
Supports breast cancer research/women's health groups

Workplace Record on Sexual Orientation
Diversity training inclusive of sexual orientation
Full domestic-partnership health care benefits
Gay and lesbian employee group
Written sexual orientation nondiscrimination policy statement

Company Overview
J.P. Morgan is a premier multinational banking company with about 16,000 employees worldwide. The company's services include well as investment banking, brokerage services, and asset management. It advises corporate clients on business strategies such as mergers and acquisitions. There are also reportedly out gay employees at the highest levels of the company.

Kinder, Lydenberg, Domini, & Co.

129 Mount Auburn St.
Cambridge, MA 02138
(617) 547-7479
(617) 354-5353 (fax)
www.kld.com

Author's Overall Appraisal
Progressive

Consumer Cautions
Invests in companies that do not offer domestic partner health insurance

Important Considerations
Diversity training inclusive of people with disabilities
Listed on GLV 100 Index
Supporter of ENDA
Supports AIDS services/men's health groups
Supports breast cancer research/women's health groups

Workplace Record on Sexual Orientation
Diversity training inclusive of sexual orientation
Full domestic-partnership health care benefits
Gay and lesbian employee group
Written sexual orientation nondiscrimination policy statement

Company Overview
Kinder, Lydenberg, Domini & Co. was founded in 1988. It provides social research on corporations for institutional investors. Although it is registered as an investment adviser with the U.S. Securities and Exchange Commission, it does not manage money. Instead, KLD publishes reports on 650 securities issuers and tracks the performance of more than 4,000 domestic and foreign companies. The firm is well-known for its Domini 400 Social Index, the benchmark for measuring the performance of socially screened portfolios. (A listing of the DSI 400 is provided in the appendix.) KLD provides social research to the no-load Domini Social Equity Fund, managed by Mellon Equity Associates. KLD also produces Socrates software, a corporate social ratings monitor program.

In 1992 *The Social Investment Almanac*, edited by Peter D. Kinder, Steven D. Lydenberg, and Amy L. Domini, was published by Henry Holt & Co. The book provides a wealth of information on practically every social issue (other than sexual orientation). Socially responsible investors will find it an invaluable resource.

Lincoln Financial Group

200 East Barry
Fort Wayne, IN 46801
(219) 455-2000
(219) 455-4268 (fax)
www.lnc.com

Author's Overall Appraisal
Progressive

Consumer Cautions
Possible overseas labor problems

Important Considerations
Affiliated with groups supportive of gay and lesbian rights
Diversity training inclusive of people with disabilities
Exceptional workplace record supporting parents
Has advertised in the gay and lesbian press
Listed as a Fortune 500 Company
Listed on Domini Social Index
Listed on Meyers Pride Value Fund
Supports AIDS services/men's health groups
Supports breast cancer research/women's health groups

Workplace Record on Sexual Orientation
Diversity training inclusive of sexual orientation
Full domestic-partnership health care benefits
Gay and lesbian employee group
Written sexual orientation nondiscrimination policy statement

Company Overview
Lincoln Financial Group, which includes Lincoln National Corp. and affiliated companies, employs about 10,000 people worldwide. It is one of the largest providers of individual annuities, life insurance, life and health reinsurance, 401(k) plans, institutional investment management, and mutual funds.

Merrill Lynch
250 Vesey St.
World Trade Center, North Tower
New York, New York 10291
(212) 449-1000
(212) 236-2363 (human resources)
www.merrilllynch.com

Author's Overall Appraisal
Progressive

Consumer Cautions
One of the last large financial institutions to implement domestic-partner health care benefits

Important Considerations
Has advertised to gay and lesbian consumers through direct mail and telemarketing

Workplace Record on Sexual Orientation
Diversity training inclusive of sexual orientation
Full domestic-partnership health care benefits
Written sexual orientation nondiscrimination policy statement

Company Overview
Merrill Lynch, one of America's largest brokerage houses, has been targeting gay and lesbian investors for about five years. However, the company's plan to implement domestic-partnership health care coverage did not go into effect until January of 1999.

Meyers Capital Management LLC/ Meyers Pride Value Fund

8901 Wilshire Blvd.
Beverly Hills, CA 90211
(800) 410-3337 (toll-free)
(310) 657-9393
(310) 657-9380 (fax)
www.pridefund.com

Author's Overall Appraisal
Very progressive

Consumer Cautions
Invests in companies that do not have domestic partner health benefits

Important Considerations
Affiliated with groups supportive of gay and lesbian rights
Early supporter of ENDA
Exceptional workplace record supporting parents
Gay- and lesbian-owned company
Has advertised in the gay and lesbian press
Has included gay- or lesbian-suggestive imagery in mainstream advertising or programming
Listed on GLV 100 Index
Supports AIDS services/men's health groups
Supports breast cancer research/women's health groups

Workplace Record on Sexual Orientation
Full domestic-partnership health care benefits
Gay and lesbian employee group
Written sexual orientation nondiscrimination policy statement

Company Overview
In the summer of 1996, Shelly J. Meyers launched the Meyers Pride Value Fund, the first world's first public gay and lesbian investment fund. The majority of the company is lesbian- and gay-owned, and over 50% of the staff is gay or lesbian. The rationale behind the Pride Value Fund is that enterprises responsive to the concerns of gays and lesbians and other socially sensitive constituencies will benefit financially from consumer loyalty generated by such social awareness. Furthermore, those companies will be less likely to incur legal liabilities that can arise as a result of discrimination.

Readers should be aware that a company does not have to have domestic-partnership benefits to be included in the Pride Fund's portfolio. But companies must prove they have a written nondiscrimination policy statement regarding sexual orientation.

Principal Financial Group

711 High St.
Des Moines, IA 50392-0300
(515) 247-5111
(515) 246-5475 (fax)
www.principal.com

Author's Overall Appraisal

Progressive

Consumer Cautions

None

Important Considerations

Affiliated with groups supportive of gay and lesbian rights
Diversity training inclusive of people with disabilities
Significantly visible supporter of ENDA
Supports AIDS services/men's health groups
Supports breast cancer research/women's health groups

Workplace Record on Sexual Orientation

Diversity training inclusive of sexual orientation
Encouraging remarks from vendors or gay and lesbian employees
Full domestic-partnership health care benefits
Gay and lesbian employee group
Written sexual orientation nondiscrimination policy statement

Company Overview

The Principal Financial Group employs approximately 18,000 people and is known as a company with strong executive leadership on HIV/AIDS and gay and lesbian workplace issues. Its lines of business include group life and health insurance, commercial banking, mutual funds, and residential mortgages.

Provident Financial Group Inc.

One E. 4th St.
Cincinnati, OH 45202
(513) 579-2000
(513) 345-7190 (fax)
www.provident-bank.com

Author's Overall Appraisal

Progressing

Consumer Cautions

No survey response

Important Considerations

Affiliated with groups supportive of gay and lesbian rights

Has included gay- or lesbian-suggestive imagery in mainstream advertising or programming

Workplace Record on Sexual Orientation

Written sexual orientation nondiscrimination policy statement

Company Overview

Provident Financial Group, the nation's 60th largest bank holding company, provides banking services to consumers and businesses through the Provident Bank and Provident Bank of Florida. The company's largest shareholder is Carl Lindner, who is chairman and CEO of three other companies: American Financial Group, chiefly involved in insurance; the food company Chiquita Brands International Inc.; and the Great American Group of Insurance Companies. Sources say Provident Financial has a written nondiscrimination policy statement on sexual orientation, but this has not been officially confirmed.

St. Paul Cos.
385 Washington St.
St. Paul, MN 55102
(612) 310-7911
(612) 221-8294 (fax)
www.stpaul.com

Author's Overall Appraisal
Progressive

Consumer Cautions
None

Important Considerations
Diversity training inclusive of people with disabilities
Listed as a Fortune 500 company
Listed on Domini Social Index
Listed on GLV 100 Index
Stock held by Meyers Pride Value Fund
Supports AIDS services/men's health groups

Workplace Record on Sexual Orientation
Diversity training inclusive of sexual orientation
Full domestic-partnership health care benefits
Gay and lesbian employee group
Written sexual orientation nondiscrimination policy statement

Company Overview
St. Paul provides property-liability and life insurance and reinsurance worldwide. It is also involved in investment management as majority owner of the John Nuveen Co.

Trillium Asset Management

711 Atlantic Ave.
Boston, MA 02111-2809
(800) 548-5684 (toll-free)
(617) 423-6655
(617) 482-6179 (fax)
www.frdc.com

Author's Overall Appraisal
Very progressive

Consumer Cautions
None

Important Considerations
Affiliated with many groups supportive of gay and lesbian rights
Early supporter of ENDA
Has advertised in the gay and lesbian press
Has lead or supported numerous shareholder resolutions on sexual orientation
Listed on GLV 100 Index
Supports AIDS services/men's health groups
Supports breast cancer research/women's health groups

Workplace Record on Sexual Orientation
Full domestic-partnership health care benefits
Written sexual orientation nondiscrimination policy statement

Company Overview

Trillium Asset Management (formerly Franklin Research and Development) provides investment services to institutional and individual clients who want their dollars to make a positive difference on social and environmental issues. Among other things, it has urged companies in which it invests to adopt policies against discrimination based on sexual orientation. Trillium's shareholder resolutions have led several Fortune 500 companies to put such policies in place.

Trillium, a majority employee- and women-owned firm, is involved in every conceivable human rights issue. The company testified in the Massachusetts and Connecticut legislatures in support of selective-purchasing laws concerning products made in Myanmar (formerly Burma), which has a poor record on human rights. This pressure resulted in decisions by Apple, Kodak, Hewlett-Packard, and Philips Electronics to cease business operations in Myanmar.

U.S. Bancorp Piper Jaffray
Piper Jaffray Tower
222 S. Ninth St.
Minneapolis, MN 55402-3804
800-468-9716 (transfer agent and registrar)
(612) 342-6000
www.piperjaffray.com/

Author's Overall Appraisal
Very progressive

Consumer Cautions
None

Important Considerations
Affiliated with groups supportive of gay and lesbian rights
Diversity training inclusive of people with disabilities
Exceptional workplace record supporting parents
Listed as a Fortune 500 Company
Listed on Domini Social Index
Significantly visible supporter of ENDA
Supports AIDS services/men's health groups

Workplace Record on Sexual Orientation
Diversity training inclusive of sexual orientation
Encouraging remarks from vendors or gay and lesbian employees
Full domestic-partnership health care benefits
Gay and lesbian employee group officially acknowledged
Written sexual orientation nondiscrimination policy statement

Company Overview
U.S. Bancorp Piper Jaffray is the 11th largest brokerage firm in the nation. Its products and services include stock and bond trades, securities analysis and research, investment banking, and venture capital funds. Formerly known as Piper Jaffray Companies Inc., it was acquired by U.S. Bancorp in 1998, with the name change coming in 1999. The company is likely to maintain its commitments to progressive workplace policies for gays and lesbians and to a wide range of civic projects. The company and its foundation have historically dedicated 5% of pretax income to charitable activities. They disbursed more than $2.5 million in 1998.

Wainwright Bank and Trust

63 Franklin St.
Boston, MA 02110
(617) 478-4000
www.wainwrightbank.com

Author's Overall Appraisal
Very progressive

Consumer Cautions
None

Important Considerations
Affiliated with groups supportive of gay and lesbian rights
Has advertised in the gay and lesbian press
Listed on GLV 100 Index
Supports AIDS services/men's health groups
Supports breast cancer research/women's health groups

Workplace Record on Sexual Orientation
Full domestic-partnership health care benefits
Written sexual orientation nondiscrimination policy statement

Company Overview
Wainwright Bank provides personal and business banking services, including checking and savings accounts, certificates of deposit, and credit cards. It also owns 30% of Trillium Asset Management. Wainwright has a socially responsible corporate agenda that embraces diversity, affordable housing efforts, community development, women's rights, advancement of people of color, and equal rights for gays and lesbians. It has offered domestic-partner benefits since 1994, and its lobbying convinced all 160 of the Massachusetts Bankers Association's member banks to offer such benefits too. It has received awards from gay rights groups such as the Human Rights Campaign and the Lesbian and Gay Political Alliance of Massachusetts as well as organizations focusing on other social issues. The Association of Affirmative Action Professionals, for instance, lauded Wainwright's "creativity and cutting-edge leadership." Half of its officers are women, and half of its directors are women, minorities, gays, or lesbians. Its retail services staff is fluent in more than a dozen languages.

Wells Fargo

420 Montgomery St.
San Francisco, CA 94163
(415) 477-1000
(415) 362-6958 (fax)
http://wellsfargo.com/home/

Author's Overall Appraisal
Progressive

Consumer Cautions
Possible overseas labor problems

Important Considerations
Affiliated with groups supportive of gay and lesbian rights
Diversity training inclusive of people with disabilities
Has advertised in the gay and lesbian press
Includes gay- or lesbian-suggestive imagery in mainstream advertising or programming
Listed on Domini Social Index
Supports AIDS services/men's health groups
Supports breast cancer research/women's health groups

Workplace Record on Sexual Orientation
Diversity training inclusive of sexual orientation
Full domestic-partnership health care benefits
Gay and lesbian employee group officially acknowledged
Written sexual orientation nondiscrimination policy statement

Company Overview
Wells Fargo is one of the largest banks in the United States, with more than $200 billion in assets, nearly 6,000 locations, and 102,000 employees. It provides a full range of consumer and business banking services, including residential mortgages, institutional investment management, venture capital, and foreign exchange, and it has the nation's largest bank-affiliated insurance agency, Norwest Insurance. Wells Fargo HSBC Trade Bank, a joint venture with HSBC Group, specializes in banking services for U.S. companies involved in international trade. Walter Annenberg and Warren Buffett are significant shareholders in Wells Fargo.

Working Assets

701 Montgomery St.
San Francisco, CA 94111
(415) 788-0777
(415) 788-7572 (fax)
www.wald.com

Author's Overall Appraisal

Very progressive

Consumer Cautions

None

Important Considerations

Affiliated with groups supportive of gay and lesbian rights
Diversity training inclusive of people with disabilities
Exceptional workplace record supporting parents
Has advertised in the gay and lesbian press
Includes gay- or lesbian-suggestive imagery in mainstream advertising or programming
Listed on Domini Social Index
Listed on GLV 100 Index
Supports AIDS services/men's health groups
Supports breast cancer research/women's health groups

Workplace Record on Sexual Orientation

Diversity training inclusive of sexual orientation
Full domestic-partnership health care benefits
Gay and lesbian employee group officially acknowledged
Written sexual orientation nondiscrimination policy statement

Company Overview

Working Assets, in business since 1985, helps consumers support non-profit groups, charities, and human rights concerns. By using the company's long-distance telephone service, Working Assets Visa card, or new online shopping service, customers can make a social impact with every phone call they make or dollar they spend. The company puts a portion of its proceeds into a pool that funds charities. The Working Assets board of directors selects each year's funding recipients based on customer nominations, and then customers vote to determine which groups will get how much of the donations pool. Most recently, Working Assets has contributed to the National Minority AIDS Council, Breast Cancer Action, and the Black Women's Health Project.

Clothing and Sportswear

The majority of clothing manufacturers, retailers, and catalog merchandisers are not progressive on issues relating to sexual orientation in the workplace. Less than 25% of the nation's largest clothing, shoe, and accessories retailers offer domestic-partner health care insurance for their gay and lesbian employees.

Furthermore, the apparel industry's record on overseas labor issues is suspect, as vendor relationships and subcontracting agreements change frequently. Consumers concerned about such issues will need to look beyond this book to adequately track each company's record on sweatshop activity.

General Industry Resources:

American Textile Manufacturers Institute
  www.atmi.org
Angel of Fashion
  www.fashionangel.com/angel.html
Fashion Planet
  www.fashion-planet.com
International Fashion and Fiber Buyers Network
  www.kenpubs.co.uk/texinst/index.html
Industrial Fabrics Association International
  www.ifai.com/
The Textile Institute
  texi.org/index-a.htm

Abercrombie & Fitch

4 Limited Parkway
Reynoldsburgh, OH 43068
(614) 577-6500
www.abercrombie.com

Author's Overall Appraisal
Progressing somewhat

Consumer Cautions
No domestic-partnership health care benefits
Possible overseas labor problems
No longer owned by The Limited, Inc.

Important Considerations
Affiliated with groups supportive of gay and lesbian rights
Has advertised in the gay and lesbian press
Has included gay- or lesbian-suggestive imagery in mainstream advertising or programming

Workplace Record on Sexual Orientation
Encouraging remarks from vendors or gay and lesbian employees
Written sexual orientation nondiscrimination policy statement

Company Overview
Sportswear retailer Abercrombie & Fitch has unabashedly placed gay-identifiable advertising in both gay and nongay magazines—with great success. The advertisements are beautiful and have been well-received by the public. The company is an aggressive supporter of the United Way, offering an employee matching funds program, but not domestic-partner health care benefits.

Adidas-Salomon AG
Adi-Dassler-Strasse 2
91074 Herzogenaurach, Germany
+49-9132-840
+49-9132-842241 (fax)
www.adidas.com

Author's Overall Appraisal
Progressing too slowly

Consumer Cautions
No survey response
Non–gay-related boycott activity

Important Considerations
Unknown

Workplace Record on Sexual Orientation
Unknown

Company Overview
Adidas-Salomon (previously known as Adidas) is one of the top five sportswear, sports equipment, and footwear providers in the United States. Its biggest competitors are Nike and Reebok. Adidas-Salomon has been targeted by the International Wildlife Coalition along with three other companies—Browning, Florsheim, and Puma—for allegedly utilizing endangered Australian kangaroo skins in shoe production.

With no survey response, it is difficult to know where the company stands on issues of interest to gay and lesbian employees and consumers.

Dayton Hudson

777 Nicollet Mall
Minneapolis, MN 55402
(612) 370-6948
(612) 370-5502 (fax)
www.dhc.com

Author's Overall Appraisal
Progressing somewhat

Consumer Cautions
Possible overseas labor problems

Important Considerations
Affiliated with groups supportive of gay and lesbian rights
Diversity training inclusive of people with disabilities
Listed as a Fortune 500 Company
Listed on Domini Social Index
Listed on Standard & Poor's Index
Supports AIDS services/men's health groups
Supports breast cancer research/women's health groups

Workplace Record on Sexual Orientation
Diversity training inclusive of sexual orientation
Gay and lesbian employee group
Mixed remarks from vendors or gay and lesbian employees
Written sexual orientation nondiscrimination policy statement

Company Overview

Contrary to previously published reports, Dayton Hudson does not provide full domestic-partnership health care coverage to its gay and lesbian employees—although such benefits are said to be under consideration.

Dayton Hudson employs approximately 214,000 people. The company owns Dayton's, Hudson's, Target, Mervyn's, and Marshall Field's. Target is huge and competes against Wal-Mart and Kmart. If you shop at big retail chains and superstores for household items and discounted merchandise, go with Dayton Hudson stores. The company may not have curiously trendy spokespeople like Rosie O'Donnell, but it has a better record than its competitors on sexual orientation issues.

Popular Name Brands or Key Industry Products
28 Shop Apparel, Baby's Favorites, Baxter, Marona, Personal Record, Good Mast, Greatland, Seaside Collection, Sostanza, Trend Basics.

Donna Karan Inc.
40 W. 40th St.
New York, NY 10018
(212) 730-5271
www.donnakaran.com

Author's Overall Appraisal

Very progressive

Consumer Cautions

None

Important Considerations

Affiliated with groups supportive of gay and lesbian rights

Exceptional workplace record supporting parents

Has advertised in the gay and lesbian press

Has included gay- or lesbian-suggestive imagery in mainstream advertising or programming

Listed on GLV 100 Index

Supports AIDS services/men's health groups

Supports breast cancer research/women's health groups

Workplace Record on Sexual Orientation

Encouraging remarks from vendors or gay and lesbian employees

Full domestic-partnership health care benefits

Gay and lesbian employee group

Written sexual orientation nondiscrimination policy statement

Company Overview

It was a principled heterosexual woman, Donna Karan, who first brought domestic-partnership health care insurance to gay and lesbian employees in the fashion industry. So if you want to be both fashionable and politically correct, you'll wear Donna Karan clothing.

Donna Karan and DKNY offer men's and women's clothing, shoes, and athletic wear. The name is also associated with licenses involving everything from home furnishings and bras to children's clothing, fragrances, and hosiery.

Federated Department Stores Inc.
7 W. 7th St.
Cincinnati, OH 45202
(513) 579-7000
(513) 579-7555 (fax)
www.federated-fds.com

Author's Overall Appraisal
Progressing somewhat

Consumer Cautions
No survey response
No domestic partner healthcare confirmed

Important Considerations
Supports AIDS services/men's health groups
Supports breast cancer research/women's health groups

Workplace Record on Sexual Orientation
Diversity training inclusive of sexual orientation
Written sexual orientation nondiscrimination policy statement

Company Overview
Federated has more than 400 stores in 33 states. Its stores include Bloomingdale's, Macy's, Bon Marché, Burdines, Stern's, Rich's, Lazarus, and Goldsmith's. It also sells merchandise through catalogs and Web sites. Federated has made limited efforts to target the gay and lesbian market through direct-mail programs.

Gap Inc.
One Harrison
San Francisco, CA 94105
(650) 952-4400
(650) 952-4069 (fax)
www.gap.com

Author's Overall Appraisal
Progressive

Consumer Cautions
Possible overseas labor problems

Important Considerations
Diversity training inclusive of people with disabilities
Has advertised in the gay and lesbian press
Has included gay- or lesbian-suggestive imagery in mainstream advertising or programming
Listed as a Fortune 500 Company
Listed on GLV 100 Index
Listed on Standard & Poor's Index
Significantly visible supporter of ENDA
Supports AIDS services/men's health groups
Supports breast cancer research/women's health groups

Workplace Record on Sexual Orientation
Encouraging remarks from vendors or gay and lesbian employees
Full domestic-partnership health care benefits
Gay and lesbian employee group
Written sexual orientation nondiscrimination policy statement

Company Overview
Gap Inc. founder Don Fisher opened his first store in 1969 on Ocean Avenue in San Francisco. In those days, he sold records and blue jeans. Now a massive retailer of trendy casual clothing, Gap operates outlets in the United States, England, France, Germany, Japan, and Canada.

Popular Name Brands or Key Industry Products
Baby Gap, GapKids, GapScents, Hemisphere, Old Navy Clothing Co., Gap, Banana Republic

Tommy Hilfiger Corp.
6/F, Precious Industrial Centre,
18 Cheung Yue St., Cheung Sha Wan
Kowloon, Hong Kong
+852-2745-7798
+852-2312-1368 (fax)
www.tommypr.com

Author's Overall Appraisal
Progressing too slowly

Consumer Cautions
No survey response

Important Considerations
Unknown

Workplace Record on Sexual Orientation
Unknown

Company Overview
Tommy Hilfiger's biggest competitors are Calvin Klein and Nautica. Hilfiger's fashions are a favorite among hip-hop youth, and the company also has a strong presence in men's and women's casual wear and athletic wear. The company is involved extensively in licensing of the Tommy Hilfiger name for fragrances, accessories, athletic bags, and sporting gear. Tommy Hilfiger brands are sold in department stores and about 50 Hilfiger branded retail outlets.

JC Penney
P.O. Box 10001
Dallas, TX 75301-4301
(800) 953-9421 (toll-free shareholder information)
(800) 222-6161 (customer service and catalog sales)
(972) 431-1000
www.jcpenney.com

Author's Overall Appraisal
Progressing too slowly

Consumer Cautions
Possible overseas labor problems
No domestic partner healthcare benefits

Important Considerations
Diversity training inclusive of people with disabilities
Listed on Domini Social Index
Listed on Standard & Poor's Index
Stock held by Meyers Pride Value Fund
Supports breast cancer research/women's health groups

Workplace Record on Sexual Orientation
Diversity training inclusive of sexual orientation
Mixed remarks from vendors or gay and lesbian employees
Written sexual orientation nondiscrimination policy statement

Company Overview
JC Penney has reinvented itself a number of times in its nearly 100-year history. It sells goods by mail order as well as its department stores. In addition to its own brands, it is a leading retailer of other clothing lines, including Nike, Warners, Vanity Fair, Oshkosh B'Gosh, and Levi's. JC Penney also operates the JC Penney Insurance Group, the nation's number one mass marketer of group life and health insurance products. Total annual sales for JC Penney have hovered around $16 billion in recent years.

Kenneth Cole

152 W. 57th St.
New York, NY 10019
(212) 265-1500
(212) 265-1662 (fax)
www.kencole.com

Author's Overall Appraisal
Progressing too slowly

Consumer Cautions
Possible overseas labor problems
Refused to participate in survey

Important Considerations
Has advertised in the gay and lesbian press

Workplace Record on Sexual Orientation
Mixed remarks from vendors or gay and lesbian employees

Company Overview
Kenneth Cole was contacted regarding this book, and a spokesperson explained that the company does not disclose information about its employment policies or employee benefits packages. The company may be perceived to be gay- and lesbian-friendly since it has advertised its products with gay-positive messages, and the company's shoe line is a favorite among gay men. Since the company won't disclose its policies, though, gay and lesbian consumers can't really know if Kenneth Cole's business practices match the gay-friendly image it projects. The company employs over 500 people and sells shoes, bags, belts, eyewear, and luggage.

Lands' End

Lands' End Lane
Dodgeville, WI 53595
(800) 356-4444 (catalog)
(608) 935-9341
www.landsend.com

Author's Overall Appraisal

Progressing too slowly

Consumer Cautions

No domestic partner healthcare benefits
No written nondiscrimination policy statement on sexual orientation

Important Considerations

Listed on Domini Social Index

Workplace Record on Sexual Orientation

Mixed remarks from vendors or gay and lesbian employees

Company Overview

Lands' End is a leading merchant of traditionally styled, casual clothing for men, women, and children. It also sells accessories, domestic furnishings, shoes, and soft luggage. The company makes its products available primarily through direct-mail solicitation with a monthly catalog. It also makes custom-designed catalogs available to specifically targeted customers. The company is a master at customer service and a primary competitor of L.L. Bean. In 1995 Lands' End launched an Internet shopping site.

Levi Strauss & Co.
1155 Battery St.
San Francisco, CA 94111
(415) 544-6000
(415) 544-1653 (fax)
www.levistrauss.com

Author's Overall Appraisal
Very progressive

Consumer Cautions
Labor operations are being moved overseas

Important Considerations
Affiliated with groups supportive of gay and lesbian rights
Contributes to gay and lesbian nonprofit groups
Contributes to gay and lesbian political organizations
Diversity training inclusive of people with disabilities
Early and significantly visible supporter of ENDA
Exceptional workplace record supporting parents
Has advertised in the gay and lesbian press
Includes gay- or lesbian-suggestive imagery in mainstream advertising or programming
Listed on GLV 100 Index
Supports AIDS services/men's health groups
Supports breast cancer research/women's health groups

Workplace Record on Sexual Orientation
Diversity training inclusive of sexual orientation
Encouraging remarks from vendors or gay and lesbian employees
Full domestic-partnership health care benefits
Gay and lesbian employee group officially acknowledged
Written sexual orientation nondiscrimination policy statement

Company Overview
Levi Strauss is widely known for blue jeans, casual wear, and Dockers brand slacks. The corporation operates company-owned Levi specialty stores in selected markets. Levi Strauss is not shy about its gay and lesbian themed advertising. The November 1998 issue of *Out* magazine contained a 12-page insert showing lesbians and gay men wearing Dockers pants. The models included actor-writer Guinevere Turner, actor Wilson Cruz, and photographer Eve Fowler.

A telling anecdote about Levi Strauss comes in the form of an unverifiable but widely circulated rumor regarding an incident that occurred just prior to the company's implementation of domestic-partnership health care coverage: A senior-level Levi's executive responded to a threatened boycott of the company by religious radicals over implementation of the new gay-friendly policy by stating, "Who do you really think supports our company? Who do you really think will buy more blue jeans over time?" Furthermore, the company ceased funding of the Boy Scouts of America after the organization declared homosexuality morally wrong.

Lillian Vernon
1 Theall Road
Rye, NY 10580
(914) 925-1300
(914) 925-1400 (fax)
www.lillianvernon.com

Author's Overall Appraisal
Very progressive

Consumer Cautions
None

Important Considerations
Affiliated with groups supportive of gay and lesbian rights
Contributes to gay and lesbian nonprofit groups
Contributes to gay and lesbian political organizations
Exceptional workplace record supporting parents
Listed on GLV 100 Index
Supports AIDS services/men's health groups
Supports breast cancer research/women's health groups

Workplace Record on Sexual Orientation
Diversity training inclusive of sexual orientation
Encouraging remarks from vendors or gay and lesbian employees
Full domestic-partnership health care benefits
Gay and lesbian employee group officially acknowledged
Written sexual orientation nondiscrimination policy statement

Company Overview

Lillian Vernon is a catalog merchandiser focusing on gift, household, gardening, kitchen, and children's products. The company does just about everything right when it comes to sexual orientation. There are reportedly out and acknowledged gay employees working at all levels of the company. The company mailed over 178 million catalogs in 1998. For that fiscal year, its revenues were approximately $258 million.

The Limited
Three Limited Parkway
Columbus, Ohio 43230
(614) 415-8000
www.limited.com

Author's Overall Appraisal
Very progressive

Consumer Cautions
No longer owns Abercrombie and Fitch

Important Considerations
Affiliated with groups supportive of gay and lesbian rights
Diversity training inclusive of people with disabilities
Has included gay- or lesbian-suggestive imagery in mainstream advertising or programming
Supports AIDS services/men's health groups
Supports breast cancer research/women's health groups

Workplace Record on Sexual Orientation
Diversity training inclusive of sexual orientation
Encouraging remarks from vendors or gay and lesbian employees
Full domestic-partnership health care benefits
Gay and lesbian employee group
Written sexual orientation nondiscrimination policy statement

Company Overview
The Limited Inc. is one of the country's largest employers, with over 131,000 employees and more than 3,400 retail outlets operating under the names Express, Lerner New York, Lane Bryant, Limited, Limited Too, Structure, Galyan's, and Henri Bendel. The company extended full domestic-partner health care benefits to its employees effective April 1, 1999. The company also extended adoption assistance benefits to all employees, gay or straight, single or partnered. The Limited is a publicly held company valued at $9.3 billion. Leslie Wexner is the CEO, founder, and largest shareholder, with 24% of the outstanding stock.

The Limited is the majority shareholder in Intimate Brands, which owns Victoria's Secret, a retailer of lingerie and personal accessories, and Bath and Body Works, which sells soaps, lotions, bath gels, and related products>. As of mid 1999 there were 849 Victoria's Secret stores and 1,101 Bath and Body Works outlets. The company also distributes apparel around the world via its popular Victoria's Secret Catalogue.

Liz Claiborne
1441 Broadway
New York, NY 07047
(212) 354-4900
(212) 626-3416 (fax)
www.lizclaiborne.com

Author's Overall Appraisal
Progressive

Consumer Cautions
None

Important Considerations
Full domestic-partnership health care benefits
Listed on Domini Social Index
Supports AIDS services/men's health groups
Supports breast cancer research/women's health groups

Workplace Record on Sexual Orientation
Gay and lesbian employee group
Encouraging remarks from vendors or gay and lesbian employees
Written sexual orientation nondiscrimination policy statement

Company Overview
Liz Claiborne, which employs over 7,000 people, manufactures and distributes merchandise including clothing, shoes, and home furnishings. It sells goods through department stores and more than 200 of its own specialty stores nationwide. It has made a name for itself by offering a variety of clothing styles at varying prices. The company is known for its support of causes related to women's health and advancement.

Nike Inc.
1 Bowerman Drive
Beaverton, OR 97005-6453
(503) 671-6453
(503) 671-6300 (fax)
http://info.nike.com

Author's Overall Appraisal
Progressing too slowly

Consumer Cautions
Affiliated with groups less than supportive of gay and lesbian rights
Non–gay-related boycott activity
Possible overseas labor problems

Important Considerations
Contributes to many groups supportive of youth

Workplace Record on Sexual Orientation
No written sexual orientation nondiscrimination policy statement
Domestic-partnership health care benefits

Company Overview
Nike, the world's biggest sportswear manufacturer, sells products in over 100 countries. The company makes nearly half of all the athletic shoes sold in the United States.

Despite Nike's progressive workplace policies, the company has refused to distance itself from one of its corporate spokespeople, antigay former Green Bay Packers football player Reggie White. White gave a well-publicized speech to the Wisconsin state legislature in 1998 in which he stated that homosexuality is sinful and that it contributes to the breakdown of the family. He also suggested that homosexuals are dishonest. Nike responded with a statement supporting White's right to freedom of speech.

Since that incident, White has continued to speak out against homosexuality, allowing pictures of himself in his Packers uniform (contrary to National Football League policy) to appear in radical right-wing fund-raising letters with headlines such as "Reggie White Toes the Line Against Homosexuality." Many gays and lesbians cannot understand why Nike has ignored this issue, especially since Nike was previously known for being diversity-conscious.

Chairman and CEO Philip H. Knight owns more than one third of the company's stock.

Nordstrom

1321 2nd Ave.
Seattle, WA 98101
(206) 628-2111
(206) 628-1795 (fax)
www.nordstrom-pta.com

Author's Overall Appraisal

Progressing somewhat

Consumer Cautions

Possible overseas labor problems

Important Considerations

Affiliated with groups supportive of gay and lesbian rights
Diversity training inclusive of people with disabilities
Listed as a Fortune 500 Company
Listed on Domini Social Index
Supports AIDS services/men's health groups
Supports breast cancer research/women's health groups

Workplace Record on Sexual Orientation

Diversity training inclusive of sexual orientation
Encouraging remarks from vendors or gay and lesbian employees
Domestic-partnership health care benefits under consideration
Written sexual orientation nondiscrimination policy statement

Company Overview

Nordstrom has approximately 40,000 employees nationwide. The company does not offer domestic-partner benefits, but several sources say such benefits are under consideration.

Reebok

100 Technology Center Drive
Stoughton, MA 02072
(781) 341-5000
(781) 341-7402 (fax)
www.reebok.com

Author's Overall Appraisal
Progressive

Consumer Cautions
Possible overseas labor problems

Important Considerations
Affiliated with groups supportive of gay and lesbian rights
Diversity training inclusive of people with disabilities
Has advertised in the gay and lesbian press
Has included gay- or lesbian-suggestive imagery in mainstream advertising or programming
Supports AIDS services/men's health groups
Supports breast cancer research/women's health groups

Workplace Record on Sexual Orientation
Diversity training inclusive of sexual orientation
Encouraging remarks from vendors or gay and lesbian employees
Full domestic-partnership health care benefits
Gay and lesbian employee group
Written sexual orientation nondiscrimination policy statement

Company Overview
Reebok, which employs approximately 7,000 people, is the world's second largest manufacturer of athletic shoes, but it's the top athletic shoe company when it comes to policies affecting gays and lesbians. Reebok was first athletic shoe manufacturer to offer domestic-partnership health care coverage to its gay and lesbian employees. Reebok products are endorsed by socially conscious athletes such as Emmitt Smith, Frank Thomas, and Michael Chang, whereas the company's main competitor, Nike, utilizes homophobic Reggie White as a spokesperson.Many athletic shoe companies have come under fire for everything from questionable celebrity endorsements to labor abuses in developing nations. Reebok, however, has largely avoided such problems. A Reebok subsidiary company, Rockport, also makes shoes—for dress and casual wear.

Sears

3333 Beverly Road
Hoffman Estates, IL 60179
(847) 286-2500
(847) 286-7829 (fax)
www.sears.com

Author's Overall Appraisal

Progressing too slowly

Consumer Cautions

Possible overseas labor problems
No domestic partner healthcare benefits

Important Considerations

Listed as a Fortune 500 Company
Listed on Domini Social Index

Workplace Record on Sexual Orientation

Diversity training inclusive of sexual orientation
Gay and lesbian employee group
Mixed remarks from vendors or gay and lesbian employees
Written sexual orientation nondiscrimination policy statement

Company Overview

With over 250,000 employees, Sears is one of the world's largest clothing and home furnishings retailers. Sears competes primarily with Wal-Mart, Kmart, and JC Penney. Most outlets are located in malls. Stock generally includes men's and women's apparel, auto parts, sporting equipment, appliances, and lawn care products.

Sears also provides in-home repair services for appliances it sells under such brand names as Kenmore. The company at one time had interests in Discover Card, Dean Witter Financial Services, and Allstate Insurance, but has divested itself of those operations, choosing to focus on its core business—retailing.

The Warnaco Group Inc.
90 Park Ave.
New York, NY 10016
(212) 661-1300
(212) 687-0480 (fax)
www.warnaco.com

Author's Overall Appraisal
Progressing too slowly

Consumer Cautions
No survey response
No domestic partner healthcare benefits

Important Considerations
Affiliated with groups supportive of gay and lesbian rights
Has included gay- or lesbian-suggestive imagery in mainstream advertising or programming
Supports AIDS services/men's health groups

Workplace Record on Sexual Orientation
Unknown

Company Overview
Warnaco Group, home of Calvin Klein briefs and menswear, is the biggest bra and underwear marketer in the United States. It is also a company thought to have one of the biggest queer followings in the retail world. Nevertheless, the company refused to divulge whether it has gay-friendly employment policies. Calvin Klein has aimed advertising at gays and lesbians, but smart spenders might benefit from comparison shopping. You could make a good start by examining the profiles in this section on Donna Karan and Gap.

Communications and Technology

The majority of communications and technology companies are exceptionally progressive on issues relating to sexual orientation in the workplace. Most have been offering domestic-partner health care insurance throughout the 1990s.

Unfortunately, some of the most progressive companies on sexual orientation issues have less than admirable records on labor conditions, ethics, and policies in Mexico, South America, and Southeast Asia.

General Industry Resources:

beyond.com
   www.beyond.com
Commercial Internet eXchange
   www.cix.org
Computerworld
   www.computerworld.com
International Data Corporation
   www.idcresearch.com
Internet Service Providers' Consortium
   www.ispc.org
Internet Society
   www.isoc.org
Internet World Daily
   www.internetworld.com/
MacWeek
   www8.zdnet.com/macweek
Network Solutions
   www.networksolutions.com
PCWeek
   www8.zdnet.com/pcweek
Shareware.com
   www.shareware.com

The Most Influential Companies / 71

Tucows Network—collection of Winsock software
 www.tucows.com
Wired
 www.wired.com/wired
ZDNet Software Library
 www.hotfiles.com

Adobe Systems

345 Park Ave.
San Jose, CA 95110-2704
(800) 833-6687 (toll-free)
(415) 536-6000
(415) 537-6000 (fax)
www.adobe.com

Author's Overall Appraisal

Progressive

Consumer Cautions

None

Important Considerations

Affiliated with groups supportive of gay and lesbian rights
Diversity training inclusive of people with disabilities
Listed on GLV 100 Index
Listed on Standard & Poor's index
Supports breast cancer research/women's health groups

Workplace Record on Sexual Orientation

Diversity training inclusive of sexual orientation
Encouraging remarks from vendors or gay and lesbian employees
Full domestic-partnership health care benefits
Gay and lesbian employee group
Written sexual orientation nondiscrimination policy statement

Company Overview

One of the largest software production companies, Adobe Systems employs approximately 2,500 people. The company develops desktop publishing software. Many of Adobe's products and software programs help consumers and businesspeople design Web pages. The company's products are also utilized in advertising agencies, design firms, and photographic production studios.

Popular Name Brands or Key Industry Products

Computer software, including Acrobat, Adobe Gallery Effects, Adobe Illustrator, Adobe Photoshop, FrameMaker, PageMaker, PostScript, Adobe PageMill, and Adobe SiteMill

Advanced Micro Devices

1 AMD Plaza
Sunnyvale, CA 94088-3453
(800) 538-8450 (toll-free)
(408) 732-2400
www.amd.com

Author's Overall Appraisal
Progressive

Consumer Cautions
None

Important Considerations
Affiliated with groups supportive of gay and lesbian rights
Diversity training inclusive of people with disabilities
Listed as a Fortune 500 company
Listed on Domini Social Index
Listed on GLV 100 Index
Listed on Standard & Poor's Index
Stock held by Meyers Pride Value Fund

Workplace Record on Sexual Orientation
Diversity training inclusive of sexual orientation
Encouraging remarks from vendors or gay and lesbian employees
Full domestic-partnership health care benefits
Gay and lesbian employee group officially acknowledged
Written sexual orientation nondiscrimination policy statement

Company Overview
Advanced Micro Devices employs more than 13,000 people. The company, which went public in 1972, is a semiconductor manufacturer with factories in the United States and Asia, and sales offices throughout the world. The company's products include a wide variety of integrated circuits used in telecommunications equipment, data and network communications equipment, consumer electronics, and personal computers and workstations. The company markets and sells its products to a broad base of customers composed primarily of distributors of computation and communication equipment. Two million shares of common stock are currently held by AMD employees.

In 1981 AMD discovered that its manufacturing facilities in Santa Clara County, Calif., were releasing carcinogenic chemicals. The company has since stopped using such chemicals.

America Online
22000 AOL Way
Dulles, VA 22182-2285
(703) 448-8700
(703) 918-1400 (fax)
www.aol.com

Author's Overall Appraisal
Progressive

Consumer Cautions
Affiliated with groups less than supportive of gay and lesbian rights
Affiliated with sales of alcoholic beverages

Important Considerations
Affiliated with groups supportive of gay and lesbian rights
Diversity training inclusive of people with disabilities
Listed on GLV 100 Index
Significantly visible supporter of ENDA
Supports AIDS services/men's health groups
Supports breast cancer research/women's health groups

Workplace Record on Sexual Orientation
Diversity training inclusive of sexual orientation
Full domestic-partnership health care benefits
Gay and lesbian employee group officially acknowledged
Written sexual orientation nondiscrimination policy statement

Company Overview
America Online employs nearly 8,000 people and has more than 14 million online customers. If you look at workplace policy, community involvement, and employee benefits packages regarding gays and lesbians, America Online is one of the most progressive multimedia/high technology service companies. The company's involvement with gay and lesbian companies and nonprofit organizations has been healthy. However, one high-profile event has marred the company's reputation.

In late 1997 Timothy R. McVeigh, a highly decorated 17-year veteran of the U.S. Navy, was outed after he E-mailed the wife of a shipmate under the screen name "Boysrch." She looked up his AOL profile and saw his marital status listed as "gay." She alerted Navy officials, and the military attempted to discharge McVeigh. Part of its case involved information provided by AOL, in violation of AOL's own privacy policy. A federal judge contended the Navy was conducting a "search and destroy" mission against McVeigh and ordered his reinstatement. AOL acknowledged it breached McVeigh's privacy and reached a financial settlement with him. McVeigh also reached an agreement with the Navy that allowed him to retire with full benefits.

Ameritech

30 W. Wacker Drive
Chicago, IL 60606
(312) 750-5000
(312) 207-0016 (fax)
www.ameritech.com

Author's Overall Appraisal
Progressing too slowly

Consumer Cautions
No domestic partner healthcare benefits

Important Considerations
Diversity training inclusive of people with disabilities
Supports breast cancer research/women's health groups

Workplace Record on Sexual Orientation
Diversity training inclusive of sexual orientation
Gay and lesbian employee group officially acknowledged
Mixed remarks from vendors or gay and lesbian employees
Written sexual orientation nondiscrimination policy statement

Company Overview

Ameritech has over 70,000 employees and provides over 10 million customers in Wisconsin, Indiana, Michigan, Ohio, and Illinois with local phone service. In addition, Ameritech has over 3 million cellular phone service subscribers.

Ameritech is one of the least pro-gay telephone companies. There is a dedicated and organized gay and lesbian employee group, but members hint at a less-than-encouraging response from management about the implementation of health care coverage for domestic partners of gay and lesbian employees. In 1998 Ameritech announced plans to merge with SBC Communications, which has pro-gay policies. The merger, which in mid-1999 was awaiting regulatory approval, could improve Ameritech's policies regarding gays and lesbians.

Ameritech has been involved in joint ventures with SBC and Disney, another pro-gay company.

Apple Computer

20525 Mariani Avenue
Cupertino, CA 95014
(408) 966-1010
(408) 996-0275 (fax)
www.apple.com

Author's Overall Appraisal

Very progressive

Consumer Cautions

None

Important Considerations

Affiliated with groups supportive of gay and lesbian rights
Diversity training inclusive of people with disabilities
Early supporter of ENDA
Good workplace record supporting parents
Has advertised in the gay and lesbian press
Has contributed to gay and lesbian nonprofit groups or political organizations
Has included gay- or lesbian-suggestive imagery in mainstream advertising or programming
Listed as a Fortune 500 company
Listed on Domini Social Index
Listed on GLV 100 Index
Listed on Standard & Poor's Index
Supports AIDS services/men's health groups
Supports breast cancer research/women's health groups

Workplace Record on Sexual Orientation

Diversity training inclusive of sexual orientation
Encouraging remarks from vendors or gay and lesbian employees
Full domestic-partnership health care benefits
Gay and lesbian employee group officially acknowledged
Written sexual orientation nondiscrimination policy statement

Company Overview

Apple has had an employee nondiscrimination policy statement including sexual orientation since 1988. One of the company's most successful advertising campaigns depicted sports stars Martina Navratilova, an out lesbian, and Art Monk, a heterosexual man of color, posing with Apple PowerBook computers. The company has recently ceased giving to charities and community groups as a cost-cutting measure. Prior to that the company had been an in-kind supporter of numerous gay and lesbian events and activities.

Popular Name Brands or Key Industry Products

Macintosh, Claris, iMac, Newton, PowerBook, Performa, PowerTalk, QuickTime, StyleWriter, LaserWriter, WorldScript

AT&T

32 Avenue of the Americas
New York, NY 10013-2412
(800) 222-0400 (toll-free)
(212) 387-5400
cerc@att.com
www.att.com

Author's Overall Appraisal

Progressing

Consumer Cautions

Affiliated with groups less than supportive of gay and lesbian rights
Affiliated with military contracts
Possible overseas labor problems

Important Considerations

Diversity training inclusive of people with disabilities
Has advertised in the gay and lesbian press
Listed as a Fortune 500 company
Listed on Standard & Poor's Index
Supports AIDS services/men's health groups
Supports breast cancer research/women's health groups

Workplace Record on Sexual Orientation

Diversity training inclusive of sexual orientation
Full domestic-partnership health care benefits announced in 1998
Gay and lesbian employee group officially acknowledged
Has had gay/lesbian discrimination lawsuits
Written sexual orientation nondiscrimination policy statement

Company Overview

AT&T has more than 90 million customers, approximately 126,000 employees, and more than $51 billion in annual sales. It runs the world's largest long-distance network and North America's largest digital wireless network. It also is a leading supplier of data and Internet services for businesses and the nation's largest direct Internet service provider to consumers. AT&T has come a long way on sexual orientation issues. Nevertheless, the company has a history of responding slowly on issues important to gay and lesbian employees, investors, and consumers, waiting until 1998 to announce its plans to extend domestic-partnership health care insurance to its gay and lesbian employees (pending union approval). In the early 1990s the company experimented with a direct marketing mail campaign designed to woo gay and lesbian long distance customers. The envelope was printed in lavender and sported a rainbow-colored phone cord with a tag stating it was "time for a change." The letter was packaged with a slip explaining the company's position on gays and lesbians in the workplace. Backlash from the religious right, however, may have scared senior management away from similar promotions.

Popular Name Brands or Key Industry Products

AT&T telecommunications devices, AT&T digital PCs, AT&T Wireless, AT&T WorldNet Services, AT&T Universal Card, AT&T Direct Services, AT&T Global Olympic Network, AT&T Personal Reach Service; AUDIX, CODE COM, COM KEY, Merlin, Princess, Ranger, Trimline, Truevoice

Autodesk
111 McIninis Parkway
San Rafael, CA 94903
(800) 228-3601 (toll-free)
(415) 507-5000
(415) 331-8003 (fax)
www.autodesk.com and www.ktx.com

Author's Overall Appraisal
Progressive

Consumer Cautions
None

Important Considerations
Diversity training inclusive of people with disabilities
Listed on Domini Social Index
Listed on GLV 100 Index
Listed on Meyers Pride Value Fund
Listed on Standard & Poor's Index

Workplace Record on Sexual Orientation
Diversity training inclusive of sexual orientation
Encouraging remarks from vendors or gay and lesbian employees
Full domestic-partnership health care benefits
Gay and lesbian employee group officially acknowledged
Written sexual orientation nondiscrimination policy statement

Company Overview
Autodesk is known primarily for its AutoCAD software, used in the design of automobiles and other large machines.

Banyan Worldwide

P.O. Box 5013
120 Flanders Road
Westboro, MA 01581-5013
(800) 222-6926
(508) 898-1000
(508) 898-1755 (fax)
www.banyan.com

Author's Overall Appraisal

Progressive

Consumer Cautions

Affiliated with the production of nuclear energy

Important Considerations

Diversity training inclusive of people with disabilities
Listed on GLV 100 Index
Supports AIDS services/men's health groups
Supports breast cancer research/women's health groups

Workplace Record on Sexual Orientation

Diversity training inclusive of sexual orientation
Encouraging remarks from vendors or gay and lesbian employees
Full domestic-partnership health care benefits
Gay and lesbian employee group officially acknowledged
Written sexual orientation nondiscrimination policy statement

Company Overview

Banyan Worldwide provides technology to help companies integrate their computer networks and to use in a variety of Internet applications. It also offers consulting services, while a subsidiary, Switchboard Inc., is an online directory service through which customers can find Web sites, E-mail and street addresses, telephone listings, and driving directions. In June of 1999 CBS agreed to acquire a 35% stake in Switchboard. Banyan employs about 700 people.

Popular Name Brands or Key Industry Products

Banyan SiteMinder, WorkTop, StreetTalk for Windows NT, VINES, BeyondMail, Banyan Intranet Connect, Banyan Intranet Protect

Bell Atlantic

1095 Avenue of the Americas
New York, NY 10036
(212) 395-2121
(800) 621-9900 (toll-free)
www.bellatlantic.com

Author's Overall Appraisal
Very progressive

Consumer Cautions
None

Important Considerations
Affiliated with groups supportive of gay and lesbian rights
Diversity training inclusive of people with disabilities
Exceptional workplace record supporting parents
Has advertised in the gay and lesbian press
Listed as a Fortune 500 company
Listed on Domini Social Index
Listed on GLV 100 Index
Listed on Standard & Poor's Index
Significantly visible supporter of ENDA
Supports AIDS services/men's health groups
Supports breast cancer research/women's health groups

Workplace Record on Sexual Orientation
Diversity training inclusive of sexual orientation
Encouraging remarks from vendors or gay and lesbian employees
Full domestic-partnership health care benefits
Gay and lesbian employee group officially acknowledged
Written sexual orientation nondiscrimination policy statement

Company Overview
Bell Atlantic and Nynex merged in 1997, keeping the Bell Atlantic name. It is now one of the largest local telephone companies in the nation, serving more than 40 million customers in 13 states and the District of Columbia. It also has 9 million wireless customers worldwide. It is the nation's largest publisher of Yellow Pages directories and is part owner of several telecommunications companies in Europe and Asia. In 1998 Bell Atlantic announced plans to merge with GTE, which is in many of the same businesses; as of the summer of 1999, the companies were still seeking regulatory approval.

Many insiders at Bell Atlantic say the giant conglomerate is run by "a bunch of good guys," and as a matter of policy the company has embraced diversity and taken stands against discrimination. Raymond W. Smith, who retired as chairman at the end of 1998, testified in 1997 to the U.S. Senate Committee on Labor and Human Resources in support of the Employment Non-Discrimination Act.

As a former paid consultant to Nynex and a current gay and lesbian community representative who sits on the Bell Atlantic Corporate Consumer Board, my only criticism of the company is that it may not be adequately developing its long term relationships with gay and lesbian labor union members and grassroots groups such as the National Gay and Lesbian Task Force.

Bell South
1155 Peachtree St. NE
Atlanta, GA 30309-3610
(404) 249-2000
(404) 249-5999 (fax)
www.bellsouthcorp.com

Author's Overall Appraisal
Progressing too slowly

Consumer Cautions
No domestic partner healthcare benefits

Important Considerations
Exceptional workplace record supporting parents
Supports AIDS services/men's health groups
Supports breast cancer research/women's health groups

Workplace Record on Sexual Orientation
Gay and lesbian employee group
Written sexual orientation nondiscrimination policy statement

Company Overview
BellSouth employs more than 80,000 people and provides local phone service to states in the Southeast. The company has significant wireless and international joint-venture communications operations in Mexico and South America, but the majority of its revenue comes from providing local telephone service in domestic markets.

Cadence Design Systems Inc.
555 River Oaks Parkway
San Jose, CA 95134
(408) 943-1234
(408) 943-0513 (fax)
www.cadence.com

Author's Overall Appraisal
Progressive

Consumer Cautions
None

Important Considerations
- Diversity training inclusive of people with disabilities
- Listed on Domini Social Index
- Listed on GLV 100 Index

Workplace Record on Sexual Orientation
- Diversity training inclusive of sexual orientation
- Encouraging remarks from vendors or gay and lesbian employees
- Full domestic-partnership health care benefits
- Gay and lesbian employee group
- Written sexual orientation nondiscrimination policy statement

Company Overview
Cadence has over 4,000 employees, and in 1998 its sales exceeded $1 billion. The company develops electronic design automation software, used by makers of semiconductors, computers and computer peripherals, telecommunications equipment, automotive systems, industrial controls, medical devices, consumer appliances, and other electronic products. It also provides consulting and design services.

Popular Name Brands or Key Industry Products
Affirma, Assura, SpecctraQuest

Cambridge Technology Partners

8 Cambridge Center
Cambridge, MA 02142
(617) 374-9800
(617) 374-8300 (fax)
www.ctp.com

Author's Overall Appraisal
Progressive

Consumer Cautions
Overseas operations may be affiliated with military contracts

Important Considerations
Diversity training inclusive of people with disabilities
Listed on Domini Social Index
Listed on GLV 100 Index
Supporter of ENDA

Workplace Record on Sexual Orientation
Diversity training inclusive of sexual orientation
Encouraging remarks from vendors or gay and lesbian employees
Full domestic-partnership health care benefits
Gay and lesbian employee group
Written sexual orientation nondiscrimination policy statement

Company Overview
Cambridge Technology Partners provides management consulting and computer systems integration services. It has more than 4,500 employees and 55 offices worldwide.

Cisco Systems Inc.

170 W. Tasman Drive
San Jose, CA 95134
(408) 526-4000
(408) 526-4100 (fax)
www.cisco.com

Author's Overall Appraisal
Progressive

Consumer Cautions
None

Important Considerations
Listed on Domini Social Index
Listed on GLV 100 Index
Listed on Standard & Poor's Index
Stock held by Meyers Pride Value Fund

Workplace Record on Sexual Orientation
Diversity training inclusive of sexual orientation
Encouraging remarks from vendors or gay and lesbian employees
Full domestic-partnership health care benefits
Gay and lesbian employee group
Written sexual orientation nondiscrimination policy statement

Company Overview
Cisco Systems, founded in 1984 by a forum of Stanford University scientists, develops networking systems for the Internet. Customers use Cisco's hardware, software, and consulting services to link computer systems more efficiently, The company employs 18,700 people worldwide, including 9,200 in the San Francisco Bay area, where it is based. It has significant operations in Research Triangle Park, N.C., and Chelmsford, Mass., and more than 225 sales and support offices in 75 countries. It sells its products in 115 countries.

Digital Origin
460 E. Middlefield Road
Mountain View, CA 94043
(650) 404-6000
www.digitalorigin.com
Author's Overall Appraisal
Progressive
Consumer Cautions
None
Important Considerations
Listed on GLV 100 Index
Workplace Record on Sexual Orientation
Domestic-partnership health care benefits
Written sexual orientation nondiscrimination policy statement
Company Overview
Digital Origin, known until 1999 as Radius, develops digital video software products used in computers and camcorders. Earlier in its history, it was best known as a developer and marketer of monitors and other hardware used with Apple Macintosh computers. It sold the monitor line to KDS America in 1998, and KDS's Miro Displays subsidiary now markets Radius brand monitors.

Egghead Software

22011 SE 51st
Issaquah, WA 98027
(800) 344-4323 (toll-free)
www.egghead.com

Author's Overall Appraisal

Progressive

Consumer Cautions

None

Important Considerations

Listed on GLV 100 Index

Affiliated with groups supportive of gay and lesbian rights

Listed on Domini Social Index

Workplace Record on Sexual Orientation

Full domestic-partnership health care benefits

Gay and lesbian employee group

Written sexual orientation nondiscrimination policy statement

Company Overview

In 1998 Egghead closed down its retail outlets and decided to sell software exclusively via the Internet. At one time the company operated over 200 stores across the nation.

Hewlett-Packard Co.
3000 Hanover St.
Palo Alto, CA 94304
(415) 857-1501
www.hp.com

Author's Overall Appraisal
Progressive

Consumer Cautions
None

Important Considerations
Affiliated with groups supportive of gay and lesbian rights
Diversity training inclusive of people with disabilities
Exceptional workplace record supporting parents
Listed as a Fortune 500 company
Listed on Domini Social Index
Listed on GLV 100 Index
Listed on Standard & Poor's index
Significantly visible supporter of ENDA
Supports AIDS services/men's health groups

Workplace Record on Sexual Orientation
Diversity training inclusive of sexual orientation
Full domestic-partnership health care benefits
Gay and lesbian employee group officially acknowledged
Written sexual orientation nondiscrimination policy statement

Company Overview
Hewlett-Packard has over 120,000 employees. It manufactures computers and computer workstations, servers, and electronic information storage devices for engineering and medicine. The company is extensively involved in the development of medical measuring equipment, medical technology products, and education systems.

Popular Name Brands or Key Industry Products
Hewlett-Packard brand PCs, LaserJet, DeskJet, ThinkJet, DeskWriter, DeskManager, ChangeVision, Bi-Tronics, Vectra, Omnibook

Honeywell

Honeywell Plaza
Minneapolis, MN 55408
(612) 951-1000
(612) 951-8537 (fax)
www.honeywell.com

Author's Overall Appraisal
Progressive

Consumer Cautions
None

Important Considerations
Diversity training inclusive of people with disabilities
Listed as a Fortune 500 company

Workplace Record on Sexual Orientation
Diversity training inclusive of sexual orientation
Full domestic-partnership health care benefits
Gay and lesbian employee group
Written sexual orientation nondiscrimination policy statement

Company Overview
Honeywell employs approximately 57,500 people. It is the world's largest manufacturer of home heating and cooling monitoring systems. It is also involved in the development of fire protection systems, and security and other control systems.

IBM
New Orchard Rd
Armonk, NY 10504
(800) 426-4968 (toll-free)
(914) 499-1900
www.ibm.com

Author's Overall Appraisal
Progressive

Consumer Cautions
Possible affiliations with military contracts
Possible affiliations with production of nuclear energy

Important Considerations
Affiliated with groups supportive of gay and lesbian rights
Diversity training inclusive of people with disabilities
Exceptional workplace record supporting parents
Has advertised in the gay and lesbian press
Includes gay- or lesbian-suggestive imagery in mainstream advertising or programming
Listed as a Fortune 500 company
Listed on Domini Social Index
Listed on GLV 100 Index
Listed on Standard & Poor's index
Significantly visible supporter of ENDA
Supports AIDS services/men's health groups
Supports breast cancer research/women's health groups

Workplace Record on Sexual Orientation
Diversity training inclusive of sexual orientation
Encouraging remarks from vendors or gay and lesbian employees
Full domestic-partnership health care benefits
Gay and lesbian employee group officially acknowledged
Written sexual orientation nondiscrimination policy statement

Company Overview
IBM is a worldwide leader in the creation, development, and manufacture of information technologies. The company only recently began offering domestic-partnership health care coverage to its gay and lesbian employees, but it was the first major corporation to adopt a written nondiscrimination policy statement regarding sexual orientation, doing so in 1974. Its act is an early milestone in the fight

for equal rights for gays and lesbians. In addition, IBM is dedicated to bettering the world's communities overall. Over the past ten years the company has contributed over $1.3 billion to nonprofit organizations and schools.

Informix Software
4100 Bohannon Drive
Menlo Park, CA 94025
(415) 926-6300
www.informix.com

Author's Overall Appraisal
Progressive

Consumer Cautions
None

Important Considerations
Affiliated with groups supportive of gay and lesbian rights
Diversity training inclusive of people with disabilities
Exceptional workplace record supporting parents
Listed on GLV 100 Index
Stock held by Meyers Pride Value Fund
Supports AIDS services/men's health groups
Supports breast cancer research/women's health groups

Workplace Record on Sexual Orientation
Diversity training inclusive of sexual orientation
Full domestic-partnership health care benefits
Gay and lesbian employee group officially acknowledged
Written sexual orientation nondiscrimination policy statement

Company Overview
Informix employs about 5,000 people and is primarily involved in network software design and implementation. One of its most popular products is the Informix-OnLine Dynamic Server, which works in conjunction with Windows and Unix operating systems. Informix also provides systems for network communications, database interfacing, and application development tools and products.

Inprise Corp.

100 Enterprise Way
Scotts Valley, CA 95066
(800) 331-0877 (toll-free)
(800) 356-2017 (shareholder inquiries)
(831) 431-1000
www.borland.com

Author's Overall Appraisal
Very progressive

Consumer Cautions
None

Important Considerations
Affiliated with groups supportive of gay and lesbian rights
Diversity training inclusive of people with disabilities
Listed on GLV 100 Index
Significantly visible supporter of ENDA

Workplace Record on Sexual Orientation
Full domestic-partnership health care benefits
Gay and lesbian employee group
Written sexual orientation nondiscrimination policy statement

Company Overview
Borland International changed its name to Inprise Corp. in April 1998, after having acquired Visigenic Software two months earlier. Inprise provides software that helps companies integrate their computer operations, bridging a variety of differing computer languages. It has significant business relationships with several industry leaders, including Oracle, IBM, Sun Microsystems, Microsoft, and Netscape. Inprise customers include AT&T, Abbott Labs, J.P. Morgan, Prudential, Xerox, and many more. It has more than 900 employees and operations in more than 20 countries. It was one of only a few corporations to send a board member to testify at the congressional hearings on the Employment Non-Discrimination Act.

Popular Name Brands or Key Industry Products
JBuilder, VisiBroker, Inprise AppCenter, Delphi, InterBase, Entera

Intel Inc.
P.O. Box 58119
2200 Mission College Blvd.
Santa Clara, CA 95052-8119
(408) 765-8080
(408) 765-9904 (fax)
www.intel.com

Author's Overall Appraisal
Progressive

Consumer Cautions
Pentium III processor allows employers to track employee usage of computers including personal email transmittal and web visits

Important Considerations
Diversity training inclusive of people with disabilities
Listed as a Fortune 500 company
Listed on Domini Social Index
Listed on GLV 100 Index
Listed on Standard & Poor's Index
Significantly visible supporter of ENDA
Stock held by Meyers Pride Value Fund
Supports AIDS services/men's health groups

Workplace Record on Sexual Orientation
Diversity training inclusive of sexual orientation
Full domestic-partnership health care benefits
Gay and lesbian employee group officially acknowledged
Written sexual orientation nondiscrimination policy statement

Company Overview
Intel is a major provider of microprocessors, which control the central processing data in personal computers, as well as networking and communications products that enhance the capabilities of PC systems and networks, and other products such as flash memory, which provides easily reprogrammable memory for computer systems and other electronic devices. The company is expanding into Brazil, China, and India.

For up-to-date information on Intel's workplace and environmental records you can check out its "Workplace of Choice" report at www.intel.com/intel/oppty/why/workplace.htm and its "Commitment Around the Globe" environmental health and safety performance report at www.intel.com/intel/other/ehs/index.htm. Printed copies are available by calling (800) 753-9754, ext. 348, or (847) 296-9333, ext. 348.

Interleaf
62 Fourth Ave.
Waltham, MA 02451
(781) 290-0710
(781) 290-4943 (fax)

Author's Overall Appraisal
Progressive

Consumer Cautions
None

Important Considerations
Diversity training inclusive of people with disabilities
Listed on GLV 100 Index
Stock held by Meyers Pride Value Fund
Supports breast cancer research/women's health groups

Workplace Record on Sexual Orientation
Diversity training inclusive of sexual orientation
Full domestic-partnership health care benefits
Gay and lesbian employee group
Written sexual orientation nondiscrimination policy statement

Company Overview
Interleaf provides software for content management and high-end publishing. Its products are designed to make it easy for companies to assemble, manage, retrieve, distribute, and publish critical information.

International Data Group
One Exeter Plaza, 15th floor
Boston, MA 02116-2851
(617) 534-1200
(617) 859-8642 (fax)
www.idg.com

Author's Overall Appraisal
Progressive

Consumer Cautions
None

Important Considerations
Listed on GLV 100 Index
Supports AIDS services/men's health groups
Supports breast cancer research/women's health groups

Workplace Record on Sexual Orientation
Diversity training inclusive of sexual orientation
Full domestic-partnership health care benefits
Gay and lesbian employee group
Written sexual orientation nondiscrimination policy statement

Company Overview
IDG employs more than 9,000 people and had revenues of $2.35 billion in 1998. Operations include book and magazine publishing, online and electronic commerce information systems, expositions, conferences, market research, and education. Its research arm, International Data Corp., provides information technology data, analysis, and consulting.

Popular Name Brands or Key Industry Products
IDG Books (including the ...For Dummies series), *Computerworld*, *InfoWorld*, *Macworld*, *NetworkWorld*, *PC World*, ExecuTrain

Lucent Technologies

600 Mountain Ave.
Murray Hill, NJ 07974
(908) 582-8500
(908) 508-2576 (fax)
www.lucent.com

Author's Overall Appraisal
Very progressive

Consumer Cautions
None

Important Considerations
Affiliated with groups supportive of gay and lesbian rights
Diversity training inclusive of people with disabilities
Exceptional workplace record supporting parents
Listed on GLV 100 Index
Listed on Standard & Poor's Index
Significantly visible supporter of ENDA
Supports AIDS services/men's health groups
Supports breast cancer research/women's health groups

Workplace Record on Sexual Orientation
Diversity training inclusive of sexual orientation
Encouraging remarks from vendors or gay and lesbian employees
Full domestic-partnership health care benefits
Gay and lesbian employee group
Written sexual orientation nondiscrimination policy statement

Company Overview

Lucent employs approximately 140,000 people. The company was part of AT&T before AT&T split into AT&T, NCR, and Lucent. Lucent makes software and networking systems for use in telephone and Internet communications, and also manufactures voice, video, and multimedia communications systems for business and government. Bell Labs is Lucent's research and development arm.

After splitting from AT&T, Lucent almost immediately offered domestic-partnership health care benefits to its gay and lesbian employees, as did NCR. AT&T did not do so until much later. Lucent also became one of the first large companies to specifically incorporate language in its nondiscrimination policy statement protecting transgendered employees.

MCI Worldcom

500 Clinton Center
Clinton, MS 39056
(800) MCI-WCOM (toll-free)
(601) 460-8350 (fax)
www.wcom.com

Author's Overall Appraisal

Progressing too slowly

Consumer Cautions

Has not publicly disclosed whether it offers domestic-partnership benefits

Important Considerations

Has advertised in the gay and lesbian press
Listed as a Fortune 500 company
Listed on Domini Social Index
Supports AIDS services/men's health groups
Supports breast cancer research/women's health groups

Workplace Record on Sexual Orientation

Diversity training inclusive of sexual orientation
Gay and lesbian employee group
No confirmed written sexual orientation nondiscrimination policy statement

Company Overview

WorldCom acquired MCI in 1998, and the combined company is AT&T's primary competitor. MCI Worldcom provides local and long-distance telephone services and Internet access. The Internet business generates annual revenues in excess of $2 billion. The company's most recognized brands include On-Net, 1-800-COLLECT, 5 Cent Sundays, 10-10-321, and UUNET.

Microsoft

One Microsoft Way
Redmond, WA 98052-6399
(800) 426-9400 (toll-free)
(445) 882-8080
(445) 936-7329 (fax)
www.microsoft.com

Author's Overall Appraisal
Progressive

Consumer Cautions
Affiliated with groups less than supportive of gay and lesbian rights
Affiliated with military contracts
Antitrust challenges
Possible overseas labor problems

Important Considerations
Diversity training inclusive of people with disabilities
Includes gay- or lesbian-suggestive imagery in mainstream advertising or programming
Listed as a Fortune 500 company
Listed on GLV 100 Index

Workplace Record on Sexual Orientation
Diversity training inclusive of sexual orientation
Full domestic-partnership health care benefits
Gay and lesbian employee group officially acknowledged
Mixed remarks from vendors or gay and lesbian employees
Written sexual orientation nondiscrimination policy statement

Company Overview
Microsoft, with over 22,000 employees, is involved in everything from home entertainment and personal shopping to online banking and multimedia education. It produces operating systems for personal computers, server applications for client/server environments, business and consumer productivity applications, interactive media programs, and Internet platform and development tools. It also offers online services, sells personal computer books and input devices, and researches and develops advanced technology software products. Microsoft products are available in more than 30 languages and are sold in more than 50 countries. Microsoft and its chairman, Bill Gates, have become highly controversial. A lawsuit by the U.S. Department of Justice and 19 states ac-

cuses Microsoft of engaging in activities designed to unfairly undermine its competitors. The legal proceedings were continuing as this book went to press.

Popular Name Brands or Key Industry Products

Access, BackOffice, Bookshelf, Chat, Encarta, Excel, Flight Simulator, FrontPage, Graphics Studio, IntelliMouse, Internet Explorer, Links LS, MSN, MSNBC, Natural Keyboard Elite, Office 2000, Outlook, Picture It!, PowerPoint, *Slate* magazine, Visual, Windows, Word, Works

NCR
1700 S. Patterson Blvd.
Dayton, OH 45479
(937) 445-5000
(937) 445-1682 (fax)
www.ncr.com

Author's Overall Appraisal
Progressive

Consumer Cautions
None

Important Considerations
Affiliated with groups supportive of gay and lesbian rights
Diversity training inclusive of people with disabilities
Exceptional workplace record supporting parents
Significantly visible supporter of ENDA
Supports AIDS services/men's health groups
Supports breast cancer research/women's health groups

Workplace Record on Sexual Orientation
Diversity training inclusive of sexual orientation
Encouraging remarks from vendors or gay and lesbian employees
Full domestic-partnership health care benefits
Gay and lesbian employee group
Written sexual orientation nondiscrimination policy statement

Company Overview
NCR was part of AT&T from 1991 until 1997, when AT&T spun off NCR and Lucent Technologies). NCR is divided into three operating units: retail systems, financial systems, and computer systems. Its products include cash register terminals, automated teller machines, bar code scanners, check-clearing equipment and data warehousing.

Nortel Networks Corp.
8200 Dixie Road
Suite 1000
Brampton, Ontario L6T 5P6, Canada
(905) 863-0000

Author's Overall Appraisal
Progressive

Consumer Cautions
None

Important Considerations
Listed on GLV 100 Index
Listed as a Fortune 500 company
Supports AIDS services/men's health groups
Supports breast cancer research/women's health groups

Workplace Record on Sexual Orientation
Full domestic-partnership health care benefits
Gay and lesbian employee group
Written sexual orientation nondiscrimination policy statement

Company Overview
Nortel, formerly Northern Telecom, provides network technologies used by local, long-distance, and cellular telephone companies; cable television carriers; Internet service providers; and utilities. It has about 75,000 employees worldwide and had revenues of $17.6 billion in 1998.

Novell

122 East, 1700 South
Provo, UT 84606
(800) 453-1267 (toll-free)
(801) 429-7000
(801) 429-5155 (fax)
www.novell.com

Author's Overall Appraisal
Progressive

Consumer Cautions
None

Important Considerations
Listed on GLV 100 Index
Listed as a Fortune 500 company
Listed on Domini Social Index

Workplace Record on Sexual Orientation
Full domestic-partnership health care benefits
Written sexual orientation nondiscrimination policy statement

Company Overview
Novell employs about 4,700 people. The company provides network services to clients around the globe. One of its most popular network operating systems is NetWare, which allows local business networks to communicate with each other. NetWare is licensed to tens of millions of users.

Oracle
500 Oracle Pkwy.
Redwood Shores, CA 94065
(650) 506-7000
(650) 506-7200 (fax)
www.oracle.com

Author's Overall Appraisal
Progressive

Consumer Cautions
None

Important Considerations
Affiliated with groups supportive of gay and lesbian rights
Diversity training inclusive of people with disabilities
Early supporter of ENDA
Exceptional workplace record supporting parents
Listed as a Fortune 500 company
Listed on GLV 100 Index
Supports AIDS services/men's health groups
Supports breast cancer research/women's health groups

Workplace Record on Sexual Orientation
Diversity training inclusive of sexual orientation
Encouraging remarks from vendors or gay and lesbian employees
Full domestic-partnership health care benefits
Gay and lesbian employee group officially acknowledged
Written sexual orientation nondiscrimination policy statement

Company Overview
Oracle, founded in 1977, is one of the largest providers of software and services for managing information. The company has 41,000 employees worldwide and does business in approximately 145 countries. Its software is designed to help businesses manage and access information quickly and easily across a variety of computer and network environments.

Oracle provides space for gay and lesbian employee meetings and offers a long list of benefits and services, including domestic-partnership health insurance and bereavement leave. Its written policy banning discrimination based on sexual orientation has been in place since 1986.

Popular Name Brands or Key Industry Products
Oracle8, Oracle Workflow, Oracle Discoverer, JDeveloper, Express

Pacific Bell

140 New Montgomery St., #2190
San Francisco, CA 94105
(415) 394-3967
(415) 824-3513 (fax)
www.pacbell.com

Author's Overall Appraisal
Progressive

Consumer Cautions
Parent company, SBC Communications, routinely declined survey participation for all other subsidiaries

Important Considerations
Affiliated with groups supportive of gay and lesbian rights
Diversity training inclusive of people with disabilities
Exceptional workplace record supporting parents
Has advertised in the gay and lesbian press
Listed as a Fortune 500 company
Listed on Domini Social Index
Significantly visible supporter of ENDA
Supports AIDS services/men's health groups
Supports breast cancer research/women's health groups

Workplace Record on Sexual Orientation
Diversity training inclusive of sexual orientation
Encouraging remarks from vendors or gay and lesbian employees
Full domestic-partnership health care benefits
Gay and lesbian employee group officially acknowledged
Has had gay/lesbian discrimination lawsuit(s)
Written sexual orientation nondiscrimination policy statement

Company Overview

Pacific Bell provides telephone services and products to more than 15.3 million customers throughout California. Its parent company is SBC Communications, based in San Antonio, which also owns Southwestern Bell and Nevada Bell.

In the early 1970s Pacific Bell had a policy of not hiring "manifest homosexuals." That policy was scrapped after the company lost an expensive lawsuit. Since that time, things have changed dramatically. The company is now a leader on gay and lesbian issues in the workplace.

Steve Colter, vice president of external affairs for Pacific Bell, was one of only a few corporate representatives to testify on Capitol Hill in support of the Employment Non-Discrimination Act.

The company has done some preliminary focus group research about including gay and lesbian imagery in mainstream advertising, but has not yet instituted any campaigns.

Paradigm
694 Tasman Drive
Milpitas, CA 95035
(800) 767-4530 (toll-free)
(408) 954-0500
(408) 954-8913 (fax)
www.prdm.com

Author's Overall Appraisal
Progressive

Consumer Cautions
Affiliated with the production of nuclear energy
Affiliated with military contracts

Important Considerations
Affiliated with groups supportive of gay and lesbian rights
Diversity training inclusive of people with disabilities
Listed on GLV 100 Index

Workplace Record on Sexual Orientation
Diversity training inclusive of sexual orientation
Encouraging remarks from vendors or gay and lesbian employees
Full domestic-partnership health care benefits
Gay and lesbian employee group
Written sexual orientation nondiscrimination policy statement

Company Overview
Paradigm specializes in standard random access memory semiconductor devices that are used in telecommunications, high-performance personal computers, advanced modems, military and aerospace applications, and other complex electronic systems. Although the company only has around 100 employees, it licenses its products to outside contractors, including National Semiconductor. In 1998 it merged with IXYS Corp., keeping the Paradigm name.

PeopleSoft Inc.
4460 Hacienda Drive
Pleasanton, CA 94588-8618
(800) 380-7638 (toll-free)
(925) 225-3000
(925) 694-4444 (fax)
www.peoplesoft.com

Author's Overall Appraisal
Progressive

Consumer Cautions
May be affiliated with military contracts

Important Considerations
Listed on GLV 100 Index

Workplace Record on Sexual Orientation
Full domestic-partnership health care benefits
Written sexual orientation nondiscrimination policy statement

Company Overview
PeopleSoft, founded in 1987, provides software used in financial and accounting applications, manufacturing, distribution, and human resources. In 1998 the company had revenues of $1.3 billion. It employs more than 6,000 people and has over 3,000 customers.

Pitney Bowes

1 Elmcroft Road, 63-09
Stamford, CT 06926-0700
(203) 351-6349
(203) 351-6835 (fax)
www.pitneybowes.com

Author's Overall Appraisal
Progressing slowly

Consumer Cautions
No survey response

Important Information:
Listed as a Fortune 500 company
Listed on Domini Social Index (DSI)

Workplace Record on Sexual Orientation
Gay and lesbian employee group
Written sexual orientation nondiscrimination policy statement

Company Overview
Pitney Bowes employs about 30,000 people. The company is the world's largest supplier of postage meters. It also makes electronic office equipment such as fax machines, weighing machines, and records management devices.

Platinum Technology

1815 S. Meyers Road
Oakbrook Terrace, IL 60181-5241
(800) 442-6861 (toll-free)
(630) 620-5000
(630) 691-0718 (fax)
www.platinum.com

Author's Overall Appraisal
Progressive

Consumer Cautions
None

Important Considerations
Affiliated with groups supportive of gay and lesbian rights
Diversity training inclusive of people with disabilities
Listed on GLV 100 Index
Significantly visible supporter of ENDA
Stock held by Meyers Pride Value Fund
Supports AIDS services/men's health groups
Supports breast cancer research/women's health groups

Workplace Record on Sexual Orientation
Diversity training inclusive of sexual orientation
Encouraging remarks from vendors or gay and lesbian employees
Full domestic-partnership health care benefits
Gay and lesbian employee group
Written sexual orientation nondiscrimination policy statement

Company Overview
Platinum provides computer software and systems solutions to assist businesses with the management of information and documentation systems. The company has worked closely with Cybercash, Hewlett-Packard, Norfolk Southern, and Ameritech. The workplace environment for gays and lesbians is quite positive. One Platinum employee stated, "I am very out at work about both my partner and our son, and have encountered no problems—everyone accepts us as a family." Computer Associates International acquired Platinum in June 1999.

Qualcomm
5775 Morehouse Drive
San Diego, CA 92121
(858) 587-1121
(858) 658-2100 (fax)
www.qualcomm.com

Author's Overall Appraisal
Progressive

Consumer Cautions
None

Important Considerations
Affiliated with groups supportive of gay and lesbian rights
Exceptional workplace record supporting parents
Listed on GLV 100 Index

Workplace Record on Sexual Orientation
Diversity training inclusive of sexual orientation
Encouraging remarks from vendors or gay and lesbian employees
Full domestic-partnership health care benefits
Gay and lesbian employee group
Written sexual orientation nondiscrimination policy statement

Company Overview
Qualcomm was founded in 1985 and currently employs about 10,500 people. The company provides digital and wireless systems, software, and communications products. Qualcomm is primarily known for its two-way mobile satellites used in commercial trucking and information management systems in the United States, Canada, Europe, Japan, Brazil, Mexico, Malaysia, and Korea.

Quark

1800 Grant Street
Denver, CO 80203
(303) 894-8888
(303) 894-3399 (fax)
www.quark.com

Author's Overall Appraisal
Very progressive

Important Considerations
Affiliated with many groups supportive of gay and lesbian rights
Diversity training inclusive of people with disabilities
Exceptional workplace record supporting parents
Has advertised in the gay and lesbian press
Includes gay- or lesbian-suggestive imagery in mainstream advertising or programming
Listed on GLV 100 Index
Significantly visible supporter of ENDA
Supports AIDS services/men's health groups
Supports breast cancer research/women's health groups

Workplace Record on Sexual Orientation
Diversity training inclusive of sexual orientation
Encouraging remarks from vendors or gay and lesbian employees
Full domestic-partnership health care benefits
Gay and lesbian employee group officially acknowledged
Written sexual orientation nondiscrimination policy statement

Company Overview
Quark was founded in 1981 by Tim Gill, who wrote the initial word-processing application and platform language for Apple before Apple became a household word. Quark is a revolutionary force in typography and professional typesetting. QuarkXPress is used by thousands of designers in hundreds of companies worldwide. The company currently employs approximately 500 people.

Gill, who is openly gay, has used a large chunk of his personal earnings to endow the Gill Foundation, which gives primarily to gay and lesbian charities.

Popular Name Brands or Key Industry Products
QuarkXPress, QuarkImmedia, Quark Publishing System, Quark Digital Media System, Avenue.Quark

Silicon Graphics Inc.
1600 Amphitheatre Parkway
Mountain View, CA 94043
(650) 960-1980
www.sgi.com

Author's Overall Appraisal
Progressive

Consumer Cautions
Affiliated with military contracts

Important Considerations
Affiliated with groups supportive of gay and lesbian rights
Diversity training inclusive of people with disabilities
Listed as a Fortune 500 company
Listed on GLV 100 Index
Significantly visible supporter of ENDA
Supports AIDS services/men's health groups
Supports breast cancer research/women's health groups

Workplace Record on Sexual Orientation
Diversity training inclusive of sexual orientation
Encouraging remarks from vendors or gay and lesbian employees
Full domestic-partnership health care benefits
Gay and lesbian employee group officially acknowledged
Written sexual orientation nondiscrimination policy statement

Company Overview
Silicon Graphics Inc. provides high-performance computing and advanced graphics technology. Its products offer such capabilities and features as 3-D special effects, computer-generated animation, and the latest in MIPS microprocessors and customized graphic design systems. Filmmaker George Lucas's Industrial Light and Magic used SGI products to animate digital characters and create special effects for *Star Wars: Episode I—The Phantom Menace*. Cray Research, a maker of supercomputers, is a subsidiary of SGI. SGI has 9,000 employees worldwide.

Popular Name Brands or Key Industry Products
Octane, Onyx, Origin, Cray

Sprint

2330 Shawnee Mission Parkway
Mail Stop # KSWESA0206
Westwood, KS 66205
(913) 624-3000
(913) 624-3281 (fax)
www.sprint.com

Author's Overall Appraisal
Progressing too slowly

Consumer Cautions
None

Important Considerations
Affiliated with groups supportive of equal rights for gays and lesbians
Diversity training inclusive of people with disabilities
Has advertised in the gay and lesbian press
Listed as a Fortune 500 company
Listed on Domini Social Index

Workplace Record on Sexual Orientation
Diversity training inclusive of sexual orientation
Encouraging remarks from vendors or gay and lesbian employees
Gay and lesbian employee group
Written sexual orientation nondiscrimination policy statement

Company Overview
Sprint is a major provider of long-distance and other telecommunications services. The company employs about 50,000 people.

Sun Microsystems

901 San Antonio Road
Palo Alto, CA 94303
(800) 555-9SUN (toll-free)
(650) 960-1300
www.sun.com

Author's Overall Appraisal
Progressive

Consumer Cautions
Affiliated with military contracts

Important Considerations
Affiliated with groups supportive of gay and lesbian rights
Diversity training inclusive of people with disabilities
Early supporter of ENDA
Listed on Domini Social Index
Listed on GLV 100 Index
Supports AIDS services/men's health groups
Supports breast cancer research/women's health groups

Workplace Record on Sexual Orientation
Diversity training inclusive of sexual orientation
Encouraging remarks from vendors or gay and lesbian employees
Full domestic-partnership health care benefits
Gay and lesbian employee group
Written sexual orientation nondiscrimination policy statement

Company Overview
Sun Microsystems makes computer workstations, servers, storage systems, and software used in business and consumer applications. The company employs approximately 20,000 people.

Popular Name Brands or Key Industry Products
Solaris, Ultra, Java, Netra

Sybase
6475 Christie Ave.
Emeryville, CA 94608
(800) 8-SYBASE (toll-free)
(510) 922-3500
(510) 658-9441 (fax)
www.sybase.com

Author's Overall Appraisal
Progressive

Consumer Cautions
None

Important Considerations
Listed on GLV 100 Index

Workplace Record on Sexual Orientation
Full domestic-partnership health care benefits
Written sexual orientation nondiscrimination policy statement

Company Overview
Sybase, which employs approximately 4,300 people, is one of the ten largest global independent software companies. Its products are used in data management and Internet applications. Customers include many of the largest banks and life insurance companies, telecommunications providers, health care organizations, and governmental bodies.

U.S. West Inc.

7800 E. Orchard Road
Englewood, CO 8011-6508
(800) 537-0222 (toll-free)
(303) 793-6500
www.uswest.com

Author's Overall Appraisal
Progressive

Consumer Cautions
None

Important Considerations
Diversity training inclusive of people with disabilities
Listed on GLV 100 Index
Listed on Domini Social Index

Workplace Record on Sexual Orientation
Diversity training inclusive of sexual orientation
Full domestic-partnership health care benefits
Gay and lesbian employee group officially acknowledged
Written sexual orientation nondiscrimination policy statement

Company Overview
U.S. West employs approximately 50,000 people and is a provider of integrated telephone, computer, and voice-mail communications systems. The company's high-capacity and broadband communications networks bring cable television, telephone, and high-speed Internet services to consumers. The company extended domestic partnership benefits to its gay and lesbian employees on January 1, 1998. In July 1999 U.S. West agreed to merge with Qwest Communications; the deal was expected to close by mid 2000, after regulatory approval was completed.

Visioneer

34800 Campus Drive
Freemont, CA 94555
(510) 608-6300
(510) 608-0305 (fax)
www.visioneer.com

Author's Overall Appraisal

Progressive

Consumer Cautions

None

Important Considerations

Listed on GLV 100 Index

Workplace Record on Sexual Orientation

Full domestic-partnership health care benefits

Written sexual orientation nondiscrimination policy statement

Company Overview

Visioneer is a small company, with slightly more than 40 employees. Its award-winning OneTouch scanners make it easy to put documents and photographs into computers. Visioneer is a subsidiary of Primax Electronics, headquartered in Taiwan.

Xerox

800 Long Ridge Road
Stamford, CT 06904
(800) 275-9376 (toll-free)
(203) 968-3000
www.xerox.com

Author's Overall Appraisal

Progressive

Consumer Cautions

None

Important Considerations

Affiliated with groups supportive of gay and lesbian rights
Diversity training inclusive of people with disabilities
Early supporter of ENDA
Exceptional workplace record supporting parents
Listed on Domini Social Index
Listed on GLV 100 Index
Supports AIDS services/men's health groups
Supports breast cancer research/women's health groups

Workplace Record on Sexual Orientation

Diversity training inclusive of sexual orientation
Encouraging remarks from vendors or gay and lesbian employees
Full domestic-partnership health care benefits
Gay and lesbian employee group officially acknowledged
Written sexual orientation nondiscrimination policy statement

Company Overview

The name Xerox is synonymous with the word "copy." But the company is rapidly becoming equally well-known for its involvement in everything from document management and processing, to color production technology, to scanning, printing, and digital graphic output. The company is involved in a number of joint ventures, and has focused on overseas marketing opportunities in South America, Japan, and China.

Popular Name Brands or Key Industry Products

Computers, photocopiers, printers, office supplies, facsimile equipment, computer software, printers, peripherals, equipment, paper, toner, inks. Reading AdvantEdge, CentreWare, ContentGuard, Xerox DocuPrint, Xerox WorkCentre

Consumer Products and Home Furnishings

The majority of consumer products and home furnishings companies have a long way to go to catch up with other industry sectors on sexual orientation policy. Most do not offer domestic-partner health care insurance to their gay and lesbian employees, and virtually none advertises to gay and lesbian consumers.

General Industry Resources:

Association of Home Appliance Manufacturers
    www.aham.org
The Consumer Electronics Manufacturers Association
    www.cemacity.org
Consumer Electronics Society
    www.ieee.org/society/ce
Electronic Industries Alliance
    www.eia.org
National Housewares Manufacturers Association
    www.housewares.org

Alberto Culver
2525 Armitage Ave.
Melrose Park, IL 60160-1163
(708) 450-3000
(708) 450-3382 (fax)

Author's Overall Appraisal
Progressing too slowly

Consumer Cautions
Animal testing

Important Considerations
Listed on Domini Social Index
Listed on Standard & Poor's Index
Supports AIDS services/men's health groups
Supports breast cancer research/women's health groups

Workplace Record on Sexual Orientation
Mixed remarks from vendors or gay and lesbian employees
Written sexual orientation nondiscrimination policy statement

Company Overview
Alberto Culver has three operating units: Alberto-Culver USA; Alberto-Culver International; and Sally Beauty Company, a retailer of beauty supplies. Alberto Culver recently acquired St. Ives Laboratories, which includes Swiss Formula Botanicals Plus. The company considers itself well-positioned for growth, despite the massive consolidation of competitors like Unilever, Dial, and Procter & Gamble>.

Popular Name Brands or Key Industry Products
Alberto VO5, Blondes American Style, Baker's Joy, Derma Fresh, Tresemmé, Molly Mcbutter seasonings, Mrs. Dash, Poppa Dash, Kleen Guard, Static Guard, Desk Guard, Sudden Silver, Sugar Twin, TCB, Upside Down

Black & Decker Corp.

701 E. Joppa Rd.
Towson, MD 21286
(410) 716-3900
(410) 716-2933 (fax)
www.blackanddecker.com

Author's Overall Appraisal
Progressing too slowly

Consumer Cautions
No survey response

Important Considerations
Unknown

Workplace Record on Sexual Orientation
Unknown

Company Overview
Black & Decker is the world's largest maker of power tools, hardware systems, and lawn care products.

Popular Name Brands or Key Industry Products
Black & Decker brand tools and appliances, Price Pfister, Kwikset, Dustbuster, SnakeLight, Emhart

Body Shop
5036 One World Way
Wake Forest, NC 27587
(919) 554-4900
(919) 554-4361 (fax)
www.the-body-shop.com

Author's Overall Appraisal
Progressing somewhat

Consumer Cautions
None

Important Considerations
Diversity training inclusive of people with disabilities
Supports AIDS services/men's health groups
Supports and lobbies for animal-free products
Supports breast cancer research/women's health groups

Workplace Record on Sexual Orientation
Diversity training inclusive of sexual orientation
Encouraging remarks from vendors or gay and lesbian employees
Written sexual orientation nondiscrimination policy statement

Company Overview
The Body Shop is the U.S. division of the U.K.-based company, the Body Shop International. The company has over 300 shops in the United States that sell environmentally safe cosmetics and toiletries. The Body Shop encourages recycling, and its animal-testing-free products use a minimum of packaging. The company has campaigned against human rights abuses in various countries, set up AIDS awareness programs in India and Nepal, and established the Body Shop Foundation to fund human rights and environmental protection groups.

Popular Name Brands or Key Industry Products
Body Butter, No Debate, Activist, Of a Woman, Super Sunnies, the Body Shop Label

Clorox Co.
1221 Broadway
Oakland, CA 94612-1888
(510) 271-7000
(510) 832-1463 (fax)
www.clorox.com

Author's Overall Appraisal
Progressing too slowly

Consumer Cautions
No survey response

Important Considerations
Unknown

Workplace Record on Sexual Orientation
Written sexual orientation nondiscrimination policy statement

Company Overview
Clorox is America's best-selling bleach brand. The company has operations in approximately 40 countries. Its biggest competitor is Procter & Gamble.

Popular Name Brands or Key Industry Products
Clorox, SOS, Pine-Sol, Armor All, Formula 409, Black Flag, Combat, Fresh Step, Scoop Away, Hidden Valley, K.C. Masterpiece, Kingsford, Match Light, Brita, Glad, STP

Colgate-Palmolive
300 Park Ave.
New York, NY 10022-7499
(800) 850-2654 (toll-free)
(212) 310-2000
www.colgate.com
Author's Overall Appraisal
Progressing somewhat
Consumer Cautions
Animal testing
Important Considerations
Diversity training inclusive of people with disabilities
Listed as a Fortune 500 Company
Listed on Domini Social Index
Listed on Standard & Poor's Index
Stock held by Meyers Pride Value Fund
Workplace Record on Sexual Orientation
Diversity training inclusive of sexual orientation
Gay and lesbian employee group
Mixed remarks from vendors or gay and lesbian employees
Written sexual orientation nondiscrimination policy statement
Company Overview
Colgate-Palmolive manufactures and distributes many personal and household products, including laundry detergents, dishwashing products, toothpastes, toothbrushes, shampoos, fabric softeners, and bleach. The company has recently developed wide-scale brand recognition of products in Russia. The company has women and people of color on its board of directors.
Popular Name Brands or Key Industry Products
Ajax, Burst, Challenge, Choice, Cashmere Bouquet, Colgate, Curad, Dynamo, AB, Hour After Hour, Murphy Oil Soap, Palmolive, Science Diet, Ultra Brite, Appeal, CongestAid, Crystal White, Purad, Purity, Dermassage, Fab, Fresh Start, Flora-Guard, Hair Defense, Handi Wipes, Irish Spring, Lady Speed Stick, Showermate, Staysoft, Sterno, Mennen

Deluxe Corp.

3680 Victoria St. N.
Shoreview, MN 55126-2966
(651) 483-7358
(651) 450-4033 (investor transfer agent fax)
www.deluxe.com

Author's Overall Appraisal

Progressing

Consumer Cautions

None

Important Considerations

Diversity training inclusive of people with disabilities

Workplace Record on Sexual Orientation

Encouraging remarks from vendors or gay and lesbian employees
Gay and lesbian employee group
Written sexual orientation nondiscrimination policy statement

Company Overview

Deluxe Corp., founded in 1915 and listed as the 640th largest U.S. company by *Fortune* magazine, provides check printing and business forms to the financial services industry, and sells checks to households and small businesses by direct mail. The company also provides check authorization, account verification, and collection services to financial institutions and retailers, as well as electronic funds transfer services to the financial and retail industries, and electronic benefit transfer services to state governments. Deluxe operates a joint venture called HCL-Deluxe with HCL Corp. of India to provide products and services to financial companies in the United States and India.

As of this writing, Deluxe was considering the implementation of domestic-partner benefits.

Dial Corp.

15501 N. Dial Blvd.
Scottsdale, AZ 85260-1619
(602) 754-3425
(602) 754-1098 (fax)
www.dialcorp.com

Author's Overall Appraisal
Progressing too slowly

Consumer Cautions
No survey response

Important Considerations
Unknown

Workplace Record on Sexual Orientation
Written sexual orientation nondiscrimination policy statement

Company Overview
Dial Corp. makes soap and other consumer products. It kept the Dial name when the earlier Dial Corp. was split in 1996 into two companies, one focusing on consumer products, the other—which took the name Viad—on financial services. Dial competes primarily with Colgate Palmolive and Procter & Gamble. Its products are sold in more than 40 countries.

Popular Name Brands or Key Industry Products
Dial, Breck, Purex, Sta-Flo, Borateem, Renuzit, Armour meats

Eastman Kodak

343 State St.
Rochester, NY 14650
(716) 724-1000
(716) 724-0663 (fax)
www.kodak.com

Author's Overall Appraisal
Very progressive

Consumer Cautions
Affiliated with military contracts

Important Considerations
Affiliated with groups supportive of gay and lesbian rights
Contributes to gay and lesbian nonprofit groups
Diversity training inclusive of people with disabilities
Exceptional workplace record supporting parents
Listed as a Fortune 500 Company
Listed on GLV 100 Index
Listed on Standard & Poor's Index
Significantly visible supporter of ENDA
Stock held by Meyers Pride Value Fund
Supports AIDS services/men's health groups
Supports breast cancer research/women's health groups

Workplace Record on Sexual Orientation
Diversity training inclusive of sexual orientation
Full domestic-partnership health care benefits
Gay and lesbian employee group officially acknowledged
Written sexual orientation nondiscrimination policy statement

Company Overview
Eastman Kodak is a major manufacturer of film and photography equipment. The company has teamed up with many high-tech development and telecommunications industry leaders—particularly those that can enhance the company's ability to compete in the exploding digital imaging business. Kodak has joint venture partnership arrangements with Microsoft, Apple, and IBM—three corporations with excellent records on gay and lesbian issues.

Eastman Kodak was among the cutting-edge companies that sent marketing analysts to Workplace/Marketplace '96 in New York City, the first gay and lesbian consumer and employee conference. Eastman

Kodak vice president of human resources Mike Morley testified in support of ENDA before a Senate committee in 1996. The company maintains an education and development center that provides a four hour class for employees titled "Sexual Orientation Issues in the Workplace."

Eastman Kodak and its gay and lesbian employee group, the Lambda Network, hosted the Family Ties photo exhibit "Love Makes a Family: Living in Lesbian and Gay Families" during National Coming Out Day last year. The display coincided with letters from Kodak management to employees making it clear that harassment or violence against gay and lesbian employees would be immediate grounds for termination.

Popular Name Brands or Key Industry Products
Colorflow, Carousel, Digital Science cameras, Ektachrome, Ektaprint copiers, Kodak cameras, Kodachrome film

The Estée Lauder Cos. Inc.
655 Madison Ave.
New York, NY 10153
(212) 786-4801
www.elcompanies.com

Author's Overall Appraisal
Very progressive

Consumer Cautions
None

Important Considerations
Listed on GLV 100 Index
Supports AIDS services/men's health groups
Supports breast cancer research/women's health groups

Workplace Record on Sexual Orientation
Diversity training inclusive of sexual orientation
Full domestic-partnership health care benefits
Written sexual orientation nondiscrimination policy statement

Company Overview
Estée Lauder is known for quality face and body care products, fragrances, and a complete line of cosmetics for women and men. Estée Lauder products are sold around the world in department stores, boutiques, and specialty retail outlets. Estée Lauder also owns several other popular cosmetics brands.

Popular Name Brands or Key Industry Products
Estée Lauder, Bobbi Brown Essentials, Jane, Clinique, Prescriptives, Origins, Aramis, M-A-C, Aveda, Tommy Hilfiger and Donna Karan fragrances

Gillette

Prudential Tower Building
Boston, MA 02199
(617) 421-7000
(617) 421-7123 (fax)
www.gillette.com

Author's Overall Appraisal
Progressing too slowly

Consumer Cautions
Animal testing
No survey response

Important Considerations
Listed as a Fortune 500 Company
Listed on Standard & Poor's Index

Workplace Record on Sexual Orientation
Mixed remarks from vendors or gay and lesbian employees
Nondiscrimination policy based on the words "sexual preference"

Company Overview
Gillette is one of the world's largest makers of batteries, razor blades, writing products, and toiletries. The company even makes small appliances. Less than half of Gillette's annual sales occur in the United States. The company employs nearly 50,000 people.

Gillette does not have a reputation for being sympathetic to gay and lesbian concerns. It reportedly pulled advertising from same-sex-themed episodes of *Golden Girls* and *L.A. Law*.

Popular Name Brands or Key Industry Products
Adorn, Agility, Atra, Bare Elegance, Braun appliances, Clear Gel, CustomPlus, Daisy, Dippity Do, Dry Idea, Dry Line correction film, Dry Look, Duracell batteries, Epic Waves, Face Saver, Foamy Gillette, Foot Guard, Good News, Lady Gillette, Liquid Paper, Micro Trac Blades, Mink Difference, Oral-B, Parker Pens, Paper Mate, Pencil Mate, Pivot Plus, Platinum Plus, Right Guard, Roller Stick, SensorExcel, Silkience, Soft and Dri, Swivel, Tame, ThermoScan ear thermometers, Toni, Trac II, Waterman pens, White Rain

Herman Miller
855 E. Main St.
P.O. Box 302
Zeeland, MI 49464-0302
(888) 874-0045 (toll-free)
www.hermanmiller.com

Author's Overall Appraisal
Progressive

Consumer Cautions
None

Important Considerations
Listed on Domini Social Index
Supports AIDS services/men's health groups
Supports breast cancer research/women's health groups

Workplace Record on Sexual Orientation
Diversity training inclusive of sexual orientation
Encouraging remarks from vendors or gay and lesbian employees
Full domestic-partnership health care benefits
Gay and lesbian employee group
Written sexual orientation nondiscrimination policy statement

Company Overview
Herman Miller is a major manufacturer of office furniture and home furnishings. The company is also involved in the manufacture of medical and health care equipment.

Home Depot
2455 Paces Ferry Road
Atlanta, GA 30339
(770) 433-8211
(770) 431-2685 (fax)
www.homedepot.com

Author's Overall Appraisal
Progressing too slowly

Consumer Cautions
No survey response

Important Considerations
Listed as a Fortune 500 Company
Listed on Standard & Poor's Index
Listed on Domini Social Index
Supports breast cancer research/women's health groups

Workplace Record on Sexual Orientation
Mixed remarks from vendors or gay and lesbian employees

Company Overview
Home Depot is a popular superstore for home improvement products. The company has over 800 stores and more than 100,000 employees.

IKEA

Ny Strandvej 21 DK-3053
Humlebaeck, Denmark
+45-49-15-50-00
+45-49-15-50-01
www.ikea.com

Author's Overall Appraisal

Progressive

Consumer Cautions

None

Important Considerations

Affiliated with groups supportive of gay and lesbian rights
Diversity training inclusive of people with disabilities
Exceptional workplace record supporting parents
Has included gay- or lesbian-suggestive imagery in mainstream advertising or programming
Listed on Domini Social Index
Listed on GLV 100 Index
Significantly visible supporter of ENDA
Supports AIDS services/men's health groups
Supports breast cancer research/women's health groups

Workplace Record on Sexual Orientation

Diversity training inclusive of sexual orientation
Encouraging remarks from vendors or gay and lesbian employees
Gay and lesbian employee group officially acknowledged
Written sexual orientation nondiscrimination policy statement

Company Overview

IKEA sells more than 10,000 home furnishing pieces ranging from furniture to dinnerware. The company sells its products in 28 countries through hundreds of stores. Ikea employs more than 40,000 people.

Ikea ran television commercials in selected American markets showing two gay men shopping for a table. The company received worldwide attention for this exciting advertising breakthrough.

Johnson & Johnson

1 Johnson & Johnson Plaza
New Brunswick, NJ 08933
(732) 524-0400
(732) 524-3300 (fax)
www.jnj.com

Author's Overall Appraisal
Progressing too slowly

Consumer Cautions
No survey response.

Important Considerations
Unknown

Workplace Record on Sexual Orientation
Written sexual orientation nondiscrimination policy statement

Company Overview
Johnson & Johnson employs nearly 100,000 people and is perhaps the world's largest manufacturer of health care products, with operations in dozens of countries. Unfortunately, it took threats from shareholders to get the company to implement a written nondiscrimination policy statement that included sexual orientation.

Popular Name Brands or Key Industry Products
Tylenol, Motrin, Band-Aid, Reach toothbrushes and dental floss, Acuvue contact lenses, Ergamisol cancer treatment therapy, Ortho-Novum oral contraceptives, Neutrogena, Monistat, OB, Stayfree

Kimberly-Clark

351 Phelps Drive
Irving, TX 75038
(972) 281-1200
(972) 281-1490 (fax)
www.kimberly-clark.com

Author's Overall Appraisal
Progressing somewhat

Consumer Cautions
Animal testing

Important Considerations
Affiliated with groups supportive of gay and lesbian rights
Listed as a Fortune 500 Company
Listed on Domini Social Index
Stock held by Meyers Pride Value Fund
Supports AIDS services/men's health groups
Supports breast cancer research/women's health groups

Workplace Record on Sexual Orientation
Diversity training inclusive of sexual orientation
Encouraging remarks from vendors or gay and lesbian employees
Written sexual orientation nondiscrimination policy statement

Company Overview
Over 55,000 people work at Kimberly-Clark, one of the world's largest providers of products manufactured with paper. Kimberly-Clark also develops hospital supplies, medical and surgical equipment, and more.

There are some ongoing environmental issues with Kimberly-Clark. For instance, according to the Center on Economic Policy, "Kimberly-Clark is one of the country's largest manufacturers of disposable diapers, which have been criticized for their contribution to municipal solid waste problems."

Popular Name Brands or Key Industry Products
Accord, Anyday, Boutique, Dawn, Kleenex, Kimbies, Security, Teri, Atta-Boy, Atta-Girl, Avert, Baby Steps, Basic, Bundle Pack, Casuals, Cellucotton, Cheer, Classic, Columns, Comfort-Designs, Command, Cottonelle, Depend undergarments, Free and Easy, Fresh Guard, Hi-Dri paper towels, Huggies, Kimwipes, Kotex, Lightdays, Neenah paper, New Freedom, Scott paper products, Softique, Thick and Thirsty paper towels, Vogue toilet paper, Viva paper towels, Tough Cat work clothes.

Kmart Corp.

3100 W. Big Beaver Rd.
Troy, MI 48084
(248) 643-1000
(248-) 643-5636 (fax)
www.kmart.com

Author's Overall Appraisal
Not progressive

Consumer Cautions
No survey response
No domestic-partner health care insurance

Workplace Record on Sexual Orientation
Nondiscrimination policy on sexual orientation not confirmed

Company Overview
Kmart, the third largest chain of retail outlets in the United States, does not offer domestic-partner benefits. Spokesperson Rosie O'Donnell's affiliation with the company has been questioned by activists. Kmart competes primarily with Sears and Wal-Mart. Numerous part-time employees work at Kmart. The company markets popular name-brand clothing, housewares, furniture, and general merchandise through some 2,000 locations nationwide. Kmart also offers grocery departments in many of its outlets.

Maytag

403 W. 4th St. N.
Newton, IA 50208
(515) 792-8000
(515) 791-8115 (fax)
www.maytagcorp.com

Author's Overall Appraisal
Progressing too slowly

Consumer Cautions
No domestic partner healthcare benefits

Important Considerations
Listed on Domini Social Index
Listed as a Fortune 500 Company
Supports breast cancer research/women's health groups

Workplace Record on Sexual Orientation
Mixed remarks from vendors or gay and lesbian employees
Written sexual orientation nondiscrimination policy statement

Company Overview
Maytag is one of the five largest manufacturers of major appliances, and has more than 20,000 employees. In the same league with General Electric and Whirlpool, the company makes washers, dryers, refrigerators, stoves, vending machines, and Hoover vacuum cleaners.

Newell Rubbermaid
29 E. Stephenson St.
Freeport, IL 61032
(815) 235-4171
(815) 381-8155 (fax)
www.newellco.com

Author's Overall Appraisal
Progressing too slowly

Consumer Cautions
No survey response

Important Considerations
Unknown

Workplace Record on Sexual Orientation
Unknown

Company Overview
Newell Rubbermaid manufactures housewares, household organization and home improvement items, and children's furnishings and toys.

Polaroid

784 Memorial Drive
Cambridge, MA 02139
(781) 386-2000
www.polaroid.com

Author's Overall Appraisal
Progressive

Consumer Cautions
Affiliated with military contracts
Possible overseas labor problems

Important Considerations
Affiliated with groups supportive of gay and lesbian rights
Diversity training inclusive of people with disabilities
Early and significantly visible supporter of ENDA
Has advertised in the gay and lesbian press
Listed as a Fortune 500 Company
Listed on Domini Social Index

Workplace Record on Sexual Orientation
Diversity training inclusive of sexual orientation
Full domestic-partnership health care benefits
Encouraging remarks from vendors or gay and lesbian employees
Gay and lesbian employee group officially acknowledged
Written sexual orientation nondiscrimination policy statement

Company Overview
Polaroid has over 10,000 employees and sells cameras around the world. Polaroid products are manufactured throughout Latin America and Europe.

Popular Name Brands or Key Industry Products
600 Business Edition, Captiva, OneStep cameras, Polaroid 600 film, Sidekick cameras, Spectra cameras, Time Zero consumer and business photography systems

Procter & Gamble
P.O. Box 599
Cincinnati, OH 45201-0599
(513) 983-1100
www.pg.com

Author's Overall Appraisal
Progressing too slowly

Consumer Cautions
Affiliated with military contracts
Possible overseas labor problems
No domestic partner healthcare benefits

Important Considerations
Diversity training inclusive of people with disabilities
Exceptional workplace record supporting parents
Listed as a Fortune 500 Company
Listed on Domini Social Index
Stock held by Meyers Pride Value Fund
Supports breast cancer research/women's health groups

Workplace Record on Sexual Orientation
Diversity training inclusive of sexual orientation
Mixed remarks from vendors or gay and lesbian employees
Written sexual orientation nondiscrimination policy statement

Company Overview
Procter & Gamble is an enormous company with over 100,000 employees and an operating cash flow nearing $6 billion. The company boasts a shareholder return of nearly 40% over the last three years. Procter & Gamble dominates the marketplace in a number of product categories, particularly those aimed at women's needs. For instance, the company has nearly 44 percent of the tampon market. The company has operations in 70 countries, and its stock is held by the Meyers Pride Value Fund. In 1999 it announced it would cease testing products on animals, except when such tests are required by law; it expected that it would be able to end animal testing on 80% of its products.

Popular Name Brands or Key Industry Products
Always, Bold, Bounce, Dash, Comet, Head and Shoulders, Ivory, Lava, Spic and Span, Pringles, Tide, Vidal Sassoon, Zest, Aleve, Attends, Banner, Big Top, Biz, Blue Ribbon Recipe, Bonus, Bounty, Bounty Microwave, Bowl Quick, BNP, Camay, Carefree Essentials, Cascade, Cer-

tain, Charmin, Cheer, Cheez'ums, Cloraseptic, Cinch, Citrus Hill, Clearasil, Coast, Creamsuds, Creamy Homestyle, Crest, Crisco, Dawn, Deep Dark Sunless, Detail, Dibs, Double Hawaiian Punch, Downy, Dreft, Duncan Hines, Duz, Encaprin, Enrichment de Pantene, Era, Fast Track, Feel Wet Liner, Fisher Favorites, Fit Produce Rinse, Fluffo, Fruitcal, Frymax, Fun Prints, Gain, Gentle Block, Giorgio Beverly Hills, Lite Natural Spray, Giorgio Red, Gleem, Glodo, Golden Nip, Gurd's, Head & Chest, Hidden Magic, High Point, Hugo Boss, Icy Hot, Impact, India Express, Jif, Joy, Kik, Kirk, Launette Special, Laura Biagiotti, Lavender & Old Lace, Lestoil, Light Duty, LO-Range, Luvs, Maximizer, Merit, Metamucil, Moist & Easy, Monchel, Mr. Clean, Navy, Necta Sweet, Night Spice, Norforms, Norwich, NP27, Nutex, Aosis, Ocusol, Off Shoot-T, Oil of Olay, Old Spice, Olean, Orange Nip, Oxydol, Oace, Pampers, Pantastic, Pantene, Pepto-Bismol, Peridex, Pert, Posh Puffs, Power Pouches, Prell, Prep, Primex, Whisper, Rejoice, Nyquil, Vicks Formula 44, Safeguard, Secret, SK-11

Revlon Inc.
625 Madison Ave.
New York, NY 10022
(212) 527-4000
(212) 527-6946 (fax)
www.revlon.com

Author's Overall Appraisal
Progressing too slowly

Consumer Cautions
No survey response

Important Considerations
Unknown

Workplace Record on Sexual Orientation
Unknown

Company Overview
Revlon is one of the largest beauty, make-up, and personal care cosmetics manufacturers and distributors in the county. Top competitors include Unilever and Procter & Gamble.

Popular Name Brands or Key Industry Products
Charlie, Flex, Mitchum, American Crew, Almay, Ultima II

Rite Aid Corp.

30 Hunter Lane
Camp Hill, PA 17011-2404
(717) 761-2633
(717) 975-5871 (fax)
www.riteaid.com

Author's Overall Appraisal
Progressing somewhat

Consumer Cautions
No survey response

Important Considerations
Provides many part-time and flextime jobs to working parents and youth

Workplace Record on Sexual Orientation
Written sexual orientation nondiscrimination policy statement

Company Overview
Rite Aid is a drugstore company operating throughout the United States in nearly 4,000 locations. Much of its growth has come through acquisitions. Its largest recent purchase was the 1,006-store Thrifty Payless chain in 1996. Rite Aid's biggest competitors are Walgreen and CVS.

Toys "R" Us
461 From Road
Paramus, NJ 07652
(201) 262-7800
(201) 262-7606 (fax)
www10.toysrus.com

Author's Overall Appraisal
Progressing too slowly

Consumer Cautions
No domestic partner healthcare benefits

Important Considerations
Diversity training inclusive of people with disabilities
Listed on Domini Social Index
Listed as a Fortune 500 Company

Workplace Record on Sexual Orientation
Gay and lesbian employee group
Written sexual orientation nondiscrimination policy statement

Company Overview
Toys "R" Us is perhaps the world's biggest retailer of games and toys. The company employs over 100,000 people and operates approximately 1,500 stores.

Unilever N.V.

Weena 455, P.O. Box 760
3000 DK Rotterdam, The Netherlands
+31-10-217-4000
+31-10-217-4798 (fax)
www.unilever.com

Author's Overall Appraisal
Progressing too slowly

Consumer Cautions
No survey response

Important Considerations
Listed as a Fortune 500 Company

Workplace Record on Sexual Orientation
Unknown

Company Overview
Unilever is a joint venture business comprised of two companies: Unilever N.V. (located in the Netherlands), and Unilever PLC (headquartered in England). These two giants make up one of the world's largest packaged goods operations, with 270,000 employees, manufacturing operations in 88 countries, and sales in a further 70. Unilever is the licensee for the Calvin Klein fragrances, Obsession and Eternity.

Popular Name Brands or Key Industry Products
Lipton, Wisk, Obsession and Eternity perfumes, Dove, Vaseline, Pepsodent, Q-Tips, Country Crock, Lifebuoy, Mentadent, Close-Up, Aim, Suave, Salon Selectives, Lever 2000, Elizabeth Taylor fragrances, Elizabeth Arden fragrances

Wal-Mart Stores Inc.
702 SW 8th St.
Bentonville, AR 72716-8611
(501) 273-4000
(501) 273-1917 (fax)
www.wal-mart.com

Author's Overall Appraisal
Progressing too slowly

Consumer Cautions
No survey response

Important Considerations
Unknown

Workplace Record on Sexual Orientation
Unknown

Company Overview
Wal-Mart is the world's largest retailer, with over 3,500 outlets and 900,000 employees worldwide. The company specializes in mass retailing of home furnishings, consumer products, clothing and accessories, lawn and garden supplies, computers, sporting and hunting equipment, jewelry, automotive maintenance items, and lighting. The company is also the second largest grocer in the United States. Wal-Mart's primary competitors are Kmart, Target, and, increasingly, Sears.

Whirlpool

2000 M-63 North
Benton Harbor, MI 49022
(616) 923-5000
www.whirlpoolcorp.com

Author's Overall Appraisal
Progressing too slowly

Consumer Cautions
Possible overseas labor problems

Important Considerations
Listed as a Fortune 500 Company
Listed on Domini Social Index

Workplace Record on Sexual Orientation
Mixed remarks from vendors or gay and lesbian employees
Written sexual orientation nondiscrimination policy statement

Company Overview
Whirlpool is a major manufacturer of major home appliances, under brand names including KitchenAid and Roper as well as Whirlpool. The company is not known for strong support of gays and lesbians, though its Whirlpool Foundation, the main philanthropic arm of the company, has given millions of dollars to the United Way. In addition, the company offers an employee matching gifts program.

Entertainment, Media, and Publishing

Every major Hollywood film studio now offers domestic-partner health coverage for gay and lesbian employees, and most cable television and new media production companies have become more progressive on sexual orientation over the past two years. Within this industry, entertainment and, increasingly, news-gathering organizations are the more progressive. Publishing and distributing companies are still a bit sluggish on gay and lesbian issues.

The Gay and Lesbian Alliance Against Defamation, the National Lesbian and Gay Journalists Association, and the Gay Financial Network are excellent sources of information on gay and lesbian issues in relation to the media.

General Industry Resources:

Amazon.com
www.amazon.com
American Booksellers Association
www.ambook.org
American Film Marketing Association
www.afma.com
Editor & Publisher Interactive
www.mediainfo.com
Gay and Lesbian Alliance Against Defamation
www.glaad.org
The Media History Project Connections Pages
www.mediahistory.com/print.html
Motion Picture Association of America
www.mpaa.org
National Lesbian and Gay Journalists Association
www.nlgja.org
Newspaper Association of America
www.naa.org
Recording Industry Association of America
www.riaa.com/
Video Software Dealers Association
www.vsda.org

Barnes and Noble

122 5th Ave.
New York, NY 10011
(212) 633-3300
www.barnesandnoble.com

Author's Overall Appraisal
Progressive

Consumer Cautions
None

Important Considerations
Affiliated with groups supportive of gay and lesbian rights
Exceptional workplace record supporting parents
Has advertised in the gay and lesbian press
Includes gay- or lesbian-suggestive imagery in mainstream advertising or programming
Listed on GLV 100 Index
Significantly visible supporter of ENDA

Workplace Record on Sexual Orientation
Diversity training inclusive of sexual orientation
Encouraging remarks from vendors or gay and lesbian employees
Full domestic-partnership health care benefits
Gay and lesbian employee group
Written sexual orientation nondiscrimination policy statement

Company Overview
Barnes and Noble is one of America's largest booksellers. It owns numerous superstores in metropolitan areas, offers online shopping, and operates Barnes and Noble College Bookstores, located at hundreds campuses throughout the United States, offering everything from textbooks to clothing. The company is privately held, growing rapidly, and making many in the bookselling industry very unhappy—particularly smaller chains and independent bookstores.

Most urban areas have at least one gay and lesbian bookstore, and many people believe that whenever possible queer books should be bought in those bookstores. The degree of importance you place on supporting gay-owned bookstores is something only you can determine. Gay and lesbian consumers should keep in mind that Barnes and Noble provides much-needed access to gay and lesbian books in areas of the country where gay and lesbian bookstores don't exist.

Bureau of National Affairs
1231 25th St., N.W.
Washington, D.C. 20037
(202) 452-4200
(202) 452-4610 (fax)
www.bna.com

Author's Overall Appraisal
Progressive

Consumer Cautions
None

Important Considerations
Affiliated with groups supportive of gay and lesbian rights
Diversity training inclusive of people with disabilities
Exceptional workplace record supporting parents
Has included gay- or lesbian-suggestive imagery in mainstream advertising or programming
Significantly visible supporter of ENDA
Supports AIDS services/men's health groups
Supports breast cancer research/women's health groups

Workplace Record on Sexual Orientation
Diversity training inclusive of sexual orientation
Encouraging remarks from vendors or gay and lesbian employees
Full domestic-partnership health care benefits
Gay and lesbian employee group
Written sexual orientation nondiscrimination policy statement

Company Overview
The Bureau of National Affairs is a publisher of periodicals, newsletters, books, and pamphlets on law, medical news, public policy, regulatory issues, and the environment. It is employee-owned and has over 1,800 workers, making it one of the major nongovernmental employers in the Washington, D.C., area. It was one of the first mainstream organizations to study and report on employers with gay-friendly workplace policies.

Gannett Co.

1100 Wilson Blvd.
Arlington, VA 22234
(800) 368-3553 (toll-free)
(703) 284-6000
(703) 558-3506 (fax)
www.gannett.com

Author's Overall Appraisal
Progressing somewhat

Consumer Cautions
Possible overseas labor problems

Important Considerations
Exceptional workplace record supporting parents
Listed as a Fortune 500 Company
Listed on Domini Social Index
Listed on GLV 100 Index
Listed on Standard & Poor's Index
Supports AIDS services/men's health groups
Supports breast cancer research/women's health groups

Workplace Record on Sexual Orientation
Diversity training inclusive of sexual orientation
Gay and lesbian employee group
Mixed remarks from vendors or gay and lesbian employees
Written sexual orientation nondiscrimination policy statement

Company Overview

Gannett employs approximately 40,000 people and is the nation's largest newspaper group in terms of circulation. The company publishes *USA Today* and 73 other daily newspapers across the United States. The company also owns 21 television stations, has a variety of nondaily publications such as the Sunday newspaper supplement *USA Weekend,* and in 1999 acquired Newsquest PLC, the largest regional newspaper publisher in England.

Reactions differ from paper to paper regarding working atmospheres for gay and lesbian employees, and the news coverage of gay issues varies by region as well. *USA Today* has helped raise gay and lesbian visibility in American society by routinely covering gay and lesbian events. In recent years it has featured many positive stories about gay and lesbian culture, marketing, and parenting.

On the other hand, in the spring of 1998 one of Gannett's papers, the *Gainesville* [Ga.] *Times,* abruptly stopped providing printing services to the Atlanta-based gay and lesbian newspaper *Southern Voice.* According to published reports, the decision to stop printing *Southern Voice* came shortly after religious leaders urged congregation members to cancel their subscriptions to the *Gainesville Times* and contact its advertisers to complain about its affiliation with *Southern Voice.*

MCA/Universal
100 Universal City Plaza
Universal City, CA 91608
(818) 777-1000
(818) 866-1402 (fax)
www.universalstudios.com

Author's Overall Appraisal
Progressive

Consumer Cautions
Affiliated with sales of tobacco
Affiliated with sales of alcoholic beverages

Important Considerations
Affiliated with groups supportive of gay and lesbian rights
Has advertised in the gay and lesbian press
Has included gay- or lesbian-suggestive imagery in mainstream advertising or programming
Listed as a Fortune 500 Company
Supports AIDS services/men's health groups
Supports breast cancer research/women's health groups

Workplace Record on Sexual Orientation
Diversity training inclusive of sexual orientation
Full domestic-partnership health care benefits
Gay and lesbian employee group officially acknowledged

Company Overview
About 15,000 people work full-time at Universal Studios, which produces and distributes major motion pictures, independent films, television shows, videos, and syndications. Seagram, which has a good record on gay and lesbian workplace issues, owns a controlling portion of stock in Universal, which, in turn, owns Spencer Gifts, Universal Studios theme parks, and a portion of Cineplex Odeon motion picture theaters.

McGraw-Hill
1221 Avenue of the Americas
New York, NY 10020
(212) 512-2000
(212) 512-4871 (fax)
www.mcgraw-hill.com

Author's Overall Appraisal
Progressing too slowly

Consumer Cautions
None

Important Considerations
Exceptional workplace record supporting parents
Listed as a Fortune 500 Company
Listed on Domini Social Index
Listed on Standard & Poor's Index
Supports AIDS services/men's health groups
Supports breast cancer research/women's health groups

Workplace Record on Sexual Orientation
Diversity training inclusive of sexual orientation
Gay and lesbian employee group
Mixed remarks from vendors or gay and lesbian employees
Written sexual orientation nondiscrimination policy statement

Company Overview

McGraw-Hill is one of the world's leading educational book publishers. It develops consumer and government educational textbooks, CD-ROMS, and videos, and it publishes *Business Week* magazine. One of McGraw-Hill's most recognizable subsidiaries is Standard & Poor's, which provides corporate credit ratings and financial information services. Approximately 17,000 people work at McGraw-Hill.

Sources say the company has been looking at the issue of domestic-partnership health care insurance for gay and lesbian employees, but an official target date for implementation was not available at the time of this writing.

New York Times Co.
229 W. 43rd Street
New York, NY 10036
(212) 556-1234
www.nytco.com

Author's Overall Appraisal
Very progressive

Consumer Cautions
None

Important Considerations
Affiliated with groups supportive of gay and lesbian rights
Diversity training inclusive of people with disabilities
Exceptional workplace record supporting parents
Has included gay- or lesbian-suggestive imagery in mainstream advertising or programming
Listed as a Fortune 500 Company
Listed on Domini Social Index
Listed on GLV 100 Index
Significantly visible supporter of ENDA
Supports AIDS services/men's health groups
Supports breast cancer research/women's health groups

Workplace Record on Sexual Orientation
Diversity training inclusive of sexual orientation
Encouraging remarks from vendors or gay and lesbian employees
Full domestic-partnership health care benefits
Gay and lesbian employee group officially acknowledged
Written sexual orientation nondiscrimination policy statement

Company Overview
The New York Times Co. publishes *The New York Times* and maintains business interests in a variety of news- and entertainment-oriented environments, including magazine publishing and television broadcasting. The company also owns *The Boston Globe,* 18 other daily newspapers, three nondailies, eight TV stations and two radio stations. It is co-owner, with the Washington Post Co., of the *International Herald Tribune.*

Scholastic
555 Broadway
New York, NY 10012
(212) 343-6100
www.scholastic.com
Author's Overall Appraisal
Progressive
Consumer Cautions
None
Important Considerations
Affiliated with groups supportive of gay and lesbian rights
Diversity training inclusive of people with disabilities
Exceptional workplace record supporting parents
Listed on Domini Social Index
Listed on GLV 100 Index
Stock held by Meyers Pride Value Fund
Supports AIDS services/men's health groups
Supports breast cancer research/women's health groups
Workplace Record on Sexual Orientation
Diversity training inclusive of sexual orientation
Encouraging remarks from vendors or gay and lesbian employees
Full domestic-partnership health care benefits
Gay and lesbian employee group
Written sexual orientation nondiscrimination policy statement
Company Overview
Scholastic is a major publisher of books for children. The company also produces educational and professional periodicals, as well as electronic media. The company is widely known for Scholastic Math Placement, the Scholastic Workshop, Scholastic Network, Scholastic News, and an animated science series on PBS, *The Magic School Bus*.
Popular Name Brands or Key Industry Products
Baby-Sitters Club, Blue Sky Press, Clifford the Big Red Dog, Goosebumps, *Instructor* magazine, *Junior Scholastic*, *The Magic School Bus*, *Parent and Child* magazine

Sony Corp.

7-35, Kitashinagawa
6-chome
Shinagawa-ku
Tokyo, MO 141, Japan
+81-3-5448-2111
+81-3-5448-2183 (fax)
www.world.sony.com

Author's Overall Appraisal
Progressing

Consumer Cautions
No survey response
Only Sony Pictures Entertainment division information was available

Important Considerations
Unknown

Workplace Record on Sexual Orientation
Full domestic-partnership health care benefits (at Sony Pictures Entertainment)
Gay and lesbian employee group
Written sexual orientation nondiscrimination policy statement

Company Overview
Sony makes home video game systems, semiconductors, LCDs, DVD players, MiniDiscs, TVs, VCRs, and sound systems. The company has a number of worldwide joint ventures, owns Columbia Records and Sony Pictures Entertainment (which includes Columbia TriStar film and TV production operations), and is involved in product insurance, licensing, and retailing. Maatsushita and Time Warner are its biggest competitors.

Popular Name Brands or Key Industry Products
Sony products, PlayStation, DVD, Columbia Records, Columbia TriStar

Time Warner

75 Rockefeller Plaza
New York, NY 10019
(212) 484-8000
(212) 956-2847 (fax)

Author's Overall Appraisal
Progressing somewhat

Consumer Cautions
None

Important Considerations
Exceptional workplace record supporting parents
Listed on GLV 100 Index
Supporter of ENDA
Supports AIDS services/men's health groups
Supports breast cancer research/women's health groups

Workplace Record on Sexual Orientation
Encouraging remarks from vendors or gay and lesbian employees
Full domestic-partnership health care benefits
Gay and lesbian employee group officially acknowledged
Written sexual orientation nondiscrimination policy statement

Company Overview
Time Warner is gigantic. It is involved with all kinds of products, licensing, and broadcasting, including television, music, motion pictures, book and magazine publishing, and video. One of the best-known entities owned by Time Warner is *Time* magazine.

Although generally moving in the right direction, Time Warner is still capable of screwing up. *Time* magazine's 75th anniversary issue, published in 1998, did not contain a single reference to the gay rights movement or AIDS. Thankfully, such oversights are not routine at Time Warner. Many of its publications have admirably covered gay and lesbian issues—often on the covers.

Popular Name Brands or Key Industry Products
Warner Bros., Home Box Office, Time Warner Cable, CNN, TNT, TBS, Castle Rock Entertainment, Atlanta Braves baseball team, Atlanta Hawks basketball team, New Line Cinema, Little, Brown and Co.

Viacom
1515 Broadway
New York, NY 10036
(212) 258-6000
(212) 258-6100 (fax)
info@viacom.com
www.viacom.com

Author's Overall Appraisal
Progressive

Consumer Cautions
Affiliated with groups less than supportive of gay and lesbian rights

Important Considerations
Affiliated with groups supportive of gay and lesbian rights
Diversity training inclusive of people with disabilities
Exceptional workplace record supporting parents
Has advertised in the gay and lesbian press
Has included gay- or lesbian-suggestive imagery in mainstream advertising or programming
Listed on Domini Social Index
Listed on GLV 100 Index
Stock held by Meyers Pride Value Fund
Supports AIDS services/men's health groups
Supports breast cancer research/women's health groups

Workplace Record on Sexual Orientation
Diversity training inclusive of sexual orientation
Full domestic-partnership health care benefits
Gay and lesbian employee group officially acknowledged
Written sexual orientation nondiscrimination policy statement

Company Overview
Viacom is a huge entertainment company that looks to get even bigger with its planned acquisition of CBS Corp., announced in September 1999. Viacom's holdings already include MTV, VH1, Nickelodeon, Nick at Nite, Showtime, Paramount Pictures, Paramount Television, Spelling Entertainment, Simon & Schuster publishing, several TV stations, half-interests in the United Paramount Network and Comedy Central, and more than 80% of Blockbuster Inc., the video-store operation. Viacom employs about 80,000 people and has senior-level managers involved in influential gay and lesbian organizations such as GLAAD.

Village Voice (Stern Publishing)

36 Cooper Square
New York, NY 10003
800-338-9508 (toll-free)
(212) 475-3333
www.villagevoice.com

Author's Overall Appraisal
  Progressive

Consumer Cautions
  Affiliated with sales of alcohol
  Affiliated with sales of tobacco

Important Considerations
  Affiliated with groups supportive of gay and lesbian rights
  Early supporter of ENDA
  Exceptional workplace record supporting parents
  Has advertised in the gay and lesbian press
  Has included gay- or lesbian-suggestive imagery in mainstream advertising or programming
  Listed on GLV 100 Index
  Supports AIDS services/men's health groups
  Supports breast cancer research/women's health groups

Workplace Record on Sexual Orientation
  Encouraging remarks from vendors or gay and lesbian employees
  Full domestic-partnership health care benefits
  Gay and lesbian employee group
  Written sexual orientation nondiscrimination policy statement

Company Overview

  The Village Voice was the first well-known newspaper to offer domestic-partnership health care benefits to its gay and lesbian employees. The paper has been championing human rights, women's rights, gay and lesbian rights, and equal opportunity actions since the 1960s.

  The Village Voice is owned by Stern Publishing, part of the Hartz Group, which also has interests in pet-care products and real estate development. Stern Publishing is privately held by billionaire Leonard Stern. He also owns other newspapers, including the *Long Island Voice, L.A. Weekly,* and *Orange County Weekly.*

Walt Disney/ABC
500 N. Buena Vista St.
Burbank, CA 91505
(818) 553-7200
http://disney.go.com

Author's Overall Appraisal
Progressive

Consumer Cautions
Possible overseas labor problems

Important Considerations
Affiliated with groups supportive of gay and lesbian rights
Diversity training inclusive of people with disabilities
Exceptional workplace record supporting parents
Has advertised in the gay and lesbian press
Has included gay- or lesbian-suggestive imagery in mainstream advertising or programming
Listed as a Fortune 500 Company
Listed on Domini Social Index
Listed on GLV 100 Index
Listed on Standard & Poor's Index
Significantly visible supporter of ENDA
Supports AIDS services/men's health groups
Supports breast cancer research/women's health groups

Workplace Record on Sexual Orientation
Diversity training inclusive of sexual orientation
Full domestic-partnership health care benefits
Gay and lesbian employee group officially acknowledged
Has had gay/lesbian discrimination lawsuits
Mixed remarks from vendors or gay and lesbian employees
Written sexual orientation nondiscrimination policy statement

Company Overview
Walt Disney was the last of the big media conglomerates to offer domestic-partnership benefits to its gay and lesbian employees. On the other hand, the company's political support of its gay and lesbian employees, and of gay and lesbian rights in general, has been rock-solid. Its contributions to organizations and charities of interest to gays and lesbians are noteworthy, as are the company's many gay- and lesbian-inclusive programming decisions.

The Most Influential Companies / 167

Popular Name Brands or Key Industry Products
Walt Disney Pictures, Touchstone Pictures, Hollywood Pictures, Miramax Films, Buena Vista Television, Touchstone Television, Walt Disney Television, ABC Television Network, ESPN, Lifetime (part owner), A&E Network, Walt Disney World, Disneyland, Tokyo Disneyland, Disneyland Paris, Hyperion Press, Anaheim Angels baseball team, Anaheim Mighty Ducks hockey team, and numerous television, cable, and radio companies throughout North America

Ziff-Davis Inc.

28 E. 28th St.
New York, NY 10016-7930
(212) 503-3500
(212) 503-4599 (fax)
www.ziffdavis.com

Author's Overall Appraisal

Progressive

Consumer Cautions

None

Important Considerations

Affiliated with groups supportive of gay and lesbian rights
Diversity training inclusive of people with disabilities
Listed as a Fortune 500 Company
Listed on GLV 100 Index

Workplace Record on Sexual Orientation

Full domestic-partnership health care benefits
Gay and lesbian employee group
Written sexual orientation nondiscrimination policy statement

Company Overview

Ziff-Davis Inc. employs approximately 3,500 people, and is the largest producer of computing and Internet-related magazines in the United States. The company maintains offices in numerous locations in the United States and abroad.

Ziff-Davis was among the early corporate fighters against Colorado's antigay Amendment 2. The company's domestic-partnership health care coverage includes a dental plan that can be applied to gay and lesbian partners' adopted children.

Popular Name Brands or Key Industry Products

Computer Gaming World, Computer Shopper, Inter@ctive Week, Expert Gamer, Family PC, MacWeek, PC Computing, PC Magazine, PC Week, Windows Sources, Yahoo! Internet Life

Food and Beverage Service

The majority of the food and beverage industry, including the restaurant and fast food sector, is not progressive on gay and lesbian issues. Almost none of the major food, beverage, and restaurant companies in the United States offer domestic-partner health care insurance for gay and lesbian employees, and many have implemented sexual orientation nondiscrimination policy statements only under the threat of shareholder action.

General Industry Resources:

American Culinary Federation
  www.acfchefs.org
Center for Food Safety and Applied Nutrition
  www.cfsan.fda.gov/list.html
The Culinary Connection
  www.culinary.com/
Diners Grapevine World Restaurant Guide
  www.dinersgrapevine.com
Food Products On-Line
  www.foodindustry.com/food/index.html
Food Pyramid Guide
  www.ganesa.com/food/index.html
Foodweb
  www foodweb.com
National Food Processors Association
  www.nfpa-food.org/
National Restaurant Association
  www.restaurant.org/
USDA Nutrient Values
  www.rahul.net/cgi-bin/fatfree/usda/usda.cgi

Adolph Coors Co.

12th and Ford Streets
Golden, CO 80401
(800) 642-6116 (toll-free)
(888) 621-3212 (toll-free)
(303) 279-6565

Author's Overall Appraisal
Progressing somewhat

Consumer Cautions
Coors family affiliated with groups less than supportive of gay and lesbian rights
Producer of alcoholic beverages

Important Considerations
Affiliated with groups supportive of gay and lesbian rights
Diversity training inclusive of people with disabilities
Has advertised in the Gay and Lesbian press
Listed on GLV 100 Index
Supports AIDS services/men's health groups

Workplace Record on Sexual Orientation
Diversity training inclusive of sexual orientation
Full domestic-partnership health care benefits
Gay and lesbian employee group officially acknowledged
Written sexual orientation nondiscrimination policy statement

Company Overview
Coors is controversial. The company is supportive of its gay and lesbian employees, providing domestic-partnership health care insurance, which its competitors do not. Coors also markets its products to gay and lesbian consumers, and sponsors gay and lesbian community events.

On the other hand, the Coors family, which owns the majority of the company's stock, has long been associated with antigay right-wing organizations such as the Heritage Foundation and the Free Congress Foundation.

Popular Name Brands or Key Industry Products
Coors beer, Coors Light, Coors Extra Gold, Coors Non-Alcoholic, Blue Moon Abbey Ale, Blue Moon Belgian White Ale, Keystone, Keystone Ice, Keystone Light, Zima Clear, Winterfest

Anheuser-Busch
One Busch Place
St. Louis, MO 63118
(314) 577-2000
(314) 577-2900 (fax)
www.anheuser-busch.com

Author's Overall Appraisal
Progressing somewhat

Consumer Cautions
Producer of alcoholic beverages

Important Considerations
Diversity training inclusive of people with disabilities
Has advertised in the gay and lesbian press
Listed as a Fortune 500 Company
Supports AIDS services/men's health groups

Workplace Record on Sexual Orientation
Diversity training inclusive of sexual orientation
Gay and lesbian employee group
Has had gay/lesbian discrimination lawsuits
Mixed remarks from vendors or gay and lesbian employees
Written sexual orientation nondiscrimination policy statement

Company Overview
Anheuser-Busch makes beer and owns the Sea World and Busch Gardens theme parks. The company has a written nondiscrimination policy statement inclusive of the words sexual orientation, but its actual implementation date is still in question. Busch has advertised extensively to gay and lesbian consumers, and has sponsored gay pride events around the country. In the spring of 1999 it ran a print ad featuring two men holding hands. Like many of its competitors, Busch gives equally to Republican and Democratic candidates.

Popular Name Brands or Key Industry Products
Budweiser, Bud Light, Michelob, Busch, ZiegenBock Amber, Red Wolf, O'Doul's (nonalcoholic)

Archer Daniels Midland Co.
4666 Faries Parkway
Decatur, IL 62526
(217) 424-5200
(217) 424-6196 (fax)
www.admworld.com

Author's Overall Appraisal

Not progressing

Consumer Cautions

No survey response

Nongay boycott activity

Important Considerations

Unknown

Workplace Record on Sexual Orientation

Unknown

Company Overview

Archer Daniels Midland, which processes grains and other agricultural commodities into ingredients used in food production, likes to refer to itself as the "supermarket to the world." The company is a political favorite of many conservative groups and provided a private jet to Bob Dole for use during his presidential bid. In 1996 ADM was convicted of price fixing and received a $100 million fine.

Ben & Jerry's Homemade
30 Community Drive
South Burlington, VT 05403-6828
(802) 651-9600
(802) 651-9751 (fax)
www.benjerry.com

Author's Overall Appraisal
Very progressive

Consumer Cautions
None

Important Considerations
Affiliated with groups supportive of gay and lesbian rights
Contributes to gay/lesbian nonprofit groups and political organizations
Exceptional workplace record supporting parents
Has advertised in the gay and lesbian press
Listed on Domini Social Index
Listed on GLV 100 Index
Significantly visible supporter of ENDA
Stock held by Meyers Pride Value Fund
Supports AIDS services/men's health groups
Supports breast cancer research/women's health groups

Workplace Record on Sexual Orientation
Full domestic-partnership health care benefits
Gay and lesbian employee group officially acknowledged
Written sexual orientation nondiscrimination policy statement

Company Overview
Ben & Jerry's employs approximately 700 people and manufactures the second–best-selling ice cream in the United States (after Häagen-Dazs). It sells its ice cream through company-owned outlets, franchised retail locations, and grocery and convenience stores.

Ben & Jerry's contributes a sizable portion of its profits (7.5%) to charity. The company also sponsors the gay and lesbian pride parade in Burlington, Vt.

Burger King (Diageo PLC)

17777 Old Cutler Road
Miami, FL 33157
(305) 378-3000
(305) 378-7219
www.burgerking.com

Author's Overall Appraisal

Not Progressing

Consumer Cautions

No survey response
Producer of alcoholic beverages

Important Considerations

Unknown

Workplace Record on Sexual Orientation

Unknown

Company Overview

Burger King, a subsidiary of London-based Diageo PLC, owns and operates or franchises restaurants throughout the United States and in 54 countries around the world. Diageo is one of the world's largest consumer products companies. Burger King serves approximately 1,400 customers per day in each of its restaurants. The company employs 28,000 people, a figure that balloons to more than 300,000 when its franchise operations are included.

Popular Name Brands or Key Industry Products

Diageo's portfolio of international food and drinks brands includes Guinness, Pillsbury, Green Giant, Häagen-Dazs, Old El Paso, Progresso, Burger King, Smirnoff Vodka, Bailey's Original Irish Creme, and J&B Rare Scotch Whisky

Campbell Soup Co.
Campbell Place
Camden, NJ 08103-1799
(609) 342-4800
(609) 342-3878 (fax)
www.campbellsoups.com
Author's Overall Appraisal
Progressing
Consumer Cautions
None
Important Considerations
Affiliated with groups supportive of gay and lesbian rights
Exceptional workplace record supporting parents
Listed on GLV 100 Index
Significantly visible supporter of ENDA
Supports AIDS services/men's health groups
Supports breast cancer research/women's health groups
Workplace Record on Sexual Orientation
Gay and lesbian employee group
Written sexual orientation nondiscrimination policy statement
Company Overview
Campbell Soup Co. manufactures soups, sauces, juices, and other food products. The company chose to not renew its endorsement contract with former NFL football player Reggie White after he repeatedly made insulting and bigoted comments about gay and lesbian Americans. Other companies, such as Nike, defended White's "freedom of speech."
Popular Name Brands or Key Industry Products
Campbell's Soups, Pace, Prego, Pepperidge Farm, Godiva, SpaghettiOs, V8, others

Celestial Seasonings
4600 Sleepytime Drive
Boulder, CO 80301
(800) 351-8175 (toll-free)
(303) 581-1249
(303) 581-1249 (fax)
www.celestialseasonings.com

Author's Overall Appraisal
Progressive

Consumer Cautions
None

Important Considerations
Exceptional workplace record supporting parents
Has advertised in the gay and lesbian press
Listed on GLV 100 Index
Supports AIDS services/men's health groups
Supports breast cancer research/women's health groups

Workplace Record on Sexual Orientation
Diversity training inclusive of sexual orientation
Full domestic-partnership health care benefits
Written sexual orientation nondiscrimination policy statement

Company Overview
Celestial Seasonings makes 53 different kinds of beverages, which it distributes to hundreds of stores nationwide. It also has a joint venture with Perrier to market ready-to-drink iced teas.

Popular Name Brands or Key Industry Products
Sleepytime, Wild Cherry Blackberry, Red Zinger, Raspberry Zinger, Morning Thunder, Lemon Zinger, Cinnamon Apple Spice, Fast Lane, others

Cracker Barrel Old Country Store

106 Castle Heights Ave. N.
Lebanon, TN 37087
(615) 444-5533
(615) 443-9480 (fax)
www.crackerbarrelocs.com

Author's Overall Appraisal

Not progressive

Consumer Cautions

Has fired gay and lesbian employees based on sexual orientation

Has refused to rehire or compensate fired gay and lesbian employees

Company Overview

Cracker Barrel Old Country Store is one of the worst examples of how to run a company when it comes to sexual orientation issues. It has fired gay employees simply for being gay, and it has steadfastly refused to acknowledge that its policy is discriminatory, despite shareholder resolutions, boycotts, and public demonstrations across the country. Gay consumers would be well advised to not patronize any of its 405 eating and gift establishments.

Darden Restaurants Inc.

P.O. Box 953330
Orlando, FL 32859-3330
(407) 245-6789 (investor relations)
(407) 245-5114 (fax)
www.darden.com

Author's Overall Appraisal
Not progressive

Consumer Cautions
Diversity training program installed only after a court order required it

Important Considerations
Unknown

Workplace Record on Sexual Orientation
Has had gay/lesbian discrimination lawsuits

Company Overview
Darden Restaurants Inc., owner of Red Lobster, Olive Garden, and Bahama Breeze, was sued by an assistant manager of a Red Lobster in suburban Chicago who contended he was fired for being gay. The Cook County Commission on Human Rights in 1998 ruled in the employee's favor, awarded him damages, and ordered him reinstated; it also mandated diversity training at all Red Lobster restaurants in Cook County. The company drew additional fire from gay rights groups because it challenged the constitutionality of Cook County's human rights ordinance; it quickly withdrew the challenge. Darden has 1,100 restaurants around the world. The company claims to have a written nondiscrimination policy inclusive of sexual orientation, but as of this writing had yet to provide proof. Human Rights Campaign officials, however, said Darden has been responsive to concerns raised by HRC.

Popular Name Brands or Key Industry Products
Red Lobster, Olive Garden, Bahama Breeze

Denny's Restaurants

203 E. Main St.
Spartanburg, SC 29319
(864) 597-8000
(864) 597-7538 (fax)

Author's Overall Appraisal

Progressing too slowly

Consumer Cautions

No survey response

Non–gay-related boycott activity

Was sued by customers for sexual orientation discrimination

Company Overview

In 1998 three people filed suit against Denny's claiming they were given intentionally poor service at one of the chain's Northern California restaurants because they were gay. Other customers have filed lawsuits claiming they were denied service because of their race. Denny's paid $45.7 million to settle a suit by black customers in 1994. The company contends it does not tolerate discrimination of any type but also is taking a "strong stand against frivolous lawsuits."

Domino's Pizza

30 Frank Lloyd Wright Drive
P.O. Box 997
Ann Arbor, MI 48106-0997
(734) 930-3030
(734) 669-3657 (fax)
www.dominos.com

Author's Overall Appraisal
Not progressive

Consumer Cautions
No survey response
Non–gay-related boycott activity

Important Considerations
Unknown

Workplace Record on Sexual Orientation
·Unknown

Company Overview
Domino's is a pizza delivery company with more than 6,000 locations and 120,000 employees. The company has been the subject of boycotts by feminists and pro-choice advocates because of founder Tom Monaghan's antiabortion activism. In 1988 Monaghan, then Domino's majority owner and chief executive, gave a personal—not corporate—contribution of $50,000 to the Michigan Committee to End State-Funded Abortions. Monaghan retired in 1998 and sold 93% of the company to Bain Capital Inc.

General Mills

P.O. Box 1113
Minneapolis, MN 55440
(612) 764-2311
www.generalmills.com

Author's Overall Appraisal
Progressing somewhat

Consumer Cautions
None

Important Considerations
Listed as a Fortune 500 Company
Listed on Domini Social Index
Listed on Standard & Poor's Index
Supporter of ENDA
Supports AIDS services/men's health groups
Supports breast cancer research/women's health groups

Workplace Record on Sexual Orientation
Encouraging remarks from vendors or gay and lesbian employees
Gay and lesbian employee group officially acknowledged
Written sexual orientation nondiscrimination policy statement

Company Overview
General Mills has over 10,000 employees and is one of America's leading providers of food. The company has a joint venture with PepsiCo to market snack foods in Europe and an alliance with Nestlé to sell cereal in more than 70 international markets.

The company has been very receptive regarding sexual orientation education and awareness programs and makes grants to gay and lesbian organizations. General Mills' CEO has publicly stated that gay and lesbian employees are valuable and necessary to the company's future success, and the company's diversity department is said to be working on bringing domestic-partnership health care coverage to the organization.

Popular Name Brands or Key Industry Products
Bac-Os, Betty Crocker, Bisquick, Bugles, Cheerios, Chex Mix, Chicken Helper, Cocoa Puffs, Gold Medal Flour, Lucky Charms, Trix, Wheaties, Yoplait, Robin Hood Flour, Hamburger Helper, Oatmeal Crisp, Frankenberry, Fiber One, Kaboom, Kix, Nature Valley, Pop Secret, Potato Buds, Raisin Nut Bran, Reese's Peanut Butter Puffs, Stir N Bake, SuperMoist, Total, Tuna Helper

Hershey Foods Corp.
100 Crystal A Drive
Hershey, PA 17033
(717) 534-6799
(717) 534-6760 (fax)
www.hersheys.com

Author's Overall Appraisal
Progressing too slowly

Consumer Cautions
No survey response

Important Considerations
Exceptional workplace record supporting parents

Workplace Record on Sexual Orientation
Unknown

Company Overview
Controlled by the Milton Hershey School Trust, Hershey manufactures chocolate and a variety of other foods. The company employs approximately 17,000 people.

Popular Name Brands or Key Industry Products
Hershey candy bars, syrups, and baking products; Sweet Escapes, TasteTations, Hershey's Kisses, Reese's Peanut Butter Cups, York peppermint patties, Twizzlers, Kit Kat, Skor, Jolly Rancher, Mounds, Milk Duds, Mr. Goodbar, Caramello, Heath, Almond Joy

Hormel Foods Corp.
One Hormel Place
Austin, MN 55912-3680
(507) 437-5611
(507) 437-5489 (fax)
www.hormel.com

Author's Overall Appraisal
Progressing somewhat

Consumer Cautions
None

Important Considerations
Affiliated with groups supportive of gay and lesbian rights
Exceptional workplace record supporting parents
Listed as a Fortune 500 Company
Supports AIDS services/men's health groups
Supports breast cancer research/women's health groups

Workplace Record on Sexual Orientation
Gay and lesbian employee group
Written sexual orientation nondiscrimination policy statement

Company Overview
Hormel Foods is a major manufacturer of canned and fresh meat products and dry foodstuffs. The company employs approximately 11,000 people.

James Hormel, heir to the Hormel family fortune, is an out gay man and a staunch supporter of gay and lesbian causes. He is a founding member of the Human Rights Campaign, and in 1999 he became the United States's first openly gay ambassador. He is not, however, involved in the management of Hormel, nor does he own a controlling interest in the company.

Popular Name Brands or Key Industry Products
Dinty Moore, Spam, Mary Kitchen, Peloponnese olive oil, Chi-Chi's Mexican foods, House of Tsang cooking oils

Kellogg Co.

1 Kellogg Square
Battle Creek, MI 49016-3599
(616) 961-2000
(616) 961-2871 (fax)
www.kelloggs.com

Author's Overall Appraisal
Progressing somewhat

Consumer Cautions
None

Important Considerations
Unknown

Workplace Record on Sexual Orientation
Written sexual orientation nondiscrimination policy statement

Company Overview
Kellogg is the nation's largest maker of prepared cereals, breads, and pastries. Kellogg sells it products in two dozen countries. The company's primary competitors are Quaker Oats and General Mills. The W.K. Kellogg Foundation owns 30% of the company.

Popular Name Brands or Key Industry Products
All-Bran, Apple Jacks, Corn Flakes, Froot Loops, Frosted Flakes, Rice Krispies, Special K, Eggo, Nutri-Grain, Pop-Tarts, Lender's, Rice Krispies Treats

McDonald's

McDonald's Plaza
Oak Brook, IL 60523
(630) 623-3000
(630) 623-5004 (fax)
www.mcdonalds.com

Author's Overall Appraisal

Progressing too slowly

Consumer Cautions

No survey response

Important Considerations

Diversity training inclusive of people with disabilities
Listed as a Fortune 500 Company
Listed on Domini Social Index
Supports breast cancer research/women's health groups
Supports children's groups

Workplace Record on Sexual Orientation

Mixed remarks from vendors or gay and lesbian employees
Written sexual orientation nondiscrimination policy statement (does not apply to franchises)

Company Overview

In April of 1999, McDonald's agreed to implement a written sexual orientation nondiscrimination policy statement when faced with a shareholder resolution by gay and lesbian investors who own stock in the company.

With nearly 25,000 restaurants and more than 250,000 employees, McDonald's is the biggest fast food chain in the world. McDonald's accounts for about half of all fast-food hamburgers sold in America. Statistics reflect that children motivate at least half of all sales made at McDonald's. About 61% of the restaurants are franchised, 22.5% are company-owned, and the remainder run by affiliates. The company did $35 billion in systemwide sales in 1998.

Nabisco Group Holdings Corp.

1301 Avenue of the Americas
New York, NY 10119
(212) 258-5777
(212) 969-9173 (fax)
www.rjrnabisco.com

Author's Overall Appraisal
Progressing somewhat

Consumer Cautions
Affiliated with groups less than supportive of gay and lesbian rights

Important Considerations
Listed as a Fortune 500 Company
Supporter of ENDA

Workplace Record on Sexual Orientation
Mixed remarks from vendors or gay and lesbian employees
Written sexual orientation nondiscrimination policy statement

Company Overview
In 1999 RJR Nabisco split up its food and tobacco businesses, with the food company becoming known as Nabisco Group Holdings Corp. and the tobacco company as R.J. Reynolds Tobacco. Nabisco Group Holdings owns 80% of Nabisco Holdings Corp., which in turn is the parent of Nabisco Inc., maker of crackers, cookies, snacks, and other grocery products. Before the split, a healthy portion of RJR Nabisco's sales come from tobacco—which the company marketed to gays and lesbians. Before Joe Camel was retired, he routinely appeared on billboards and in magazines dressed like a gay "clone."

Popular Name Brands or Key Industry Products
Cream of Wheat, Milk-Bone, Life Savers, SnackWell's, Grey Poupon, A.1. Steak Sauce, Oreos, Chips Ahoy, Nilla Wafer, Nutter Butter, Honeymaid Graham Crackers, Planters nuts and snacks, Fig Newtons, Teddy Grahams, Ritz crackers, Triscuit

Naya Inc.

Naya Inc.
255 Daniel Johnson Blvd.
Labal, Quebec H722L1 Canada
or
1200 High Ridge Road
Stamford, CT 06905
(800) 566-6292 (toll-free)
(203) 321-4808 (fax)
www.naya.com

Author's Overall Appraisal
Very progressive

Consumer Cautions
No confirmed domestic partner healthcare insurance

Important Considerations
Affiliated with groups supportive of gay and lesbian rights
Has advertised in the gay and lesbian press
Supporter of ENDA
Supports AIDS service/men's health groups
Supports breast cancer research/women's health groups

Workplace Record on Sexual Orientation
Diversity training inclusive of sexual orientation
Written sexual orientation nondiscrimination policy statement

Company Overview
Naya Inc. distributes premium-quality spring water in bottles made of recyclable material. The water comes from sources in the Canadian provinces of Quebec and British Columbia. Naya water is sold in 30 countries.

Nestlé S.A.
Avenue Nestlé 55
Case Postale 353
CH-1800
Vevey, Switzerland
41-21-921 2111
41-21-921 1885 (fax)
or
Nestlé USA Inc.
800 N. Brand Blvd.
Glendale, CA 91203
(818) 549-6000
(818) 549-6952 (fax)

Author's Overall Appraisal
Progressing too slowly

Consumer Cautions
Possible overseas labor problems

Important Considerations
Listed as a Fortune 500 Company
Supports breast cancer research/women's health groups

Workplace Record on Sexual Orientation
Diversity training inclusive of sexual orientation
Gay and lesbian employee group
Mixed remarks from vendors or gay and lesbian employees
Written sexual orientation nondiscrimination policy statement

Company Overview
Nestlé is the world's largest food company. The company markets nearly 10,000 products ranging from dog food to candy bars. Nestlé's biggest competitors are Mars and Philip Morris.

Popular Name Brands or Key Industry Products
Carnation Evaporated Milk, Coffee-mate, Nescafé, Taster's Choice, Hills Bros., Nesquik, Nestea, Juicy Juice, Nestlé Crunch, Butterfinger, Contadina, Drumstick, Fancy Feast, Libby's, Lean Cuisine, Mighty Dog, Stouffer's, Turtles, Arrowhead, Calistoga, Poland Spring, Perrier, San Pellegrino

The Most Influential Companies / 189

PepsiCo Inc.
700 Anderson Hill Road
Purchase, NY 10577
(914) 253-2000
(914) 253-2070 (fax)
www.pepsico.com

Author's Overall Appraisal
Progressing too slowly

Consumer Cautions
Affiliated with companies or groups less than supportive of gay and lesbian rights
Affiliated with sales of alcoholic beverages
No domestic partner healthcare benefits

Important Considerations
Listed as a Fortune 500 Company
Listed on Domini Social Index

Workplace Record on Sexual Orientation
No confirmed written sexual orientation nondiscrimination policy statement

Company Overview
PepsiCo employs nearly half a million people, and manufactures and sells soft drinks and snack foods.

Popular Name Brands or Key Industry Products
Pepsi, Mountain Dew, Mug Root Beer, Slice, Tostitos, Smartfood, Fritos, Cheetos, Doritos, Munchos, Rold Gold, Sun Chips, Ruffles, Lays, Funyons, Lipton prepared teas, Aquafina water, Tropicana Dole juices, Grandma's cookies

Philip Morris Cos. Inc.

120 Park Avenue
New York, NY 10017
(800) 442-0077 (shareholder information)
(212) 663-5000
(212) 878-2167 (fax)
pmfct@em.fcnbd.com (shareholder e-mail address)

Author's Overall Appraisal
Progressing too slowly

Consumer Cautions
Affiliated with groups less than supportive of gay and lesbian rights
Affiliated with the production of tobacco
No domestic partner healthcare benefits

Important Considerations
Affiliated with groups supportive of gay and lesbian rights
Has advertised in the Gay and Lesbian press
Supports AIDS services/men's health groups
Supports breast cancer research/women's health groups

Workplace Record on Sexual Orientation
Written sexual orientation nondiscrimination policy statement

Company Overview
Many people think only of tobacco when they hear the name Philip Morris. In reality, over the past 20 years, the company has moved aggressively into food production. The company now owns General Foods, which it acquired in 1985, and Kraft, which it purchased three years later.

Philip Morris has incurred the wrath of the gays and lesbians over such issues as campaign contributions to ultraconservative Senator Jesse Helms of North Carolina—leading to a boycott of Marlboro cigarettes and Miller beer by AIDS activists. The company continues to fund right-wing political campaigns, but has increased its funding to AIDS organizations, which led to the boycott being called off.

Philip Morris occasionally advertises its brands in gay and lesbian publications, and, through Miller beer and Benson & Hedges cigarettes, the company supported a California state gay and lesbian rights ordinance. Yet the company's Kraft food division would not allow its brands to be advertised during *Roseanne*'s famous lesbian kiss episode.

Popular Name Brands or Key Industry Products
Marlboro, Benson & Hedges, Virginia Slims, Merit, Parliament, Cambridge, Basic, Alpine, Players, Bucks, Bristol, Lark, L&M, Next, Miller, Red Dog, Icehouse, Southpaw Light, Leinenkugel's, Meister Brau, Milwaukee's Best, Molson, Foster's, Sharp's nonalcoholic, Magnum, Presidente, Maxwell House, Sanka, General Foods International Coffees, Maxim, Country Time, Crystal Light, Kool-Aid, Tang, Capri Sun, Alpha Bits, Banana Nut Crunch, Shredded Wheat, Grape Nuts, Honeycomb, Raisin Bran, Miracle Whip, Good Seasons, Velveeta, DiGiorno, Jell-o, Oscar Mayer, Philadelphia Cream Cheese, Stove Top

Quaker Oats

P.O. Box 049001
Chicago, IL 60604-9001
(312) 222-7111
(312) 222-8532 (fax)
www.quakeroats.com

Author's Overall Appraisal

Progressing somewhat

Consumer Cautions

None

Important Considerations

Affiliated with groups supportive of gay and lesbian rights
Diversity training inclusive of people with disabilities
Listed as a Fortune 500 Company
Listed on Domini Social Index
Supporter of ENDA
Supports AIDS services/men's health groups
Supports breast cancer research/women's health groups

Workplace Record on Sexual Orientation

Diversity training inclusive of sexual orientation
Gay and lesbian employee group acknowledged
Mixed remarks from vendors or gay and lesbian employees
Written sexual orientation nondiscrimination policy statement

Company Overview

Quaker Oats has nearly 12,000 employees and is said to be "considering" domestic-partnership health care benefits, but no definitive date for implementation has been set. Quaker no longer owns Snapple, but it does own many other popular brands such as Gatorade.

Popular Name Brands or Key Industry Products

Cap'n Crunch, Crunch Berries, Gatorade, Life, Quaker Cereals, Quaker Chewy granola bars, Mother's cereals, Quisp, Rice-A-Roni, Pasta Roni, Near East, Aunt Jemima

Ralston Purina

Checkerboard Square
St. Louis, MO 63164
(314) 982-1000
(314) 982-2752 (fax)
www.ralston.com

Author's Overall Appraisal
Progressing somewhat

Consumer Cautions
None

Important Considerations
Listed as a Fortune 500 Company
Listed on Domini Social Index
Supports breast cancer research/women's health groups

Workplace Record on Sexual Orientation
Encouraging remarks from vendors or gay and lesbian employees
Written sexual orientation nondiscrimination policy statement

Company Overview
Ralston Purina, with over 20,000 employees and 26 plants worldwide, is one of the largest manufacturers of pet products. In the past few years it has been getting out of unrelated businesses to focus on this one. It announced plans in June 1999 to spin off its Eveready battery division as a separate company. It spun off its international animal feed and agricultural products businesses in 1998 and sold its soy products division to DuPont in 1997. Ralston Purina had sales of $4.6 billion for the fiscal year that ended September 30, 1998.

Popular Name Brands or Key Industry Products
Alley Cat, Beggin' Strips, Bonz, Butcher's Blend, Cat Chow, Dog Chow, Eveready, Energizer, Fit & Trim, Happy Cat, Kibbles and Bits, Kitten Chow, Kit'NKaboodle, Meow Mix, Purina One, T Bonz, Tender Vittles, Tidy Cat, Whisker Lickin's

Safeway Inc.

5918 Stonebridge Mall Road
Pleasanton, CA 94588
(925) 467-3000
(925) 467-3323 (fax)
www.safeway.com

Author's Overall Appraisal
Progressing too slowly

Consumer Cautions
Affiliated with groups less than supportive of gay and lesbian rights
Affiliated with sales of alcoholic beverages
Affiliated with sales of tobacco

Important Considerations
Affiliated with groups supportive of gay and lesbian rights
Diversity training inclusive of people with disabilities
Listed as a Fortune 500 Company
Stock held by Meyers Pride Value Fund

Workplace Record on Sexual Orientation
Gay and lesbian employee group
Mixed remarks from vendors or gay and lesbian employees
Nondiscrimination policy based on the words "sexual preference"

Company Overview
Safeway operates over 1,500 grocery stores in the United States and Canada. The Vons supermarket group merged with Safeway in 1997. Safeway acquired the Dominick's chain in the Chicago area in 1998, and it announced plans in 1999 to acquire Texas-based Randall's Food Markets. An affiliated company, Casa Ley, operates 77 food stores in Mexico.

Safeway has a good record on diversity in the workplace, and an especially good history in helping people with disabilities. In addition, the company is proud of the fact that 25% of eligible U.S. employees participate in the company's payroll-deduction stock purchase plan. Safeway has been a leading corporate sponsor of the National Easter Seal Society since the mid 1980s, raising close to $50 million.

Sara Lee
Three First National Plaza
Chicago, IL 60602
(312) 726-2600
(312) 558-8567 (fax)
www.saralee.com

Author's Overall Appraisal
Progressive

Consumer Cautions
None

Important Considerations
Affiliated with groups supportive of gay and lesbian rights
Diversity training inclusive of people with disabilities
Exceptional workplace record supporting parents
Listed as a Fortune 500 Company
Listed on GLV 100 Index
Listed on Standard & Poor's Index
Supports AIDS services/men's health groups
Supports breast cancer research/women's health groups

Workplace Record on Sexual Orientation
Diversity training inclusive of sexual orientation
Gay and lesbian employee group officially acknowledged
Written sexual orientation nondiscrimination policy statement
Domestic partner benefits under consideration

Company Overview
Sara Lee manufactures food and clothing. The company the largest in the world named for a woman and is committed to the workplace advancement of women and minorities. Gay and lesbian employees are present in senior management, and had comforting things to say about Sara Lee, including that the company is considering implementation of domestic-partnership health care benefits.

Each year the company's philanthropic arm, the Sara Lee Foundation, presents its annual Frontrunner Awards for accomplishments by notable women in business, government, the arts, and the humanities. Past winners have included Dr. Susan Love, Sarah Brady, Sandra Day O'Connor, and Ruth Bader Ginsburg. In addition, the foundation annually presents the Sara Lee Leadership Awards, which recognize and support nonprofit organizations that are demonstrating innovative leadership in addressing the problems of disadvantaged people in areas where Sara Lee has facilities. The award carries with it a $25,000 grant. Recipients in 1998 included Bread & Roses Inc., providing services to people with HIV or AIDS in Connecticut; and Children's Hope Foundation, a New York City organization providing services to children with HIV or AIDS. The company is also a strong supporter of the Women's National Basketball Association.

Popular Name Brands or Key Industry Products

Sara Lee foods, Bali, Playtex, Wonderbra, Champion, Coach accessories, Beefy-T's, Donna Karan legwear, Hanes, Just My Size, L'eggs, Sheer Energy, Superior Coffee, Ball Park, Jimmy Dean, Hillshire Farms, Sinai 48, Endust, Ty-D-Bol, Aqua Velva, Brylcreem, Kiwi and Meltonian shoe polishes

The Seagram Company Ltd.
375 Park Ave.
New York, NY 10052
(212) 572-7000
(212) 572-1080 (fax)
www.seagram.com

Author's Overall Appraisal
Progressive

Consumer Cautions
Producer of alcoholic beverages

Important Considerations
Affiliated with groups supportive of gay and lesbian rights
Contributes to gay and lesbian nonprofit groups
Diversity training inclusive of people with disabilities
Early supporter of ENDA
Has advertised in the gay and lesbian press
Includes gay- or lesbian-suggestive imagery in mainstream advertising or programming
Listed on Domini Social Index
Listed on GLV 100 Index
Supports AIDS services/men's health groups
Supports breast cancer research/women's health groups

Workplace Record on Sexual Orientation
Diversity training inclusive of sexual orientation
Full domestic-partnership health care benefits
Gay and lesbian employee group officially acknowledged
Written sexual orientation nondiscrimination policy statement

Company Overview

Seagram employs approximately 30,000 people and is one of the world's largest producers and distributors of alcoholic beverages. It owns an 80% share of Universal Studios and a minority percentage of Time Warner. It acquired PolyGram in 1998.

Seagram is generally considered one of the most progressive alcoholic beverage companies when it comes to gay and lesbian issues. Seagram has long supported AIDS causes, and was one of the first companies to support the Gay and Lesbian Alliance Against Defamation. It also was one of the first alcoholic beverage companies to provide domestic-partnership heath insurance benefits to its gay and lesbian employees.

Popular Name Brands or Key Industry Products
Seagram's 7 Crown, Seagram's V.O., Seagram's Extra Dry Gin, Captain Morgan, Château Margaux, Chivas Regal, Crown Royal, Four Roses, Glenlivet, Martell

7-Eleven Inc.
2711 N. Haskell Ave.
Dallas, TX 75204
(800) 255-0711 (toll-free)
(214) 828-7011
www.7-eleven.com

Author's Overall Appraisal
Progressing somewhat

Consumer Cautions
Affiliated with sales of alcoholic beverages
Affiliated with sales of tobacco

Important Considerations
Affiliated with groups supportive of gay and lesbian rights
Diversity training inclusive of people with disabilities
Has advertised in the gay and lesbian press
Supports AIDS services/men's health groups
Supports breast cancer research/women's health groups

Workplace Record on Sexual Orientation
Written sexual orientation nondiscrimination policy statement

Company Overview
The world's largest convenience store chain, 7-Eleven Inc. (formerly Southland Corp.) has 5,600 stores in the United States, of which 3,000 are operated by franchisees and 450 by licensees. Also, 7-Eleven, its licensees, and its affiliates operate another 12,500 convenience stores around the world. Although the company culture is admittedly conservative, Southland is regarded by franchisers as a defender and advocate of workplace diversity.

Starbucks Coffee Co.

2401 Utah Avenue South
Seattle, WA 98124
(800) 344-1575 (toll-free)
(206) 447-1575
(206) 447-3029 (fax)
www.starbucks.com

Author's Overall Appraisal
Progressive

Consumer Cautions
Affiliated with groups less than supportive of gay and lesbian rights
Canada trade problems

Important Considerations
Affiliated with groups supportive of gay and lesbian rights
Contributes to gay/lesbian nonprofit groups and political organizations
Diversity training inclusive of people with disabilities
Listed on Domini Social Index
Listed on GLV 100 Index
Stock held by Meyers Pride Value Fund
Supports AIDS services/men's health groups
Supports breast cancer research/women's health groups

Workplace Record on Sexual Orientation
Diversity training inclusive of sexual orientation
Full domestic-partnership health care benefits
Gay and lesbian employee group officially acknowledged
Written sexual orientation nondiscrimination policy statement

Company Overview
Starbucks has 2,200 coffee shops around the world. Starting with one store in Seattle in 1971, it has grown to become the largest retailer of custom and gourmet blend coffees in the United States. It also sells whole bean coffees through a specialty sales group, a direct-response business, supermarkets, and its Web site. It has joint-venture partnerships to sell bottled coffee drinks and ice creams, and it markets premium teas through a subsidiary, Tazo Tea Co. Starbucks has made signification contributions to children's groups and AIDS housing organizations.

Popular Name Brands or Key Industry Products
Caffé Verona, Starbucks Breakfast Blend, Frappucino, Yukon Blend, Espresso Roast, Italian Roast, Gold Coast Blend

Tyson Foods

P.O. Box 2020
Springdale, AR 72765-2020
(501) 290-4000
(501) 290-4061 (fax)
www.tyson.com

Author's Overall Appraisal
Progressing too slowly

Consumer Cautions
No survey response

Important Considerations
Unknown

Workplace Record on Sexual Orientation
Unknown

Company Overview
Tyson is the world's largest poultry producer. It also produces frozen foods through Culinary Foods Inc., tortillas, taco shells, and chips through Mexican Original, and hogs through its Pork Group subsidiary. It sold off its seafood operations in 1999. Tyson employs 66,000 people and had sales of $7.4 billion in 1998. Tyson's principal competitor is Perdue Farms.

Wendy's International Inc.

4288 W. Dublin Granville Rd.
Dublin, OH 43017-0256
(614) 764-3100
(614) 764-3330 (fax)
www.wendysintl.com

Author's Overall Appraisal
Not progressive

Consumer Cautions
Affiliated with groups less than supportive of gay and lesbian rights

Important Considerations
Supports breast cancer research/women's health groups

Workplace Record on Sexual Orientation
No written sexual orientation nondiscrimination policy statement

Company Overview
Wendy's has more than 5,400 fast-food locations worldwide. The company often wins consumer kudos as having the best-tasting burger. Wendy's primarily competes with McDonald's and Burger King. The company also owns Tim Hortons, one of the largest doughnut retailers in Canada, which is expanding into the United States. Wendy's left a bad taste with gays and lesbians when it failed to advertise on *Ellen*'s coming-out episode in 1997, despite having been a regular advertiser on the show. Company officials said Wendy's simply wasn't scheduled to have commercials on *Ellen* that particular week

Insurance and Health Care

Insurance providers are more progressive than they were just two years ago, but many pharmaceutical companies still do not provide domestic-partner health care benefits, even though some produce medical supplies, life-extending drugs, and other products used in the fight against HIV and AIDS.

General Industry Resources:

American Association of Pharmaceutical Scientists
  www.aaps.org
American Pharmaceutical Association
  www.aphanet.org
Association of Clinical Research Professionals
  www.acrpnet.org/index2.html
Consumer Healthcare Products Association
(formerly Nonprescription Drug Manufacturers Association)
  http://ndmainfo.org
Drug Information Association
  www.diahome.org
Food and Drug Administration
  www.fda.gov

Aetna
151 Farmington Ave.
Hartford, CT 06156
(860) 273-0123
(860) 275-2677 (fax)
www.aetna.com

Author's Overall Appraisal
Progressive

Consumer Cautions
None

Important Considerations
Affiliated with groups supportive of gay and lesbian rights
Diversity training inclusive of people with disabilities
Exceptional workplace record supporting parents
Listed as a Fortune 500 Company
Supports AIDS services/men's health groups
Supports breast cancer research/women's health groups

Workplace Record on Sexual Orientation
Diversity training inclusive of sexual orientation
Encouraging remarks from vendors or gay and lesbian employees
Full domestic-partnership health care benefits
Gay and lesbian employee group officially acknowledged
Written sexual orientation nondiscrimination policy statement

Company Overview
Aetna has three core businesses: Aetna U.S. Healthcare, which offers health insurance plans; Aetna Retirement Services, offering retirement, financial planning, and investment products to individuals and employers; and Aetna International, which offers life insurance, pension management, health products, and limited property-casualty insurance in 16 countries. In 1999 Aetna acquired Prudential HealthCare, making Aetna the largest U.S. provider of health benefits. Aetna's record on paying for experimental AIDS and cancer treatment therapies is mixed.

Allstate

Allstate Plaza
2775 Sanders Road
Northbrook, IL 60062-6127
(847) 402-5000
(847) 836-3998 (fax)
www.allstate.com

Author's Overall Appraisal
Progressing too slowly

Consumer Cautions
None

Important Considerations
Exceptional workplace record supporting parents
Supports AIDS services/men's health groups
Supports breast cancer research/women's health groups

Workplace Record on Sexual Orientation
Diversity training inclusive of sexual orientation
Gay and lesbian employee group
Has had gay and lesbian discrimination lawsuits
Mixed remarks from vendors or gay and lesbian employees
Written sexual orientation nondiscrimination policy statement

Company Overview
Allstate sells life, home, and auto insurance through 15,000 agents. It has 39,000 non-agent employees. It has more than 20 million policyholders in the United States and Canada, and it has some international operations. It has won several awards for philanthropy and employee volunteerism.

American Home Products

5 Giralda Farms
Madison, NJ 07940
(973) 660-5013
(973) 660-7026 (fax)
www.ahp.com

Author's Overall Appraisal

Progressing somewhat

Consumer Cautions

None

Important Considerations

Diversity training inclusive of people with disabilities
Listed as a Fortune 500 Company
Listed on Standard & Poor's Index
Supports breast cancer research/women's health groups

Workplace Record on Sexual Orientation

Gay and lesbian employee group
Written sexual orientation nondiscrimination policy statement

Company Overview

American Home Products employs about 60,000 people and manufactures health care products. Its international sales nearly equal its domestic sales. The company does not have domestic-partnership health care insurance, but sources say those benefits are "just around the corner." American Home Products has subsidiaries with connections to AIDS treatment and research, including Wyeth-Ayerst Laboratories, Genetics Institute, and Immunex.

Popular Name Brands or Key Industry Products

Advil, Anacin, Anbesol, Caltrate, Centrum, Chap Stick, Dimetapp, Denorex, FiberCon, Dristan, Preparation H, Primatene, Robitussin, Norplant, Premarin, Leukin, Ativan, Effexor, Acel-Imune, Bicillin, Surpax, Phenergan

Bayer Corp.

100 Bayer Road
Pittsburgh, PA 15205-9741
(412) 777-2000
(412) 777-2034 (fax)
www.bayerus.com

Author's Overall Appraisal
  Progressive

Consumer Cautions
  Animal testing

Important Considerations
  Diversity training inclusive of people with disabilities
  Exceptional workplace record supporting parents
  Has included gay- or lesbian-suggestive imagery in mainstream advertising or programming
  Listed on GLV 100 Index
  Supports AIDS services/men's health groups
  Supports breast cancer research/women's health groups

Workplace Record on Sexual Orientation
  Diversity training inclusive of sexual orientation
  Encouraging remarks from vendors or gay and lesbian employees
  Full domestic-partnership health care benefits
  Written sexual orientation nondiscrimination policy statement

Company Overview
  If you get a headache after reading about the employee benefit policies of some other major pharmaceutical companies, you'll be happy to know that you can, in good conscience, take an analgesic from one of the world's most popular aspirin makers. Bayer Corp., with 26,000 employees, is the U.S. subsidiary of Bayer AG, based in Germany, which has 145,000 workers worldwide. Bayer has huge sales overseas, but its research and development spending in the United States is quite high. Although primarily known for health care products, Bayer is also involved in the manufacture of farming and business construction machinery, as well as electrical technology and plastics.

Blue Cross/Blue Shield of Massachusetts

100 Summer St.
Boston, MA 02110
(617) 832-5000
(617) 832-4832 (fax)
www.bcbsma.com

Author's Overall Appraisal

Progressive

Consumer Cautions

None

Important Considerations

Diversity training inclusive of people with disabilities
Exceptional workplace record supporting parents
Listed on GLV 100 Index
Supports AIDS services/men's health groups
Supports breast cancer research/women's health groups

Workplace Record on Sexual Orientation

Diversity training inclusive of sexual orientation
Encouraging remarks from vendors or gay and lesbian employees
Full domestic-partnership health care benefits
Gay and lesbian employee group
Written sexual orientation nondiscrimination policy statement

Company Overview

Blue Cross/Blue Shield of Massachusetts provides health insurance and health maintenance services to Massachusetts residents. It offers indemnity insurance plans, as well as HMO and preferred provider plans. BCBSMA offers domestic-partnership health insurance to its gay and lesbian employees, but some of its affiliated agencies do not.

The politics and competitive maneuvers of Blue Cross organizations around the country are constantly changing, as are the rules and policies regarding coverage of HIV and experimental cancer therapies.

Bristol-Myers Squibb
345 Park Ave.
New York, NY 10154-0037
(212) 546-4000
(212) 546-4020 (fax)
www.bms.com
Author's Overall Appraisal
Progressive
Consumer Cautions
Animal testing
Important Considerations
Affiliated with groups supportive of gay and lesbian rights
Diversity training inclusive of people with disabilities
Exceptional workplace record supporting parents
Has advertised in the gay and lesbian press
Listed as a Fortune 500 Company
Supports AIDS services/men's health groups
Supports breast cancer research/women's health groups
Workplace Record on Sexual Orientation
Diversity training inclusive of sexual orientation
Encouraging remarks from vendors or gay and lesbian employees
Full domestic-partnership health care benefits
Gay and lesbian employee group
Written sexual orientation nondiscrimination policy statement
Company Overview
Bristol-Myers Squibb employs more than 54,000 people. Known primarily as a drug manufacturer, the company also makes many personal products, including shampoos, creams, and more.
Popular Name Brands or Key Industry Products
Excedrin, Taxol, Ban, Clairol, Sea Breeze, Fostex, Nice N Easy, Frost N Tip, Comtrex, Fisherman's Friend, Bufferin, Nuprin, Excedrin, No-Doz, Biolage, Keri, Herbal Essences, 4-Way, Theragran M, Trimax, Sustacal, Zerit

Chiron

4560 Horton St.
Emeryville, CA 94608
(510) 655-8730
(510) 655-9910 (fax)
www.chiron.com

Author's Overall Appraisal
Progressive

Consumer Cautions
Animal testing

Important Considerations
Diversity training inclusive of people with disabilities
Listed on Domini Social Index
Listed on GLV 100 Index

Workplace Record on Sexual Orientation
Diversity training inclusive of sexual orientation
Encouraging remarks from vendors or gay and lesbian employees
Full domestic-partnership health care benefits
Gay and lesbian employee group officially acknowledged
Written sexual orientation nondiscrimination policy statement

Company Overview
Chiron employs about 7,500 people and is the second largest biotechnology firm (after Amgen). It makes drugs to treat cancer and other illnesses; products to test blood supplies for HIV and other blood-borne infectious diseases; and vaccines for both adults and children.

Popular Name Brands or Key Industry Products
Proleukin, Betaseron

Cigna

1 Liberty Place
1650 Market St.
Philadelphia, PA 19192-1550
(215) 761-1000
(215) 761-5510 (corporate communications department)
www.cigna.com

Author's Overall Appraisal
Progressing too slowly

Consumer Cautions
Confidentiality issues regarding HIV testing

Important Considerations
Exceptional workplace record supporting parents
Listed as a Fortune 500 Company
Listed on Domini Social Index
Listed on Standard & Poor's Index
Stock held by Meyers Pride Value Fund
Supports AIDS services/men's health groups
Supports breast cancer research/women's health groups

Workplace Record on Sexual Orientation
Diversity training inclusive of sexual orientation
Written sexual orientation nondiscrimination policy statement

Company Overview
Cigna is a major insurance provider, with assets of $115 billion. Its family of companies includes Cigna Healthcare, which provides managed medical and dental care; Cigna Group Insurance, providing life, disability, and accident insurance through employers and associations; Cigna International, offering employee benefits and financial services overseas; Cigna Investment Management, which manages money for institutions; and Cigna Financial Services, a discount broker.

Glaxo Wellcome Inc.

5 Moore Drive
Research Triangle Park, NC 27709
(919) 248-2100
(919) 248-2381 (fax)
www.glaxowellcome.com

Author's Overall Appraisal
Progressive

Consumer Cautions
Animal testing

Important Considerations
Affiliated with groups supportive of gay and lesbian rights
Diversity training inclusive of people with disabilities
Has advertised in the gay and lesbian press
Has included gay- or lesbian-suggestive imagery in mainstream advertising or programming
Listed on GLV 100 Index
Supports AIDS services/men's health groups
Supports breast cancer research/women's health groups

Workplace Record on Sexual Orientation
Diversity training inclusive of sexual orientation
Full domestic-partnership health care benefits
Gay and lesbian employee group
Mixed remarks from vendors or gay and lesbian employees
Written sexual orientation nondiscrimination policy statement

Company Overview
Glaxo Wellcome manufactures over-the-counter and prescription drugs, including AZT, which is used in the treatment of AIDS and HIV. The U.S. company is a subsidiary of London-based Glaxo Wellcome PLC, formed in 1995 from the merger of Glaxo and Wellcome, the latter being the parent of American company Burroughs Wellcome. The company's AIDS policy history is checkered. In April 1989 AIDS activists broke into Burroughs Wellcome offices and bolted themselves to the fixtures to protest the high price of AZT. In September of that year, there was a civil disobedience action at the New York Stock Exchange with ACT UP protesters encouraging stockholders to sell Burroughs Wellcome stock. The company subsequently lowered the prize of AZT 20% and made a grant to ACT UP's campaign for community-based AIDS research.

The Hartford

200 Hopmeadow St.
Simsbury, CT 06089
(860) 843-7716
(860) 843-3528 (fax)
www.thehartford.com

Author's Overall Appraisal

Very progressive

Consumer Cautions

None

Important Considerations

Advertises in gay and lesbian media
Diversity training inclusive of people with disabilities
Exceptional workplace record supporting parents
Listed on GLV 100 Index
Supports AIDS services/men's health groups
Supports breast cancer research/women's health groups

Workplace Record on Sexual Orientation

Diversity training inclusive of sexual orientation
Encouraging remarks from vendors or gay and lesbian employees
Full domestic-partnership health care benefits
Gay and lesbian employee group
Written sexual orientation nondiscrimination policy statement

Company Profile:

The Hartford provides a broad selection of insurance, personal annuity, savings, and investment services. The company recognizes that gay and lesbian domestic partners have different needs than single customers, that they have different ways of saving, and that they tend to be safer drivers. The company takes these issues into consideration when it comes to customer service, coverage plans, and pricing guidelines.

The Hartford has advertised its auto insurance policies in *The Advocate* and *Out*, explaining that there would be a reduction in premiums of "up to 25 percent for committed couples of all kinds." The ad included a humorous parenthetical aside: "Heck, we even offer discounts to heterosexual couples. (Not that there's anything wrong with that.)"

Hoffman-LaRoche

340 Kingsland St.
Nutley, NJ 07110
(973) 235-5000

Author's Overall Appraisal

Progressing too slowly

Consumer Cautions

Animal testing

No survey response

Important Considerations

Unknown

Workplace Record on Sexual Orientation

Diversity training inclusive of sexual orientation

Has had gay/lesbian discrimination lawsuits

Mixed remarks from vendors or gay and lesbian employees

Written sexual orientation nondiscrimination policy statement

Company Overview

Hoffman-LaRoche, the U.S. subsidiary of Switzerland-based Roche Holding Ltd., manufactures prescription drugs used in the treatment of AIDS, stroke, acne, and numerous other diseases.

Popular Name Brands or Key Industry Products

Versed, Dormicum, Klonopin, Accutane, Rocephin, Valium, Cytovene, Invirase, Fortovase, Roferon-A, Hivid

Merck

P.O. Box 100
Whitehouse Station, NJ 08889
(908) 423-1000
(908) 594-4662 (fax)
www.merck.com

Author's Overall Appraisal

Progressing too slowly

Consumer Cautions

Animal testing
No domestic partner healthcare benefits

Important Considerations

Exceptional workplace record supporting parents
Listed as a Fortune 500 Company
Listed on Domini Social Index
Listed on Standard & Poor's Index

Workplace Record on Sexual Orientation

Diversity training inclusive of sexual orientation
Gay and lesbian employee group
Mixed remarks from vendors or gay and lesbian employees
Written sexual orientation nondiscrimination policy statement

Company Overview

Merck is a drug manufacturer that had sales of $26.9 billion in 1998. Much of that derives from products used in the treatment of HIV and AIDS, such as the protease inhibitor Crixivan.

Mylan Laboratories

1030 Century Building
130 7th St.
Pittsburgh, PA 15222
(412) 232-0100
(412) 232-0123 (fax)
www.mylan.com

Author's Overall Appraisal
Progressive

Consumer Cautions
Animal Testing

Important Considerations
Affiliated with groups supportive of gay and lesbian rights
Has advertised in the gay and lesbian press
Has included gay- or lesbian-suggestive imagery in mainstream advertising or programming
Listed on Domini Social Index
Listed on GLV 100 Index
Supports AIDS services/men's health groups
Supports breast cancer research/women's health groups

Workplace Record on Sexual Orientation
Diversity training inclusive of sexual orientation
Encouraging remarks from vendors or gay and lesbian employees
Full domestic-partnership health care benefits
Gay and lesbian employee group
Written sexual orientation nondiscrimination policy statement

Company Overview
Mylan Laboratories has over 2,000 employees and produces more than 100 pharmaceutical products, including drugs to treat Parkinson's disease, drugs to treat ulcers, antipsychotics and antidepressants, diuretics, beta blockers, and more. The company is an innovator in wound and burn treatment products. Its divisions include Bertek Pharmaceuticals UDL Laboratories, Mylan Pharmaceuticals, and Mylan Technologies.

Pfizer

235 E. 42nd St.
New York, NY 10017-5755
(212) 573-2323
(212) 573-7851 (fax)
www.pfiz

Author's Overall Appraisal

Progressing

Consumer Cautions

Animal testing

Important Considerations

Listed as a Fortune 500 Company

Workplace Record on Sexual Orientation

Written sexual orientation nondiscrimination policy statement
Domestic partner healthcare insurance

Company Overview

Pfizer, with approximately 48,000 employees, is one of the five largest manufacturers of prescription drugs. Cholesterol-lowering drugs, drugs used in the treatment of heart disease (such as Norvasc), drugs used in the treatment of mental illness (such as Zoloft), and antibiotics make up a large portion of the company's sales. The company also manufacturers a number of over-the-counter products.

Popular Name Brands or Key Industry Products

BenGay, Visine, Bain de Soleil, Viagra, Barbasol, Cortisone 10

Schering-Plough

One Giralda Farms
Madison, NJ 07940-1010
(973) 822-7000
(973) 822-7048 (fax)
www.sch-plough.com

Author's Overall Appraisal
Progressing too slowly

Consumer Cautions
Animal testing

Important Considerations
Has advertised in the gay and lesbian press
Listed on Domini Social Index
Supports AIDS services/men's health groups
Supports breast cancer research/women's health groups

Workplace Record on Sexual Orientation
Diversity training inclusive of sexual orientation
Mixed remarks from vendors or gay and lesbian employees
Written sexual orientation nondiscrimination policy statement

Company Overview
Schering-Plough, with approximately 21,000 employees and $8.1 billion in 1998 sales, makes and sells over-the-counter and prescription drugs. Its most popular product is Claritin, a widely used antihistamine. Schering-Plough also makes numerous animal care products.

Popular Name Brands or Key Industry Products
Claritin, Afrin, Dr. Scholl's, Coppertone, Correctol, Gyne-Lotremin, Di-Gel, Drixoral, Solarcaine, Defend flea and tick remedies

SmithKline Beecham
1 New Horizons Court
Brentford, Middlesex, U.K. TW8 9EP
+44-181-975-2000
+44-181-975-2090 (fax)
www.sb.com

Author's Overall Appraisal
Progressive

Consumer Cautions
None

Important Considerations
Affiliated with groups supportive of gay and lesbian rights
Has included gay- or lesbian-suggestive imagery in mainstream advertising or programming
Supports AIDS services/men's health groups
Supports breast cancer research/women's health groups

Workplace Record on Sexual Orientation
Full domestic-partnership health care benefits
Gay and lesbian employee group
Written sexual orientation nondiscrimination policy statement

Company Overview
SmithKline Beecham is among the world's largest pharmaceutical manufacturers. In addition to vaccines, AIDS/HIV medications, antidepressants, and tranquilizers, the company manufactures vitamins, over-the-counter drugs, smoking cessation aids, and personal care products. Bristol-Myers Squibb and Novartis are its chief competitors.

Popular Name Brands or Key Industry Products
NicoDerm, Nicorette, Paxil, Aquafresh, Famvir, Avandia

Transportation and Travel

In 1999 United Airlines and American Airlines announced they would offer domestic-partner health insurance to their gay and lesbian employees beginning in spring 2000, making them the first the national airlines to do so. At press time, no trucking companies or automobile manufacturers offered such benefits. The auto rental companies are perhaps more progressive, but only because some of them offer to waive the additional driver fee for same-sex couples. Hotels are generally sluggish on issues relating to sexual orientation.

General Industry Resources:

Air Transport Association
    www.air-transport.org
American Hotel and Motel Association
    www.ahma.com/
Arthur Frommer's Budget Travel Online
    www.frommers.com
Association of International Automobile Manufacturers
    www.aiam.org
Automotive Parts and Accessories Association
    www.apaa.org/
Car-Stuff Automotive Links
    www.car-stuff.com
Federal Aviation Administration
    www.faa.gov
Is your car a lemon?
    www.lemon.org
Japan Automobile Manufacturers Association
    www.japanauto.com
The Lodging Industry on the Internet: Hotels
    www.cox.smu.edu/mis/talks/www/industry/lodging.html
National Business Travel Association
    www.nbta.org

Office of Airline Information
   www.bts.gov/programs/oai
Regional Airline Association
   www.raa.org
Travel Industry Association of America
   www.tia.org

American Airlines

P.O. Box 619616
Dallas, TX 75261-9616
(800) 433-7300 (toll-free)
(817) 963-1234
(817) 967-9641 (fax)
wwwr1.aa.com (consumer information)
www.amrcorp.com (corporate information)

Author's Overall Appraisal

Progressive

Consumer Cautions

None

Important Considerations

Affiliated with groups supportive of gay and lesbian rights
Contributes to gay/lesbian nonprofit groups and political organizations
Diversity training inclusive of people with disabilities
Early supporter of ENDA
Has advertised in the gay and lesbian press
Listed as a Fortune 500 Company
Listed on GLV 100 Index
Supports AIDS services/men's health groups
Supports breast cancer research/women's health groups

Workplace Record on Sexual Orientation

Domestic-partnership health care benefits (effective spring 2000)
Diversity training inclusive of sexual orientation
Encouraging remarks from vendors or gay and lesbian employees
Gay and lesbian employee group officially acknowledged
Has had gay and lesbian discrimination lawsuits

Company Overview

American Airlines is the most gay- and lesbian-supportive of all U.S. airlines. A number of incidents helped jolt the airline into making itself more consciously gay-friendly. One involved the forced removal of a passenger with HIV. Another, particularly embarrassing incident, occurred just after to the 1993 March on Washington, when American Airlines flight attendants had the linens changed on the seats after a flight that carried many march participants home to Texas.

What gay consumers should be most aware of is that American admitted its mistakes and took aggressive, proactive measures to correct the problems. After the march incident, the company president sent a letter to all American employees on April 29, 1993, that read in part, "American Airlines apologizes to anyone who was offended by the unfortunate actions of the few employees involved in this unhappy incident. Their actions do not reflect American Airlines' policy or practice, and everyone has my pledge that we will do everything possible to ensure such lapses in judgment do not occur in the future."

American was the second major airline to implement a sexual orientation nondiscrimination policy—three months after United Airlines did so, in 1993. Additionally, American is one of the first Fortune 100 companies to establish a high-profile marketing team to target gay and lesbian travelers. In the summer of 1999, American became the second major airline to announce it would offer domestic-partner health care benefits, coming on the heels of United's announcement that it would do so. The airline industry had been challenging a San Francisco ordinance requiring companies doing business with the city to offer the benefits, and just hours before United's announcement, an appeals court had refused to exempt the company from the ordinance.

American President Lines

1111 Broadway
Oakland, CA 94607
(800) 872-4565 (toll-free)
(510) 272-8000
(510) 272-7421 (fax)
www.apl.com
www.nol.com.sg (parent company, Neptune Orient Lines)

Author's Overall Appraisal
Progressive

Consumer Cautions
None

Important Considerations
Listed as a Fortune 500 Company
Listed on GLV 100 Index
Supports AIDS services/men's health groups
Supports breast cancer research/women's health groups

Workplace Record on Sexual Orientation
Full domestic-partnership health care benefits
Written sexual orientation nondiscrimination policy statement

Company Overview
American President Lines is second-largest shipping line in the United States, providing sea and land transportation services via more than 50 ports around the world, including in the Persian Gulf and the Pacific and Indian oceans. It has a fleet of 76 container ships. American President Lines is owned by Neptune Orient Lines Ltd. and employs approximately 4,000 people. Company sales run around $2 billion annually.

Avis

900 Old Country Road
Garden City, NY 11530
(516) 222-3000
www.avis.com

Author's Overall Appraisal

Progressing somewhat

Consumer Cautions

None

Important Considerations

Affiliated with groups supportive of gay and lesbian rights

Diversity training inclusive of people with disabilities

Has advertised in the gay and lesbian press

Supports AIDS services/men's health groups

Supports breast cancer research/women's health groups

Workplace Record on Sexual Orientation

Diversity training inclusive of sexual orientation

Encouraging remarks from vendors or gay and lesbian employees

Gay and lesbian employee group

Written sexual orientation nondiscrimination policy statement

Company Overview

Avis has car rental operations in the United States, the Caribbean, Australia, and New Zealand. It was the first car rental company to waive the additional-driver fee for gay and lesbian couples renting vehicles. Avis completes about 15 million rental transactions a year.

DaimlerChrysler

1000 Chrysler Drive
Auburn Hills, Michigan
(248) 576-5741
www.chryslercorp.com

Author's Overall Appraisal

Progressing too slowly

Consumer Cautions

Affiliated with groups less than supportive of gay and lesbian rights

Possible overseas labor problems

Important Considerations

Unknown

Workplace Record on Sexual Orientation

Gay and lesbian employee group

Has had gay and lesbian discrimination lawsuits

Mixed remarks from vendors or gay and lesbian employees

Company Overview

Chrysler Corp. merged in 1998 with German automaker Daimler-Benz AG. The combined company, DaimlerChrysler, has more than 420,000 employees around the world. The company has a history of problems when it comes to gay and lesbian issues. Chrysler's advertising suspiciously disappeared during *Ellen*'s coming-out episode in 1997 (and was replaced by a Volkswagen commercial featuring a gay-appearing couple). Chrysler officials said the decision not to advertise was based not on the show's content but on the attention it attracted. Chrysler has also fought tooth and nail with its gay and lesbian employees over the adoption of a nondiscrimination policy statement including sexual orientation. Chrysler officials said in 1996 that it did not need to add sexual orientation to its antidiscrimination policy because it already prohibited discrimination against any employee. However, on the factory floor, gay employees say they have been harassed, attacked, and had their work areas sabotaged by homophobic coworkers. Even a threatened shareholder action led by Trillium Asset Management (also profiled in this book) has failed to move Chrysler's management to address the issues of protection and equality for gay and lesbian workers. Chrysler has extended domestic-partnership benefits to workers in its Canadian operations, but only after an arbitrator ordered it to do so.

Ford Motor Co.

The American Road
Dearborn, MI 48121-1899
(313) 322-3000
(313) 323-2959 (fax)
www.ford.com

Author's Overall Appraisal

Progressing somewhat

Consumer Cautions

Affiliated with groups less than supportive of gay and lesbian rights

Important Considerations

Supports breast cancer research/women's health groups

Workplace Record on Sexual Orientation

Gay and lesbian employee group

Has had gay and lesbian discrimination lawsuits

Mixed remarks from vendors or gay and lesbian employees

Written sexual orientation nondiscrimination policy statement

Company Overview

Ford Motor Co. is the world's second largest automaker. It addition to its own brand, Ford manufactures Aston Martin, Jaguar, Lincoln, and Mercury, and it is part owner of Mazda. In 1999 Ford acquired Volvo's passenger car business. Ford also owns a majority share of Hertz car rental.

Ford is, perhaps, the least problematic U.S.-based auto manufacturer when it comes to gay and lesbian issues. Ford has supported numerous gay and lesbian community activities, including the 1995 Black Nations/Queer Nations Conference at City University of New York. However, despite a dedicated gay and lesbian employee group and a diversity and community relations history that is generally admirable, Ford also sponsored the NBC-televised 1998 St. Patrick's Day Parade in New York City—a parade that bans participation by New York's Irish Gay and Lesbian Organization.

General Motors

General Motors Building
3044 West Grand Boulevard
Detroit, MI 48202
(313) 556-5000
(313) 556-5108 (fax)
www.gm.com

Author's Overall Appraisal

Progressing too slowly

Consumer Cautions

Affiliated with groups less than supportive of gay and lesbian rights
Affiliated with military contracts
Possible overseas labor problems

Important Considerations

Exceptional workplace record supporting parents
Listed as a Fortune 500 Company
Listed on Standard & Poor's Index
Supports AIDS services/men's health groups
Supports breast cancer research/women's health groups

Workplace Record on Sexual Orientation

Diversity training inclusive of sexual orientation
Gay and lesbian employee group
Mixed remarks from vendors or gay and lesbian employees
Written sexual orientation nondiscrimination policy statement

Company Overview

General Motors' gay and lesbian employee group is to be commended for its hard work and dedication to making General Motors a more socially responsible company. But as the world's largest manufacturer of automobiles, GM needs to get its act together and extend domestic-partnership health care benefits to its gay and lesbian employees, especially since the company employs more than 647,000 people. The company produces Buick, Cadillac, Chevrolet, Chevy Trucks, GMC, Oldsmobile, Pontiac, and Saturn. It also has a joint venture to produce Saab automobiles. GM subsidiaries include Hughes Electronics Corp., which is involved in telecommunications, aerospace, defense, and automotive electronics.

Genuine Parts

2999 Circle 75 Parkway
Atlanta, GA 30339
(770) 953-1700
www.genpt.com

Author's Overall Appraisal

Progressing too slowly

Consumer Cautions

Affiliated with military contracts

Important Considerations

Listed as a Fortune 500 company
Listed on Standard & Poor's Index
Listed on Domini Social Index

Workplace Record on Sexual Orientation

Gay and lesbian employee group

Company Overview

Genuine Parts employs approximately 25,000 people. The company is a major distributor of auto parts and replacement products manufactured by dozens of suppliers and sold to major retail outlets around the world. Its 1998 sales were $6.6 billion.

Harley-Davidson

3700 W. Juno Ave.
Milwaukee, WI 53208
(877) 437-8625 (toll-free shareholder information)
(414) 342-4680
www.harleydavidson.com

Author's Overall Appraisal
Progressing somewhat

Consumer Cautions
Affiliated with groups less than supportive of gay and lesbian rights

Important Considerations
Affiliated with groups supportive of gay and lesbian rights
Early supporter of ENDA
Includes gay- or lesbian-suggestive imagery in mainstream advertising or programming

Workplace Record on Sexual Orientation
Gay and lesbian employee group
Mixed remarks from vendors or gay and lesbian employees
Written sexual orientation nondiscrimination policy statement

Company Overview
Harley-Davidson is one of the largest American-based motorcycle manufacturers. It manufactures 24 different cruiser, factory custom, and touring motorcycles, as well as police and military motorcycles. Harley-Davidson has long had a quiet but loyal gay and lesbian following, and there is a sense that senior management is aware of this, especially since the company was an early supporter of the Employment Non-Discrimination Act. Despite erroneous earlier reports and various Web site postings, the company does not currently offer domestic-partnership health care coverage, and there are conflicting reports as to whether the subject has ever seriously been placed on the table.

Hilton

9336 Civic Center Drive
Beverly Hills, CA 90210
(310) 278-4321
(310) 205-4599 (fax)
www.hilton.com

Author's Overall Appraisal

Progressing too slowly

Consumer Cautions

Affiliated with companies or groups less than supportive of gay and lesbian rights
Affiliated with sales of alcoholic beverages
Possible overseas labor problems

Important Considerations

Diversity training inclusive of people with disabilities
Listed on Standard & Poor's Index

Workplace Record on Sexual Orientation

Written sexual orientation nondiscrimination policy statement

Company Overview

In 1994 Dieter Huckestein, who was then a Hilton senior vice president and chair of the Hawaii Visitors Bureau, sent an aide to testify before a state senate committee that gay marriage would be detrimental to Hawaii's economy. Huckestein also sent a letter to the legislature emphasizing his opposition to same-sex marriage. The company has repeatedly stated that Huckestein's position was misrepresented in the press, and that he was not speaking on behalf of the company. Huckestein, now a Hilton executive vice president, has since reportedly apologized for any offense to gay and lesbian Americans.

The Hilton name is on about 250 hotels around the world, including the Waldorf-Astoria in New York City and the Palmer House in Chicago. The company also owns Bally Entertainment, which operates in cities known for gambling such as Las Vegas and Atlantic City. The company employs some 70,000 people worldwide. In 1999 Hilton announced plans to acquire Promus Hotel Corp., which operates the Doubletree and Embassy Suites hotels.

Marriott

Marriott Drive
Washington, DC 20058
(301) 380-3000
(301) 380-3969 (fax)
www.marriott.com

Author's Overall Appraisal

Progressing too slowly

Consumer Cautions

No survey response

Important Considerations

Diversity training inclusive of people with disabilities
Exceptional workplace record supporting parents
Listed as a Fortune 500 company
Listed on Domini Social Index
Supports AIDS services/men's health groups

Workplace Record on Sexual Orientation

Diversity training inclusive of sexual orientation
Written sexual orientation nondiscrimination policy statement

Company Overview

Marriott employs 133,000 people and operates over 1,800 hotel properties around the globe. In addition to hotels bearing the Marriott name, the company's properties include Fairfield Inns and Ritz-Carlton Hotels. Marriott also operates 113 retirement communities and a network of food distribution centers. Employees report diversity training at some properties.

Mirage Resorts

3400 Las Vegas Blvd. S.
Las Vegas, NV 89109
(702) 791-7111
(702) 792-7676 (fax)
www.mirageresorts.com

Author's Overall Appraisal

Progressing too slowly

Consumer Cautions

No survey response

Important Considerations

Unknown

Workplace Record on Sexual Orientation

Unknown

Company Overview

Mirage Resorts own and manages casino-based resorts including the Mirage, Bellagio, Treasure Island, and the Golden Nugget in Las Vegas, the Golden Nugget in Laughlin, Nev., and the Beau Rivage in Biloxi, Miss. It also owns 50% of the Monte Carlo hotel-casino in Las Vegas and plans to open a resort in Atlantic City. Its primary competitors include Harrah's and Hilton.

National Car Rental

7700 France Ave. S.
Minneapolis, MN 55435
(612) 830-2121
(612) 830-2921 (fax)
www.nationalcar.com

Author's Overall Appraisal
Progressing somewhat

Consumer Cautions
None

Important Considerations
Diversity training inclusive of people with disabilities
Has advertised in the gay and lesbian press

Workplace Record on Sexual Orientation
Diversity training inclusive of sexual orientation
Encouraging remarks from vendors or gay and lesbian employees
Gay and lesbian employee group
Written sexual orientation nondiscrimination policy statement

Company Overview
National rents and leases automobiles, and employs more than 17,000 people. It has nearly 3,000 locations in 75 countries. The company will waive the additional-driver fee for gay and lesbian couples. National, along with Avis, is considered a decent choice, from a gay and lesbian standpoint, for renting cars. The company has partial domestic-partnership benefits for its gay and lesbian employees—which basically means bereavement leave.

Ryder System

3600 NW 82nd Ave.
Miami, FL 33166
(305) 500-3726
(305) 500-3203 (fax)
www.ryder.com

Author's Overall Appraisal
Progressing too slowly

Consumer Cautions
None

Important Considerations
Listed on Domini Social Index
Listed as a Fortune 500 company

Workplace Record on Sexual Orientation
Gay and lesbian employee group
Written sexual orientation nondiscrimination policy statement

Company Overview
Ryder employs 45,000 people. Its primary business is truck leasing, rental, and maintenance. It has operations in North America, South America, and Europe. Ryder is heavily involved in the movement of goods for businesses. In 1999 it agreed to sell its public transportation business, which operates school buses, to FirstGroup PLC, the largest bus operator in the United Kingdom.

Subaru (Fuji Heavy Industries Ltd.)

1-7-2 Nishi-Shinjuku
Shinjuku-ku
Tokyo 160, Japan
+81-3-3347-2111
+81-3-3347-2126 (fax)
www.subaru-fhi.co.jp/fhi.htm

Author's Overall Appraisal
Progressive

Consumer Cautions
Possible overseas labor problems

Important Considerations
Affiliated with groups supportive of gay and lesbian rights
Has advertised in the gay and lesbian press
Has included gay- or lesbian-suggestive imagery in mainstream advertising or programming
Significantly visible supporter of ENDA
Supports AIDS services/men's health groups
Supports breast cancer research/women's health groups

Workplace Record on Sexual Orientation
Encouraging remarks from vendors or gay and lesbian employees
Written sexual orientation nondiscrimination policy statement

Company Overview
Subaru manufactures automobiles, focusing on off-road and four-wheel-drive vehicles. The company has targeted the gay and lesbian marketplace, as witnessed by print display ads in gay and lesbian media. (Subaru and Saab are about the only auto manufacturers to ever do so.) Reportedly, sales have responded, with Subaru among the most popular cars with American lesbians. Subaru is also a sponsor of the Rainbow Card, a Visa card that donates a portion of profits to gay and lesbian organizations.

United Airlines

P.O. Box 66100
Chicago, IL 60666
(800) 241-6522 (toll-free)
(847) 700-4000
(847) 700-5229 (fax)

Author's Overall Appraisal

Progressing too slowly

Consumer Cautions

Affiliated with groups less than supportive of gay and lesbian rights
Gay and lesbian boycott activity
Possible overseas labor problems

Important Considerations

Affiliated with groups supportive of gay and lesbian rights
Has advertised in the gay and lesbian press
Listed as a Fortune 500 company
Listed on Domini Social Index

Workplace Record on Sexual Orientation

Domestic-partnership health care benefits (effective spring 2000)
Gay and lesbian employee group officially acknowledged
Has had gay/lesbian discrimination lawsuits
Written sexual orientation nondiscrimination policy statement

Company Overview

United Airlines, principal subsidiary of the holding company UAL Corp., is the largest airline in the world. It has nearly 2,300 flights a day to 135 destinations around the world. It has alliances that allow travelers to earn and redeem United frequent flier miles when they use Germany's Lufthansa and take certain flights on other airlines (frequent flyer miles can be shared between the airlines). The company employs more than 90,000 people and had sales of approximately $17.5 billion in 1998.

In the summer of 1999 United made history by announcing it would offer domestic-partnership health care benefits to gay and lesbian employees beginning in the spring of 1999, making it the first major U.S. airline to do so; a few days later American Airlines and US Airways announced they would do so as well. United and the airline industry as a whole had been challenging a San Francisco ordinance requiring companies doing business with the city to offer such benefits. United's challenge led some gay activists to call for a boycott. United contended the issue was not about gay rights, but about the city mandating company policy. However, on July 30, 1999, an appeals court refused to exempt United from the ordinance, and a few hours after the ruling, United made its announcement. While the airline industry is continuing its appeal, other airlines may well decide to offer the benefits due to competitive pressures and as they negotiate new leases with the San Francisco airport.

Virgin Atlantic Airlines

747 Belden Avenue
Norwalk, CT 06850
(203) 750-2000
(203) 750-6460 (fax)
www.virgin-atlantic.com

Author's Overall Appraisal

Progressive

Consumer Cautions

None

Important Considerations

Affiliated with groups supportive of gay and lesbian rights
Diversity training inclusive of people with disabilities
Has advertised in the gay and lesbian press
Has included gay- or lesbian-suggestive imagery in mainstream advertising or programming
Listed on GLV 100 Index
Supporter of ENDA
Supports AIDS services/men's health groups
Supports breast cancer research/women's health groups

Workplace Record on Sexual Orientation

Diversity training inclusive of sexual orientation
Encouraging remarks from vendors or gay and lesbian employees
Gay and lesbian employee group
Written sexual orientation nondiscrimination policy statement
Domestic partner healthcare benefits

Company Overview

Virgin is known for its diversified business operations, which include airline services, book and software publishing, nightclubs, film and video editing, hotels, and retail music outlets.

Although smaller than most American air carriers, Virgin has a superior reputation among gay and lesbian professionals in the travel industry. According to Billy Kolber-Stuart, editor of the "Out & About" travel newsletter, Virgin has one of the best, most progressive employee and customer relations records for gay men and women. It also advertises regularly in the various gay and lesbian media in the United States, Europe, and Australia.

Volkswagen

3800 Hamlin Rd., Mail Code 4D01
Auburn Hills, MI 48326
(248) 340-5000
(248) 340-4960 (fax)
www.vw.com

Author's Overall Appraisal
Progressive

Consumer Cautions
None

Important Considerations
Diversity training inclusive of people with disabilities
Exceptional workplace record supporting parents
Has included gay- or lesbian-suggestive imagery in mainstream advertising or programming

Workplace Record on Sexual Orientation
Diversity training inclusive of sexual orientation
Encouraging remarks from vendors or gay and lesbian employees
Written sexual orientation nondiscrimination policy statement

Company Overview

Volkswagen of America is a subsidiary of the German company Volkswagen AG. The Volkswagen Group is the largest European automaker. Volkswagen of America makes Volkswagen and Audi vehicles. Other brands in the Volkswagen Group include Rolls Royce, Lamborghini, and Bugatti.

Volkswagen, notably, was the only auto manufacturer to advertise on the coming-out episode of *Ellen*. Advertising representatives claimed the ad was not specifically a "gay ad," but the spot featured two cute, hip, young guys riding around in a VW and picking up old furniture, and the ad reminded viewers that Volkswagen fits "your life."

Utilities, Chemicals, Materials, and Engineering

The majority of raw material production companies, engineering firms, and utilities have a long way to go on issues relating to gays and lesbians in the workplace.

General Industry Resources:

Aerospace Industries Association of America
   www.aia-aerospace.org
Aviation Week and Space Technology
   www.awstonline.com
Defence Systems Daily
   http://defence-data.com
Defense News
   www.defensenews.com
NASA
   www.nasa.gov
Space News
   www.spacenews.com

3M

3M Center
St. Paul, MI 55144
(800) 364-3577 (toll-free)
(612) 733-1893
(612) 733-9973 (fax)

Author's Overall Appraisal
Progressing somewhat

Consumer Cautions
Animal testing

Important Considerations
Exceptional workplace record supporting parents
Listed on Domini Social Index
Stock held by Meyers Pride Value Fund

Workplace Record on Sexual Orientation
Diversity training inclusive of sexual orientation
Gay and lesbian employee group officially acknowledged
Written sexual orientation nondiscrimination policy statement

Company Overview
The maker of Scotch tape and Post-it Notes, 3M (which stands for Minnesota Mining and Manufacturing Company) is also a noted gay- and-lesbian supportive company. It employs about 50,000 people in the United States and manufactures a variety of products, including adhesives and cleaning supplies.

Popular Name Brands or Key Industry Products
3M, Post-it, Scotch, Scotchgard, Scotch-Brite, Highland

Boeing

P.O. Box 3707
Seattle, WA 98124
(206) 665-0968
www.boeing.com

Author's Overall Appraisal
Progressing somewhat

Consumer Cautions
Affiliated with military contracts
Affiliated with nuclear energy
Possible overseas labor problems

Important Considerations
Diversity training inclusive of people with disabilities
Listed as a Fortune 500 Company
Listed on Standard & Poor's Index

Workplace Record on Sexual Orientation
Diversity training inclusive of sexual orientation
Gay and lesbian employee group
Has had gay/lesbian discrimination lawsuits
Mixed remarks from vendors or gay and lesbian employees

Company Overview
Boeing is the world's largest aerospace manufacturer, with approximately 205,000 full-time employees and 1998 sales of $56.2 billion. McDonnell Douglas, another major aircraft manufacturer, merged with Boeing in 1997. Boeing makes commercial planes such as the 747, 757, 767, and 777, and military aircraft such as the F-22 fighter, the V-22 Osprey tilt-rotor aircraft, the RAH-66 Comanche helicopter, the F/A-18 Hornet, and the F-15 Eagle war planes. In addition, the company has a multibillion dollar network of satellite ventures with various communications companies. Boeing offers financial accounts to employees' domestic partners through the company credit union, and is currently evaluating offering domestic-partnership health care coverage.

Chevron

575 Market St.
San Francisco, CA 94105-2856
(415) 894-7700
(415) 894-0583 (fax)
www.chevron.com

Author's Overall Appraisal
Progressive

Consumer Cautions
Possible overseas labor problems

Important Considerations
Listed on GLV 100 Index
Listed as a Fortune 500 Company
Listed on Standard & Poor's Index

Workplace Record on Sexual Orientation
Diversity training inclusive of sexual orientation
Full domestic-partnership health care benefits
Gay and lesbian employee group officially acknowledged
Has had gay and lesbian discrimination lawsuits
Written sexual orientation nondiscrimination policy statement

Company Overview
Chevron was the first major oil company to extend domestic-partnership health insurance to its gay and lesbian employees. Chevron employs approximately 33,000 people and has approximately 6.2 billion barrels of oil and equivalent gas in reserve. Its 1998 sales were $29.4 billion. Chevron also manufactures and sells chemicals. Chevron's senior leadership has taken a positive stance on gay and lesbian issues in comparison to many of its competitors.

Dow Chemical Co.

2030 Dow Center
Midland, MI 48674
(800) 422-8193 (toll-free)
(517) 636-1463
www.dow.com

Author's Overall Appraisal
Progressing somewhat

Consumer Cautions
Affiliated with groups less than supportive of gay and lesbian rights
Animal testing

Important Considerations
Affiliated with groups supportive of gay and lesbian rights
Exceptional workplace record supporting parents
Listed as a Fortune 500 Company
Listed on Standard & Poor's Index
Stock held by Meyers Pride Value Fund

Workplace Record on Sexual Orientation
Diversity training inclusive of sexual orientation
Gay and lesbian employee group
Written sexual orientation nondiscrimination policy statement

Company Overview
Dow Chemical is a manufacturer and supplier of chemicals, plastics, energy, agricultural products, consumers goods, and environmental services. The company serves customers in 168 countries and employs 39,000 people. Its annual sales exceed $18 billion. Dow incorporated in 1897 and began the world's first commercial-scale production of bleach in 1898. The company entered the agricultural chemicals market shortly after the turn of the century and hired its first woman researcher, Sylvia Stoesser, in 1929. The company announced in August 1999 that it would merge with Union Carbide Corp.

The federal government has named Dow as the potentially responsible party by the federal government at 45 Superfund environmental clean-up sites, so it is no surprise the company is not always a favorite of environmental groups. Dow's record on gay and lesbian and workplace issues, however, is acceptable.

DuPont

Nemours Building 9420
Wilmington, DE 19898
(302) 774-6088
(302) 774-7321 (fax)
www.dupont.com

Author's Overall Appraisal
Progressing somewhat

Consumer Cautions
None

Important Considerations
Exceptional workplace record supporting parents
Listed as a Fortune 500 Company
Listed on Standard & Poor's Index
Supports AIDS services/men's health groups
Supports breast cancer research/women's health groups

Workplace Record on Sexual Orientation
Diversity training inclusive of sexual orientation
Gay and lesbian employee group officially acknowledged
Written sexual orientation nondiscrimination policy statement

Company Overview
With operations in about 70 countries, approximately 84,000 employees, and 1998 sales of $24.8 billion, DuPont is one of the world's largest producers of chemicals and related products. Some of its best-known products are Lycra spandex fiber, Dacron polyester fiber, Teflon resins, SilverStone nonstick finish, Mylar polyester film, Antron carpet fiber, and Stainmaster stain-resistant carpet. The company says domestic-partnership health care benefits are currently "being considered." DuPont owned Conoco for a time, but spun it off as a separate company in 1999.

Edison International

2244 Walnut Grove Ave.
Rosemead, CA 91770
(626) 302-1212
(626) 302-2517 (fax)
www.edisonx.com

Author's Overall Appraisal

Progressive

Consumer Cautions

None

Important Considerations

Diversity training inclusive of people with disabilities
Exceptional workplace record supporting parents
Has advertised in the gay and lesbian press
Supports breast cancer research/women's health groups

Workplace Record on Sexual Orientation

Diversity training inclusive of sexual orientation
Encouraging remarks from vendors or gay and lesbian employees
Full domestic-partnership health care benefits
Gay and lesbian employee group officially acknowledged
Written sexual orientation nondiscrimination policy statement

Company Overview

Edison International is the parent company of Southern California Edison, the nation's second-largest electric utility, which provides electricity to 4.2 million customers. Edison International's holdings also include Edison Mission Energy, which operates power plants, and Edison Capital, which finances energy projects and low-income housing. Edison International is one of the more progressive utility companies where gay and lesbian issues are concerned.

Exxon
5959 Las Colinas Blvd.
Irving, TX 75039-2298
(972) 444-1000
(972) 444-1882 (fax)
www.exxon.com

Author's Overall Appraisal
Not progressive

Consumer Cautions
No survey response

Important Considerations
Unknown

Workplace Record on Sexual Orientation
Gay and lesbian employee group

Company Overview
Exxon is involved in oil drilling, refining, shipping, and sales. The company operates drilling rigs in about 30 countries around the world. Its biggest competitor is Shell. Exxon is also majority owner of a Chinese power plant. In 1989 one of the company's ships, the Exxon Valdez, spilled millions of gallons of oil into Prince William Sound off the coast of Alaska. The incident cost the company billions of dollars in fines and cleanup costs, and a lengthy, still-continuing legal battle with the state of Alaska.

In 1999 Trillium Asset Management and other shareholders submitted a proposal to add sexual orientation to Exxon's nondiscrimination policy. The votes in favor of the proposal represented 6% of Exxon's shares, enough to allow it to be reintroduced in 2000. Exxon management urged shareholders to vote against the proposal, contending the present policy already bans discrimination based on sexual orientation, although it does not contain those words. Exxon is planning to merge with Mobil, which explicitly bans such discrimination and offers domestic-partner benefits. Shareholders approved the merger at their 1999 meeting; the transaction is still awaiting regulatory approval.

General Electric

3135 Easton Turnpike
Fairfield, CT 06431
(203) 373-2211
(203) 373-3497 (fax)
www.ge.com

Author's Overall Appraisal

Not progressive

Consumer Cautions

Affiliated with groups less than supportive of gay and lesbian rights

Affiliated with military contracts

Affiliated with production of nuclear energy

No survey response

Possible overseas labor problems

Important Considerations

Listed as a Fortune 500 Company

Listed on Standard & Poor's Index

Supports breast cancer research/women's health groups

Workplace Record on Sexual Orientation

Mixed remarks from vendors or gay and lesbian employees

Company Overview

General Electric employs 293,000 people worldwide and produces appliances, aircraft engines, locomotives, lighting products, and a host of other goods. It also offers financial services and owns NBC, which in recent years has become somewhat more progressive in gay and lesbian news coverage but still lags behind ABC and PBS.

At GE's 1999 shareholder meeting, a proposal—sponsored in part by the Equality Project—that the company add sexual orientation to its written nondiscrimination policy statement, attracted 8.6% of the vote, an impressive amount for a for such a resolution in its first year of introduction. As a result of the vote, GE executives agreed to meet with backers of the proposal.

GE has drawn the ire of other social activists for everything from its environmental record to coercive relationships with small governments.

Illinois Tool Works

3600 W. Lake Ave.
Glenview, IL 60025
(630) 773-9300
www.itwinc.com

Author's Overall Appraisal
Progressive

Consumer Cautions
Affiliated with groups less than supportive of gay and lesbian rights

Important Considerations
Affiliated with groups supportive of gay and lesbian rights
Listed as a Fortune 500 Company
Listed on Domini Social Index
Listed on GLV 100 Index
Listed on Standard & Poor's Index
Stock held by Meyers Pride Value Fund

Workplace Record on Sexual Orientation
Full domestic-partnership health care benefits
Gay and lesbian employee group
Written sexual orientation nondiscrimination policy statement

Company Overview
Illinois Tool Works manufactures fasteners, components, assemblies, industrial fluids and adhesives, consumer and industrial packaging, and a variety of other products. The company is growing rapidly, with acquisitions since 1996 of Medalist Industries, Comet, SA, Gerrard Strapping, and Hobart Brothers.

Popular Name Brands or Key Industry Products
Ramset/RedHead tools, E-Z Ancor, Trugrip, Dec-King, Rock-On, Hobart, Trimark, Plexus, FlexTyer, Curastat

Lockheed Martin

6801 Rockledge Drive
Bethesda, MD 20817
(301) 897-6000
(301) 897-6704 (fax)
www.lmco.com

Author's Overall Appraisal

Progressing too slowly

Consumer Cautions

Affiliated with nuclear energy
Affiliated with military contracts
Affiliated with groups less than supportive of gay and lesbian rights

Important Considerations

Listed as a Fortune 500 Company
Listed on Standard & Poor's Index
Supports AIDS services/men's health groups
Supports breast cancer research/women's health groups

Workplace Record on Sexual Orientation

Diversity training inclusive of sexual orientation
Gay and lesbian employee group
Mixed remarks from vendors or gay and lesbian employees
Written sexual orientation nondiscrimination policy statement

Company Overview

Lockheed Martin has nearly 170,000 employees in the United States and over 5,500 employees working internationally. It has 939 U.S. facilities as well as operations in 56 other nations and territories. It is the largest U.S. military contractor; the Defense Department accounted for nearly half of its $26.2 billion in 1998. Lockheed Martin is involved in everything from missile development to space vehicle technology, and has extensive joint venture operations in Asia. Numerous gay and lesbian employees have approached the company about domestic-partnership health care insurance, but as of this writing the company has not given any indication that it might be extending such benefits.

Mobil

3225 Gallows Road
Fairfax, VA 22037
(703) 846-3000
(703) 846-4669 (fax)
www.mobil.com

Author's Overall Appraisal
Progressive

Consumer Cautions
Possible overseas labor problems

Important Considerations
Affiliated with groups supportive of gay and lesbian rights
Diversity training inclusive of people with disabilities
Exceptional workplace record supporting parents
Listed as a Fortune 500 Company
Listed on GLV 100 Index
Supports AIDS services/men's health groups
Supports breast cancer research/women's health groups

Workplace Record on Sexual Orientation
Diversity training inclusive of sexual orientation
Full domestic-partnership health care benefits
Gay and lesbian employee group
Written sexual orientation nondiscrimination policy statement

Company Overview
With 43,000 employees in more than 125 countries, Mobil is the second-largest oil company in the world. In addition to its oil and gas interests, the company is also involved in chemical integration technology, petrochemical production, and polymers/plastics. It is planning to merge with Exxon; the deal is awaiting regulatory approval. Mobil and Chevron are the most progressive oil companies regarding issues of sexual orientation.

Monsanto

800 N. Lindbergh Blvd.
St. Louis, MO 63167
(314) 694-1000
(314) 694-6572 (fax)
www.monsanto.com

Author's Overall Appraisal
Progressing too slowly

Consumer Cautions
Makers of bovine growth hormone
No survey response

Important Considerations
Unknown

Workplace Record on Sexual Orientation
Unknown

Company Overview
Monsanto has 30,600 employees and makes agricultural products such as crop seeds and weed killers in addition to prescription drugs and other health care products. The company's best-known products may be the artificial sweeteners Equal and NutraSweet, but in 1999 it announced plans to sell off its sweetener business, as it has done with others not considered crucial to its long-term strategy. Monsanto's biggest competitors are DuPont and Pioneer Hi-Bred.

Popular Name Brands or Key Industry Products
Ambien, Daypro, Arthrotec, Ortho, Roundup

Owens-Corning

One Owens-Corning Parkway
Toledo, OH 43659
419-248-8000
www.owenscorning.com

Author's Overall Appraisal

Progressing somewhat

Consumer Cautions

None

Important Considerations

Listed as a Fortune 500 Company

Workplace Record on Sexual Orientation

Written sexual orientation nondiscrimination policy statement

Encouraging remarks from vendors or gay and lesbian employees

Company Overview

Owens-Corning has more than 20,000 employees around the world and with manufacturing, sales and research facilities in more than 30 countries on six continents. The company invented glass fiber, marketed under the trade name Fiberglas. Its materials are used in construction, insulation, and a variety of consumer products.

Pacific Gas and Electric

77 Beale St.
San Francisco, CA 94177
(415) 973-7000
(415) 543-7830 (fax)
www.pge.com

Author's Overall Appraisal
Progressing somewhat

Consumer Cautions
Affiliated with military contracts
Affiliated with the production of nuclear energy

Important Considerations
Affiliated with groups supportive of gay and lesbian rights
Diversity training inclusive of people with disabilities
Listed as a Fortune 500 Company
Listed on GLV 100 Index
Significantly visible supporter of ENDA
Supports AIDS services/men's health groups

Workplace Record on Sexual Orientation
Diversity training inclusive of sexual orientation
Encouraging remarks from vendors or gay and lesbian employees
Gay and lesbian employee group officially acknowledged
Written sexual orientation nondiscrimination policy statement

Company Overview
Pacific Gas and Electric, a subsidiary of PG&E Corp., is among America's largest utilities, employing 21,500 people and supplying gas and electricity to about 12 million residents of Northern and Central California. PG&E was among the first companies to recognize its gay, lesbian, and bisexual employee group. The company's written nondiscrimination policy statement on sexual orientation has been in effect since 1982, and its corporate diversity training program includes information relative to gay and lesbian culture. In addition, PG&E gives generously to local causes, including AIDS organizations and children's groups.

Shell Oil Co.

One Shell Plaza
Houston, TX 77002
(281) 241-6161
(281) 241-6781 (fax)
www.countonshell.com

Author's Overall Appraisal
Progressing

Consumer Cautions
Possible overseas labor problems

Important Considerations
Affiliated with groups supportive of gay and lesbian rights
Listed as a Fortune 500 Company
Supports AIDS services/men's health groups
Supports breast cancer research/women's health groups

Workplace Record on Sexual Orientation
Diversity training inclusive of sexual orientation
Full domestic-partnership health care benefits
Gay and lesbian employee group
Has had gay/lesbian discrimination lawsuit(s)
Written sexual orientation nondiscrimination policy statement

Company Overview
Shell is in the crude oil, natural gas, and chemical products business. Its parent company is Royal Dutch/Shell Group, the largest petroleum company in the world. Shell has lagged behind its competitors, Mobil and Chevron, on addressing sexual orientation issues, but has improved significantly in recent years. In April 1996 Shell changed its equal employment statement to include sexual orientation, and in January 1998 it extended domestic-partnership benefits to eligible employees. The gay and lesbian employee network, SEAShell (Support, Equality, and Awareness at Shell), was instrumental in bringing about these changes.

Part Three

*Resources and Stock Options for
Gay and Lesbian Investors*

Socially Responsible Investing

Socially responsible investing is the practice of placing self-imposed restrictions called "screens" on the stocks and other investments you are willing to buy. Screens are set according to individual investors' chosen guidelines. Put simply, socially responsible investing means taking a stand on the politics of companies you choose to invest in.

Changes in corporate policies regarding sexual orientation have recently occurred at enough American corporations that organized gay and lesbian investors can use screen strategies to support companies that recognize gays and lesbians as workers and consumers, while at the same time drawing critical attention to those that do not.

Some financial managers roll their eyes when you mention socially responsible investing, claiming it limits investors' ability to realize the greatest possible return. This line of reasoning has merit if your *only* concern is profit. But a socially responsible investor's motives extend beyond profit. The socially responsible investor worries about how his or her profit might adversely effect other people's lives and jobs, and the environment.

Fortunately, socially responsible investment leaders and gay and lesbian rights activists have recently discovered each other. And their willingness to work together is creating new advancement opportunities for gays and lesbians as citizens and consumers—a trend that should bring smiles to the faces of business leaders who take gay and lesbian issues seriously.

In the early 1980s there were fewer than ten socially responsible investment funds. Today, however, there are over 200. Some funds screen tobacco- or alcohol-related enterprises, others invest only in companies with a certain percentage of women or racial minorities on staff, and still others refrain from investing in businesses tied to nuclear energy or the military. There are also religion-oriented funds, some based on fundamentalist Christian ideologies that are often antigay. Thus, it behooves gay and lesbian investors to invest with a pro-gay agenda.

The main activities screened by socially responsible investment funds include:

- production, distribution, or advertising of alcohol
- gambling, lottery, or gaming
- nuclear technology
- military contracting and/or subcontracting
- production, distribution, or advertising of tobacco

Other factors considered by socially responsible investment funds include:

- environmental protection
- labor or union relations
- diversity in the workplace, including gays and lesbians
- executive compensation
- community relations and outreach, including charitable giving
- animal testing
- foreign relations (principally with China, Myanmar, Pakistan, and Mexico)
- product safety

To Screen or Not to Screen

As mentioned, there are investment managers who believe social screening cuts into profit. And there is little doubt that the more screens you apply, the harder it is to maximize your return. Most financial counselors will initially advise against socially responsible investing or will suggest that if your principles demand it, you begin by setting aside only a portion of your money for such investments.

The good news for socially responsible gay and lesbian investors is that there are plenty of "good" companies from which to choose. Thus, cries of reduced profit are more likely reflective of an uninformed financial adviser than a true expectation of return. Still, as always with investments, let the buyer beware. Just like voting, shopping, volunteering, or even being civilly disobedient, socially responsible investing is a matter of making choices along a continuum of options. Risk is *always* part of the equation.

If gay and lesbian activism is your primary social concern, corporate policy on sexual orientation should be the screen you consider before any other. Balancing this with other concerns, however, is a thorny, complicated process.

I, for instance, will not knowingly invest in a company that is involved with nuclear technology or the employment of children overseas regardless of how progressive that company is on issues regarding sexual orientation. Each investor must develop his or her own sense of policy, priority, and balance.

Common Sense

Whatever your political views, priorities, or ethics, there are certain things you should *never* do when investing:

- Don't buy based on tips from friends or rumors circulating at work
- Don't buy based on information from Internet chat rooms, Web sites, or unsolicited E-mail

Following these guidelines may seem like common sense, but plenty of intelligent investors have acted imprudently based on unverified information.

The best investment advice might be to follow the philosophy of Wall Street leader Warren Buffett: Invest in what you know. In other words, ask yourself how much you know about the company and its products. Have you or your broker researched the management of the company? What is the company's record on the issues that are most important to you? Sometimes confidential discussions with staff members can provide the insight you seek. You should also keep in mind that a company with a good record on gay and lesbian issues is not necessarily a good investment. Invest in companies you understand and believe in, or based on what you believe to be competent, professional financial advice.

Sexual Orientation and the Socially Responsible Company

As a socially responsible gay or lesbian investor, three factors should most influence your investing habits:

- Does the company have a written nondiscrimination policy that includes sexual orientation?
- Are domestic-partnership benefits available to gay and lesbian employees? If not, is there a plan to install them?
- Does the workplace environment support the company's nondiscrimination policy by providing diversity or sensitivity training inclusive of sexual orientation, and by allowing and officially recognizing a gay and lesbian employee group?

One of the first attempts to establish investment principles and guidelines regarding gay and lesbian issues was the Wall Street Project, a corporate watchdog on sexual orientation policies, founded in 1993 and now known as the Equality Project (equalityproject.org). At its founding, the group estimated that only about 25% of American companies had sexual orientation nondiscrimination policy statements.

The Equality Project's greatest work to date involves the research and dissemination of information about companies that are abiding by the Equality Principles—the first benchmarks on sexual orientation issues in corporate America. Those principles are:

- Prohibitions against discrimination based on sexual orientation will be included in the company's written employment policy statement.
- Discrimination against HIV-positive employees or those with AIDS will be prohibited.
- Employee groups, regardless of sexual orientation, will be given equal standing with other employee associations.
- Diversity training will include sexual orientation issues.
- Spousal benefits will be offered to domestic partners of employees, regardless of sexual orientation, on an equal basis with those granted to legally married employees.
- Company advertising policy will ban negative sexual orientation stereotypes and will not discriminate against advertising in publications on the basis of sexual orientation.
- Companies will not discriminate in the sale of goods or services on the basis or sexual orientation.
- Written nondiscrimination policies on sexual orientation must be disseminated throughout the company. A senior company official will be appointed to monitor compliance corporatewide.

In addition, two for-profit firms are primarily responsible for bringing socially responsible gay and lesbian oriented investment vehicles to the market based on exceptionally strict guidelines: the Meyers Pride Value Fund, established in 1996 and managed by Shelly J. Meyers in Los Angeles, and V Management, established in 1993 and managed by Howard Tharsing in San Francisco.

About 500 companies currently meet the Meyers Pride Value Fund criteria. The Pride Fund staff works with the companies it invests in to bring about more comprehensive and gay-friendly workplace policies. The minimum investment to participate in the Pride Fund is $1,000 (or $250 for individual retirement accounts). In 1998 Meyers teamed up with BankBoston, connecting gay and lesbian financial planning to the world's oldest commercial bank.

V Management is a registered investment adviser dedicated to serving gays and lesbians and whose mission is to seek superior returns for investors concerned about issues of gay and lesbian equality. V Management is the home of the Lavender Screen, a comprehensive database of corporate policies on sexual orientation. V Management offers investment management services for institutions and high–net-worth individuals.

In 1996 Howard Tharsing and I merged information from our corporate databases in an effort to develop a specialized ten-point rating system to help institutional investors and money managers scrutinize a company's record on sexual orientation in relation to its competitors by industry. Out of this partnership grew the GLV 100 Index, an annual report on the most socially responsible companies for gays and lesbians. A list of the companies that made the 1999 GLV 100 Index appears in the appendix.

Description of the GLV Rating Scale and System

Companies using terms "sexual status" or "sexual preference" in description of nondiscrimination policy statements and materials about gay and lesbian employees	2.0
Companies using term "sexual orientation" in description of nondiscrimination policy statements and materials about gay and lesbian employees	3.0

Companies using transgender-inclusive wording in written nondiscrimination policy statements	1.0
No significant third-party support, or major stockholder affiliation (51% or more of voter shares) or ties to groups aggressively seeking to overturn or prevent passage of gay and lesbian protections	1.0
Corporate giving to nonprofit gay and lesbian organizations or events	0.5
Corporate giving to politically identified gay or lesbian organizations or events	0.5
Corporate giving to any AIDS charity or organization recognized for its support of men's health and education	0.5
Corporate giving to any breast cancer charity or organization recognized for its support of women's health and education	0.5
Diversity training inclusive of sexual orientation	0.5
Diversity training inclusive of people with disabilities	0.5
Company policy allowing gay and lesbian employee groups	0.5
Company officially recognizes gay and lesbian employee groups	0.5
Full gay and lesbian domestic-partnership health coverage program	1.0
Total Available Credit	10.00

(since the first two options are mutually exclusive)

Other important gay- and lesbian-oriented vehicles exist, such as Walter Schubert's Gay Financial Network, which offers a wealth of information, tools, and programs to help gay and lesbian consumers, employees, and investors track companies, stocks, and funds that may be of interest. The company's Web site (www.gfn.com) also offers online trading maintains one of the most comprehensive daily updates on gay- and lesbian-oriented news and financial information.

In addition, consumer-oriented gay and lesbian information appears on Planet Out, OnQ, and other queer-related Web sites. Other investment funds with specific goals that gay and lesbian investors may find attractive include the Women's Equity Fund, which provides a means for investors to build their assets and simultaneously promote leadership opportunities for women.

Activism and Politics on Wall Street

When a significant social issue arises in relation to a company's policies and practices, concerned shareholders can bring the problem to the attention of the company's other shareholders. Such action is known as a "shareholder resolution."

Issues, procedures, and politics related to shareholder resolutions are complex and tedious. Still, it's important to be aware of the basics, because any shareholder owning a minimum of 1,000 shares in a company and who meets the published requirements of the Securities and Exchange Commission can file a shareholder resolution.

In recent years, changes that have been brought about by shareholder resolutions (or the threat of shareholder resolutions) include:

- an agreement by Johnson & Johnson to include the words "sexual orientation" in its nondiscrimination policy;
- independent monitoring of textile laborers contracted by The Gap in El Salvador;
- agreement by 3M Media to cease all tobacco advertising on American billboards;
- divestment by PepsiCo of its bottling interest in Myanmar (Burma).

Other shareholder issues have revolved around nuclear power operations and disputes, dioxin releases into the atmosphere by large industrial plants, and issues related to racism and sexism in the workplace.

Socially Responsible Case Studies

As a means of better understanding how individuals might go about investing while applying socially responsible screens to their portfolios, I've included these eight case studies. I am extremely grateful to Patrick McVeigh of Trillium Asset Management for his input and written analysis based on each individual's stated requirements. (Please keep in mind that Patrick made his analyses at the time of this writing. The market will have changed, perhaps significantly, by the time you read his recommendations.)

Case #1

> Identifies self as: Single lesbian mother; nurse; age 32
> Screens: No tobacco companies; no companies with a history of employment discrimination problems of any kind for at least five years; sexual orientation policy statement not mandatory; alcohol, nuclear, or military affiliations are OK
> Goals: Aggressive growth; thinking of college tuition for ten-year-old daughter
> Available cash: $42,000
> Monthly contribution: $250

This individual is in a better position than most parents in having planned ahead for her daughter's college education. With $42,000 already saved and another eight years to go before her daughter is of college age, she is doing well. She can plan, with a return of 10% per year, which has been the historical average for growth-oriented stocks, on her savings growing to approximately $130,000 by the time her daughter turns 18. She might want to consider investing her funds in a host of socially screened growth mutual funds. Some to consider would include the Parnassus Fund, Citizens Emerging Growth, the Dreyfus Third Century Fund, the Domini Social Equity Fund, and Calvert World Values. All of these funds meet her stated social criteria.

Keeping the savings in her name rather than her daughter's name will prove beneficial when it comes time to apply for college financial aid. Colleges expect a higher percentage of a child's savings to go toward tuition.

To make sure she is maximizing her savings, it is important that she make full use of any retirement options available. Her monthly savings of $250 could be about one-third greater if the savings were accomplished through pretax deductions from her paycheck into a 401(k) plan. (It is allowable to withdraw money from retirement plans for educational needs without any penalty.)

She should plan to increase her monthly contribution to her savings as her income grows. Being 32 and in a career that remains in demand in the job market, she can expect regular salary increases.

Case #2

> Identifies self as: Gay white male; advertising executive; age 48
> Screens: No tobacco companies; no nuclear; no oil; companies do not have to have a sexual orientation policy, but cannot have had any major court battles over employment issues surrounding race, sex, or sexual orientation for five years
> Goals: Aggressive growth; thinking of retirement income
> Available cash: $80,000
> Monthly contribution: $1,000

As he is 48 years old, it is good that this individual is thinking of retirement income. He has made a good start by saving $80,000, but he will need considerably more than this to retire comfortably within 20 years. His monthly contributions of $1,000 are a sizable amount and will help him catch up to what he needs for retirement. If he continues to make these contributions until the age of 65 and averages a 10% annual return on his investments, his pool would grow to nearly $1 million. Along with Social Security and any other retirement plan he has, this should be more than adequate to ensure a comfortable retirement. As a result, his choice of investments does not need to be as aggressive as he might think.

He should sit down with a stockbroker or financial planner and design a portfolio consisting of high-quality growth stocks. Given his age and the good start he has made on setting money aside, he would do better to stick primarily with high-quality companies and only dabble with smaller, more aggressive stocks. Some larger companies experiencing high levels of sustainable growth and selling for reasonable valuations include Bank of America, Colgate-Palmolive, Eastman Kodak, McGraw-Hill, McKesson, Sears, and Xerox. A few midsize growth companies to round out the portfolio could include Lewis Galoob Toys, Silicon Graphics, and Chiron.

Case #3

> Identifies self as: Bisexual Hispanic male; graphic designer; age 23
> Screens: No investing in any company without a written policy banning discrimination based on sexual orientation; no nuclear technology or military; no investing in cotton; liquor and tobacco are OK
> Goals: Aggressive growth; risk taker with no experience in market and little market knowledge or understanding of investments
> Available cash: $2,500
> Monthly contribution: $100

Given that this individual is just starting out in the work world, he would benefit from sitting down with a financial planner to develop his long-term financial goals and strategies. Such a meeting would also help him better understand the financial options available to him. Since he has an extensive list of social concerns, I suggest that he call the Social Investment Forum, (202) 872-5319. This is an organization of financial professionals involved in socially responsible investing. They can provide him with the names of financial planners involved with social investing in his area.

Because he has small amount of cash available for investments, he should go in the direction of a mutual fund. There is no mutual fund available that meets all of his social criteria, as his interest in not investing in cotton is not a concern covered by any fund. If he is willing to loosen this restriction, the Pride Fund would be an option. This is the only mutual fund that requires a written policy banning discrimination based on sexual orientation from companies it invests in. If he does not want to drop his restriction on firms in the cotton business, he then could start buying stock directly in some companies. A stockbroker familiar with social investing would be able to help him. Interesting stocks for him to consider could include H.B. Fuller, Graco, and Solectron.

Case #4

Identifies self as: Asian-American lesbian; novelist; age 52
Screens: Sexual orientation nondiscrimination policy required
Goals: Security and income
Available cash: $340,000
Monthly contribution: $1,500

Given this person's age and the relative uncertainty of income from her job as a novelist, she is wise to be aiming toward security and income from her investments. If she can continue to contribute $1,500 per month to her savings, her retirement pool will increase rapidly. Assuming a modest 6% annual return on her investments, she will have amassed nearly $750,000 by the time she turns 60.

She would be best advised to invest most of her money in conservative stocks that pay a good yield and in municipal bonds. The bonds should be targeted to mature on a staggered basis, based on when she expects to need the income. For example, she could plan to have bonds maturing every year or two after she turns 65.

She could keep a smaller portion of her assets invested in high-yield stocks such as utility, energy, drug, and banking stocks. Companies in these industries that have sexual orientation policies nondiscrimination include Amoco, Baltimore Gas and Electric, Eastern Utilities, Associates, Merck, and Norwest.

Case #5

Identifies self as: Strict vegetarian; feminist; nutritionist; age 29
Screens: No oil, chemical, alcohol, nuclear, military, international investing, dairy, or meat
Goals: Income
Available cash: $50,000
Monthly contribution: $0

Given the description of this individual, it seems as if her job as a nutritionist does not cover all her living expenses. As a result, despite her young age, she relies on income from her savings. Her $50,000 in savings will only create about $3,000 a year in income. If possible, she would be better off in the long term if she could reduce her living expenses somewhat in order to let her savings grow.

If maximizing her income now is the most important goal, she should invest her cash in a bond, which in today's market will yield between 6% and 7%. Given her extensive list of restrictions based on ethical considerations, she should consider bonds issued by agencies of the federal government. Bonds issued by the Federal National Mortgage Association go to support housing, while those issued by the Student Loan Marketing Association support education. She should stick with bonds maturing between five and ten years given that her financial situation is likely to change during that time frame.

Case #6

> Identify selves as: African-American male couple; own carpet cleaning business; ages 44 and 57
> Screens: No tobacco companies
> Goals: Aggressive growth and retirement income
> Available cash: $50,000 (combined)
> Monthly contribution: $875 (combined)

Given this couple's disparity in age, it is not surprising that there is also a divergence in their financial goals. They state that they are seeking aggressive growth and retirement income, two goals that do not normally go together. While one individual has 20 years until retirement and could afford to invest aggressively, the other is only eight years from retirement and should be more concerned with income and safety.

Unfortunately, the $50,000 in cash already amassed will not have much of a chance to grow in only eight more years. With a combined monthly contribution of $875 and assuming a 7% annualized return (reflective of a somewhat conservative investment posture), the funds will grow to only $200,000 in eight years. Thus the couple will really be counting on the success of their carpet cleaning business and the earning power of the younger individual to carry them as they age.

Having their own business is a risky investment, and this should be seen as the more aggressive part of their overall financial portfolio. Their cash should be invested more conservatively. My financial advice depends on how solid their business is. Many cleaning businesses are relatively insecure. If that is true in this case, I would recommend keeping up to six months' worth of personal expenses in a money market account. Additional cash could be invested in very solid growth stocks such as Johnson & Johnson, Procter & Gamble, and Wells Fargo.

Given that they own their own business, these two should also make sure that they have set up an IRA and KEOGH plan that would allow them to each save up to $30,000 or 25% of their incomes, whichever is less, on a tax-deferred basis.

Case #7

> Identify selves as: Lesbian couple; veterinarian and advertising copywriter; ages 32 and 47
> Screens: None
> Goals: Aggressive growth.
> Available cash: $35,000 (combined)
> Monthly contribution: $400 (combined)

This couple, like the previous pair, have a wide disparity in age, but these two are quite a bit younger, which has significant implications for their investment decisions. Though they are starting with less cash than the previous couple and have less than half as much to contribute to their savings on a monthly basis, their money should grow to be two to three times as large by retirement age. This is due to the power of compound interest over time. Whereas the previous couple had only about eight years before one reached the age of 65, this couple has 18 years. As a result, they can pursue a more aggressive investment style. Projecting annualized returns of 8 to 10% will turn their $35,000 initial investment into $400,000 to $550,000 over 20 years.

Given the size of their initial investment, they would be best served by starting with mutual funds. I would recommend the same batch of growth mutual funds that I mentioned in Case #1. They should probably choose three funds from among the Parnassus Fund, Citizens Emerging Growth, Domini Social Equity, Dreyfus Third Century, and Calvert World Values.

Case #8

Identifies self as: Gay man; computer consultant; age 38
Screens: No tobacco companies; no nuclear or military; no companies with a history of employment discrimination problems of any kind for at least five years; sexual orientation nondiscrimination policy statement not mandatory; alcohol is OK
Goals: Aggressive growth.
Available cash: $10,000
Monthly contribution: $250

Here is an individual with a good job as a computer consultant who has relatively limited savings of $10,000. As a consultant, he may not have any established retirement program. If not, this is something he should immediately create.

Despite having savings of only $10,000, he is only saving $3,000 per year. At his age, he will need to save more to build funds for retirement. An aggressive investment portfolio built on these figures can probably only grow to the $400,000 to $500,000 range by the time he reaches 65.

The size of his initial investment would be best served in a mutual fund. Both Calvert and Citizens offer families of mutual funds that screen on all the issues of importance mentioned. In addition, they both offer growth and aggressive growth funds.

Part Four

Gay and Lesbian Desk Reference

Key Employers with No Written Sexual Orientation Nondiscrimination Policy

Cracker Barrel Old Country Store
Exxon
General Electric
Lands' End
McDonald's franchises
Wendy's

Employers with Domestic-Partnership Health Care Plans, as of April 1999

(Does not include municipalities, universities, labor unions, or law firms)

Adobe Systems, San Jose, Calif.
Adolph Coors Co., Golden, Colo.
Advanced Micro Devices, Sunnyvale, Calif.
Aetna Inc., Hartford, Conn.
Agouron Pharmaceuticals, La Jolla, Calif.
Akron Beacon Journal, Akron, Ohio
Allina Health Systems, Minneapolis
America Online, Dulles, Va.
American Express Co., New York City
American President Lines, Oakland, Calif.
Apple Computer, Cupertino, Calif.
Arizona Cable, Payson, Ariz.
Arizona Public Service, Phoenix
AT&T, New York City

Atlanta Braves, Atlanta
Atlanta Hawks, Atlanta
Atlantic Records & Pictures, Los Angeles
Autodesk Inc., San Rafael, Calif.
Avon Products, New York City
Bain & Co., Boston
Bank of America, Charlotte, N.C.
BankBoston Corp., Boston
Bankers Trust, New York City
Banyan Worldwide, Westboro, Mass.
Barnes & Noble, New York City
Barra Inc., New York City
Bay Area Rapid Transit, Oakland, Calif.
Bay Networks Inc., Santa Clara, Calif.
BBN Advanced Computers Inc., Mount Airy, Md.
BEA Systems Inc., San Jose, Calif.
Bell Atlantic, Philadelphia
Bell Northern Research, Norcross, Ga.
Ben & Jerry's Homemade, South Burlington, Vt.
Beth Israel Medical Center, Boston
Beth Israel Medical Center, New York City
Bisys Cinti Regional Center, Cincinnati
Blue Cross/Blue Shield of Connecticut, North Haven, Conn.
Blue Cross/Blue Shield of Massachusetts, Boston
Blue Cross/Blue Shield of New York, Syracuse, N.Y.
Bose Corp., Framingham, Mass.
Boston Consulting Group, Boston
Boston Globe Co., Boston
BP Amoco Corp., Chicago
Bristol-Myers Squibb Co., New York City
Bureau of National Affairs, Washington, D.C.
Business for Social Responsibility, San Francisco
Cadence Design Systems Inc., San Jose, Calif.
California Pacific Medical Center, San Francisco
Calloway Golf, Carlsbad, Calif.
Cambridge Technology Group, Cambridge, Mass.
Cambridge Technology Partners, Needham, Mass.
Candle Corp., Santa Monica, Calif.

Cape Air, Hyannis, Mass.
Carroll, Burdick, & McDonough, San Francisco
Cartoon Network, New York City
Celestial Seasonings, Boulder, Colo.
Centigram Communications Corp., San Jose, Calif.
Centura Software Corp., Redwood City, Calif.
Ceridian Corp., Minneapolis
Chadbourne & Parke, New York City
Chapman & Cutler, Chicago
Charles Schwab and Co., San Francisco
Chase Manhattan, New York City
Chevron Corp., San Francisco
Children's Healthcare Center, Laguna Hills, Calif.
Children's Hospital of Boston, Boston
Chiron Corp., Emeryville, Calif.
Choate, Hall, & Stewart, Boston
Chubb Corp., Warren, N.J.
Cisco Systems, San Jose, Calif.
Cleary, Gottlieb, Steen, & Hamilton, New York City
Clorox Co., Oakland, Calif.
CMP Media Inc., Manhasset, N.Y.
CNN, New York City
Codman Square Health Center, Dorchester, Mass.
Communications Management Associates, California
Compaq Computer Corp., Houston,
Computer Associates International, Islandia, N.Y.
Computer Graphics, St. Louis
Consumers Union, Yonkers, N.Y.
Corel Corp., Orem, Utah
Costco Wholesale, Issaquah, Wash.
Coudert Brothers, New York City
Council on Foundations, Washington, D.C.
Covington & Burling, Washington, D.C.
Cravath, Swain, & Moore, New York City
Creative Artists Agency Inc., Beverly Hills
Crum and Forster Insurance, Morristown, N.J.
D'Ancoma & Pflaum, Chicago
Dana-Farber Cancer Institute, Boston

David Sarnoff Research Center, Princeton, N.J.
Debevoise & Plimpton, New York City
Deluxe Corp., Shoreview, Minn.
Democratic National Committee, Washington, D.C.
Dewey Ballantine, New York City
Digital Equipment Corp., Maynard, Mass
Digital Origin, Mountain View, Calif.
Directors Guild Industry Health Fund, Los Angeles
Discovery Channel, Bethesda, Md.
District Council 1707
Donna Karan, New York City
DreamWorks SKG, Universal City, Calif.
E! Entertainment Television, Los Angeles
Eastern Mountain Sports, Peterborough, N.H.
Eastman Kodak Co., Rochester, N.Y.
EES Consulting Inc., Bellevue, Wash.
Egghead Software, Issaquah, Wash.
Electronic Data Systems Corp., Plano, Tex.
Entertainment Radio Network, Malibu, Calif.
ENTEX, Rye Brook, N.Y.
Estée Lauder Companies Inc., New York City
Fannie Mae, Washington, D.C.
First Tech Computer, Minneapolis
Fish & Richardson PC, Boston
Fleishman Hillard Inc., St. Louis
Ford Foundation, New York City
Forte Software, Wakefield, Mass.
Fox Broadcasting, New York City
Frame Relay Technologies Inc., Costa Mesa, Calif.
Fred Hutchinson Cancer Research Center, Seattle
Freddie Mac, McLean, Va.
Fried, Frank, Harris, Shriver, & Jacobson, New York City
Gap Inc., San Francisco
Gardener's Supply Co., Burlington, Vt.
Gardner, Carton, & Douglas, Chicago
Gay and Lesbian Advocates and Defenders, Boston
Gay and Lesbian Alliance Against Defamation, New York City
Gay and Lesbian Medical Association, San Francisco

Gay and Lesbian Victory Fund, Washington, D.C.
Genentech, San Francisco
Gibson, Dunn, & Crutcher LLP, Los Angeles
Gill Foundation, Colorado Springs, Colo.
Glaxo Wellcome, Research Triangle Park, N.C.
Golsten, Storrs, Boston
Goodwill Games, New York City
Greenpeace, Washington, D.C.
Group Health Cooperative of Puget Sound, Seattle
Hale & Door, Boston
Hartford Financial Services Co., Hartford, Conn.
Harvard Pilgrim Health Care Inc., Quincy, Mass.
Hearst Corp., New York City
Hewitt Associates, Lincolnshire, Ill.
Hewlett-Packard, Palo Alto, Calif.
Hill & Knowlton, New York City
Home Box Office, New York City
Human Rights Campaign, Washington, D.C.
IBM, Armonk, N.Y.
ICM Mortgage Corp., Greenwood Village, Colo.
IDG, Roanoke, Va.
IDS Financial Services, Minneapolis
Illinois Masonic Medical Center, Chicago
Imation Corp., Oakdale, Minn.
Immunex Corp., Seattle
Informix Software, Menlo Park, Calif.
Inprise Corp., Scotts Valley, Calif.
Insurance Co. of the West, Arlington, Tex.
Intel Inc., Santa Clara, Calif.
Interleaf, Waltham, Mass.
Intermedia Partners, San Francisco, Calif.
Isis Pharmaceuticals Inc., Carlsbad, Calif.
J.P. Morgan & Co., New York City
Jackson Labs, Northridge, Calif.
Jackson, Tufts, Cole, & Black, San Jose, Calif.
James Irvine Foundation, San Francisco, Calif.
Jeffer, Mangels, Butler, & Marmaro, Los Angeles
Jenner & Block, Chicago

Jet Propulsion Laboratory, Pasadena, Calif.
John D. & Catherine T. MacArthur Foundation, Chicago
John Hancock Mutual Life Insurance, Boston
Joyce Mertz-Gilmore Foundation, New York City
Kaiser Permanente Foundation Health Plan Inc., Oakland, Calif.
Keynote Systems Inc., Pittsburgh
Knight-Ridder, San Jose, Calif.
KQED Radio, San Francisco
Lambda Legal Defense and Education Fund, New York City
Lawrence Berkeley Laboratory, Berkeley, Calif.
Lawrence Livermore National Laboratory, Livermore, Calif.
Learning Company, Cambridge, Ill.
Legal Aid, Elmira, N.Y.
Levi Strauss & Co., San Francisco
The Limited Inc., Columbus, Ohio
Lincoln Financial, Fort Wayne, Ind.
Local Initiatives Support Corp., Washington, D.C.
Los Alamos National Laboratory, Los Alamos, N.M.
Los Angeles Philharmonic Association, Los Angeles
Lotus Development, Cambridge, Mass.
LucasFilm, San Rafael, Calif.
Lucent Technologies, Murray Hill, N.J.
Macmillan Publishing Co., New York, N.Y.
Maine Medical, Portland, Maine
Mark Hopkins Intercontinental Hotel, San Francisco
Mark Shale Outlet, Naperville, Ill.
Market News Service, Washington, D.C.
Marriott International, Bethesda, Md.
Mattel Inc., El Segundo, Calif.
MCA/Universal, Universal City, Calif.
McGraw-Hill, New York City
Mentor Graphics Corp., Wilsonville, Ore.
Merrill Lynch, New York City
Metro-Goldwyn-Mayer Inc./United Artists, Santa Monica, Calif.
Meyers Pride Value Fund, Beverly Hills
The Miami Herald, Miami
Microsoft Corp., Redmond, Wash.
Milbank, Tweed, Hadley, & McCloy, New York City

Millipore Corp., Bedford, Mass.
Star Tribune, Minneapolis
Minnesota Public Radio, St. Paul
Mobil Corp., Fairfax, Va.
Monitor Advertising, Houston
Monsanto Co., St. Louis
Montefiore Medical Center, Bronx, N.Y.
Museum of Modern Art, New York City
National Association of Socially Responsible Organizations, Washington, D.C.
National Audubon Society, New York City
National Center for Lesbian Rights, San Francisco
National Conference for Community and Justice, New York City
National Equity Fund, Chicago
National Gay and Lesbian Task Force, Washington, D.C.
National Grocers Association, Reston, Va.
National Organization for Women, Washington, D.C.
National Public Radio, Washington, D.C.
Nature Conservancy, Arlington, Va.
NCR Corp., Dayton, Ohio
Netscape Communications Corp., Mountain View, Calif.
Nevada Bell, Reno, Nev.
New England Medical Center, Boston
New York Times Guild Benefits Plan, New York City
Newspaper Guild of Greater Philadelphia
NeXT Software Inc., Redwood City, Calif.
Nike Inc., Beaverton, Ore.
Nortel Networks Corp., Brampton, Canada
Northern States Power, Minneapolis
Northern Trust Co., Chicago
Nossaman, Guthner, Knox, & Elliot, Los Angeles
Novartis Pharmaceutical Corp., East Hanover, N.J.
Novell, Provo, Utah
NW Ayer & Co., New York City
O'Melveny & Meyers, Los Angeles
Oakland Children's Hospital, Oakland, Calif.
Octel America Inc., Newark, Del.
Oil and Chemical Atomic Workers, Rahway, N.J.
Oracle Corp., Redwood Shores, Calif.

Organic Online, San Francisco
Pacific Bell, San Francisco
Pacific Enterprises, Los Angeles
Pacific Gas & Electric, San Francisco
Pacific Stock Exchange, San Francisco
Pacificare Health Systems, Santa Ana, Calif.
Pacificorp, Portland, Ore.
Para Transit, Sacramento
Paradigm, San Francisco
Paramount Pictures, Los Angeles
Park Nicollet Medical Center, St. Louis Park, Minn.
Patagonia Inc., Ventura, Calif.
Patton Boggs LLP, Washington, D.C.
Paul, Hastings, Janofsky, & Walker, Los Angeles
Paul, Weiss, Rifkind, Wharton, & Garrison, New York City
PE Corp., Norwalk, Conn.
Peabody & Arnold, Boston
PeopleSoft Inc., Pleasanton, Calif.
Pew Charitable Trusts, Philadelphia
Pillsbury Co., Minneapolis
Planned Parenthood Federation of America, New York City
Portland Cable Access, Portland, Ore.
Primix Solutions, Watertown, Mass.
Principal Financial Group, Des Moines, Iowa
Principal Mutual Life Insurance, Des Moines, Iowa
Public Broadcasting Service, Alexandria, Va.
Qualcomm, San Diego
Quark Inc., Denver
Reader's Digest Association, Pleasantville, N.Y.
Recreational Equipment Inc., Sumner, Wash/
Reebok, Stoughton, Mass.
Remedy Corp., Mountain View, Calif.
Reuters America Holdings Inc., New York, N.Y.
Rhode Island Counseling Associates., Warwick, R.I.
RSVP Travel Productions Inc., Minneapolis
Rudnick & Wolfe, Chicago
Safeco, Seattle, Wash.
San Francisco 49ers, San Francisco

San Francisco Chronicle, San Francisco
Santa Cruz Operations, Santa Cruz, Calif.
SAS Institute Inc., Cary, N.C.
Scripps Research Institute, La Jolla, Calif.
Scudder Kemper Investments, New York, N.Y.
Seagate Technology Inc., Scotts Valley, Calif.
The Seagram Company Ltd., New York City
Seattle City Light, Seattle
Seattle Mental Health Institute, Seattle
Seattle Symphony Orchestra, Seattle
Seattle Times, Seattle
Segal Co., New York City
Shell Oil Co., Houston
Sherman & Sterling, New York City
Showtime Networks Inc., New York City
Sidley & Austin, Chicago
Silicon Graphics Inc., Mountain View, Calif.
Smith & Hawken, Acton, Mass.
Smith Kettlewell Eye Institute, San Francisco
SmithKline Beecham, Philadelphia
Sony Pictures Entertainment, New York City
Southern California Gas Co., Los Angeles
Space Telescope Science Institute, Baltimore
Springs Industries, New York City
St. Paul Companies, St. Paul, Minn.
St. Petersburg Times, St. Petersburg, Fla.
St. Vincent Hospital, Santa Fe, N.M.
Starbucks Coffee Co., Seattle
State Bar of California, Los Angeles
Sun Microsystems, Mountain View, Calif.
Supermac Technology, Sunnyvale, Calif.
Sybase, Emeryville, Calif.
TBS, New York City
Teachers Insurance and Annuity Association, New York City
Tech Data Corp., Clearwater, Fla.
Telecommunications Inc., Denver
Teradyne, Somerville, Mass.
Testa, Hurwitz, & Thibeault LLP, Boston

Thinking Machines, Cambridge, Mass.
Ticketmaster Group Inc., West Hollywood, Calif.
Timberland Co., Stratham, N.H.
Time Warner, New York City
Times Mirror Co., Los Angeles
TNT, New York City
Tower Records and Video Stores, West Sacramento, Calif.
Tropicana/Dole Beverages, Bradenton, Fla/
Trillium Asset Management, Boston
Tufts Healthcare Plan, Waltham, Mass.
Turner Broadcasting System, Atlanta
Turner Classic Movies, New York City
Union of American Hebrew Congregations, New York City
Unisys, Blue Bell, Pa.
Unitarian Universalist Committee, Boston
United Church Board Homeland, Cleveland
United University Professors, Albany, N.Y.
United Way of the Bay Area, San Francisco
Urban Institute, Washington, D.C.
US Healthcare, Wilmington, Del.
U S West Inc., Englewood, Colo.
Veritas Software Corp., Mountain View, Calif.
Vermont Girl Scouts Council, Essex Junction, Vt.
Viacom, New York City
Vignette Corp., Austin, Tex.
Village Voice, New York, NY
Visa International, Foster City, Calif.
Vision Services Plan, Tamaqua, Pa.
Visioneer, Fremont, Calif.
Wainwright Bank and Trust, Boston
Walker Art Center, Minneapolis
Walt Disney, Burbank, Calif.
Wang Global, Billerica, Mass.
Warner Brothers, Burbank, Calif.
Washington Post Co., Washington, D.C.
Watson Wyatt & Co., Bethesda, Md.
Weil, Gotshal, & Manges, New York City
Wells Fargo & Co., San Francisco, CA

WGBH Public Television, Boston
White & Case, New York City
White & Williams, McLean, Va.
Whitman-Walker Clinic, Washington, D.C.
Whole Foods Market Inc., Austin, Tex.
Wilder Foundation, St. Paul, Minn.
William Morris Agency, New York City
Worcester Telegram, Worcester, Mass.
Working Assets, San Francisco
World Championship Wrestling, New York City
WQED-FM, Pittsburgh
Writers Guild of America West, Los Angeles
WRQ Inc., Seattle
Xerox Corp., Stamford, Conn.
Ziff-Davis Publishing, New York City

This list represents the best efforts of the Human Rights Campaign to track employers that offer domestic-partner health coverage. Because of the proprietary nature of human resource information and because there is no centralized place where employers must report such policies, some companies that offer domestic-partner health coverage may not appear. Also, while every effort is made to confirm the existence of these policies, some employers may have been included in error. We encourage readers with additions, corrections, questions or comments to contact: Daryl Herrschaft, research coordinator, at:

daryl.herrschaft@hrc.org, Human Rights Campaign, http://www.hrc.org

Gay and Lesbian Corporate Employee Groups

3M
People Like Us
A Group of Groups Coalition
(612) 737-3228
Regional Network—Northern California
Phil James
Pjames@HTG.com

Adolph Coors Co.
LAGER
P.O. Box 643
Golden, CO 80403
Steve Kelliher
(303) 277-3417

Aetna
1000 Middle Street
Convery MA-22
Middletown, CT 06457
Rick Balmer
(203) 636-4691

Air Products and Chemicals
GLEE
7201 Hamilton Blvd.
Allentown, PA 18195
Dale Miller
(610) 481-8212

American Airlines
GLEAM
PO Box 619616, MD 5575
DFW airport, TX 75261-9616
Tim Kincaid
Tim_Kincaid@amrcorp.com

Amoco Corp.
B.T. GLASS
c/o Amoco Diversity Group
200 E Randolph, MC 3501
Chicago, IL 60601
(312) 856-3442
glass@amoco.com

American College Personnel Association
Standing Committee for Lesbian, Gay, Bisexual and Transgendered Awareness
One Dupont Circle, Suite 300 NW
Washington, DC 20035-1110
(202) 835-ACPA (2272)
www.acpa.nche.edu/comms/Scomma/sclgbta.htm

AMR Corporation (American Airlines, American Eagle, The SABRE Group)
GLEAM
(214) 521-5342, ext.812
gleam@poboxes.com
http://web.webvis.net/gleam/

AT&T
LEAGUE
2020 K St., NW
Washington, DC 20006
John Klenert
(202) 776 5685
Jklenert@attmail.com
http://www.league-att.org/

Atlantic Executive Network
P.O. Box 8924
Atlanta, GA 31106
(404) 814-1418
(404) 873-0125 (fax)

Apple Computer
Apple Lambda
20525 Mariani Ave.
Cupertino, CA 95014

Autodesk
111 McInnis Pkwy
San Rafael, CA 94903
Pat Keaney
(415) 507 8506

Bank of America
1655 Grant Street Building
Concord, CA 94520
Daniel Ray-Carothers
(510) 675 1621

284 / Smart Spending

BankBoston
GLOE
100 Federal St.
Boston, MA 02110-1802
Chris Palmer
(617) 434-8772

Bankers Association for Gay & Lesbian Equality
BAGLE
P.O. Box 06325
Wacker Drive Post Office
Chicago, IL 60606
BAGLEHQ@aol.com

Baxter Healthcare
1430 Waukegan
McGaw Park, IL 60085
Jonathan Hnilicka
(847) 578-6682

Bell Atlantic
GLOBE
5428 Braddock Ridge Dr.
Centerville, VA 22020-3313
Sandy Strauss
(703) 830-4668

Bellcore
Outreach
331 Newman Springs Road, Room 1F-229
Red Bank, NJ 07701
Jack Zatz
(908) 758-5044
jzatz@notes.cc.bellcore.com

Boeing
BEAGLES
P.O. Box 1733
Renton, WA 98057
Ed Gentzler
(206) 781-3587

Chase Bank of Texas
PRIDE
People Recognizing Individual Differences Equally
Harold Shultz
(713) 216-6740
harold.shultz@chase.com
Richard Bielec
(713) 655-5423
richard.bielec@chase.com
Paula Andries
(713) 262-1567
paula.andries@chase.com

Chase Manhattan
Gay & Lesbian Friends @ Chase (GLFC)
New York City
Chase Hawkins (212) 493-4623
Nancy DiDia (212) 622-8999

Chevron
GLGEA
100 Chevron Way
Richmond, CA 94802
Kirk Nass
(510) 242 -932
CLGEA@aol.com

Chubb Corp.
15 Mountainview Rd.
Warren, NJ 07059
Joan Caputo
(908) 903-7373
jcaputo@chubb.com

Citicorp Citibank
Lesbian and Gay Employee Group
Doug Robinson
(718) 248-8073
doug.robinson@citicorp.com
http://www.lesbigayradio.com/citibank

The Coca-Cola Company
KOLAGE
1 Coca-Cola Plaza
Atlanta, GA 30313
Michael Wright
(404) 676-7530
mwright@na.ko.com
kolage@mindspring.com

Commonwealth Edison
CEEGLO
125 S. Clark, Room 1100
Chicago, Il 60603
Tim Hickerness
(312) 394-8391

Corestates Financial
MOSAIC
FC: 1 8 14 2
Broad and Chestnut Sts.
Philadelphia, PA 19107
Pat Quigley
(215) 375-3087

DaimlerChrysler
People of Diversity
Michelle Marquis
(313) 252-6025
mm87@chrysler.com
Michelle Waters
(248) 576-0909
mmw@chrysler.com

Dayton-Hudson
P.O. Box 859
Minneapolis, MN 55402
Nancy Landis
(612) 375 3087

Digital Queers
DigiQueers@aol.com

DuPont
BGLAD
P.O. Box 2192
Wilmington, DE 19899-2192
(302) 571.9112
bglad@dol.net
http://dupontbglad.com/

DuPont/Merck Pharmaceutical Co.
Gay and Lesbian Employees of DuPont/ Merck
DuPont/Merck Plaza, LR 1S5
P.O. Box 80705
Wilmington, DE 19880-0705
(302) 992 2230

Eastman Kodak
Lambda Network at Kodak
PO Box 14067
Rochester, NY 14614-0067
David Kosel
(716) 234 4388

Exxon
EGLE
124 N. Holly Drive
Baytown, TX 77520
Linda Perry
(713) 425 4206

Farallon Communications
Out There at Farallon
2470 Mariner Square Loop
Alameda, CA 94501
Lezlie Lee
(510) 814-5288
lezliel@farallon.com

Federal Government
GLOBE
P.O. Box 45237
Washington, DC 20026-5237
Rob Sadler
Rob@fedglobe.org
http://www.fedglobe.org/index.html

Fleet Bank
Group in Progress

Ford Motor Company
GLOBE
23814 Michigan Ave. Suite 187
Dearborn, MI 48124
(313) 438-1970 (voice mail)
FordGlobe@delphi.com
http://www.people.delphi.com/fordglobe

Freddie Mac
Lambda Group
8100 Jones Branch Drive
Mailstop B39
McClean, VA 22102
Thomas Antignani
(703) 714-2953

Genentech
Gays, Lesbians, Bis, and Friends
460 Point San Bruno Blvd.
South San Francisco, CA 94080
(415) 225-6260

General Mills
Betty's Family
1 General Mills Blvd.
Minneapolis, MN 55426
Daniel Duty/Maggie George
Dutyx000@mail.genmills.com
George_maggie@mail.genmills.com

General Motors
GM Plus
(in formation stages)

GLSEN
Gay, Lesbian, and Straight Education Network
Kevin Jennings
glsen@glsen.org

The Hartford Financial Services Group
GLOBE
Jeff McCartney
(860) 547-5895
jmccartney@thehartford.com

Harvard Pilgrim Health Care Inc.
Health Triangle/Diversity Committee
1200 Crown Colony Drive
Quincy, MA 02370
Comma Williams
(800) 742-8326

Hewlett-Packard
GLEN
P.O. Box 700542
San Jose, CA 95170
Kim Harris (415) 857-7771
Greg Gloss (408) 447-6123
also: NE GLEN in Chelmsford and Andover, MA
(508) 436-4480 or (508) 659-2511

Hoechst Celanese
Gay Community at HCC
86 Morris Ave.
Summit, NJ 07901
Grietje Wybenga
(908) 522-7573
gxw@sumhcc1.hcc.com

Honeywell
Honeywell Pride Committee
MN12-5258
P.O. Box 524
Minneapolis, MN 55440
Dan Lyden
(612) 951-2057 (committee line)

IBM
EAGLE
Sharon Lane
Atlanta, GA
sjlane@us.ibm.com
(404) 373-2343
Ed McCanless
San Jose, CA
MCCANLES@us.ibm.com
(408) 256-8895

Intel
2200 Mission College Blvd.
Santa Clara, CA 95092
(408) 765-4199
liz_parrish@ccm.sc.intel.com

JC Penney Co.
EAGLe
http://home1.gte.net/djone2/eagl/

Jet Propulsion Laboratory
4800 Oak Grove Drive, MS 249 104
Pasadena, CA 91109
Randy Herrera
(818) 393-0664
rgh@godzilla.jpl.nasa.gov

Kaiser Permanente
KP Pride
P.O. Box 31651
Oakland, CA 94604
(510) 987-4148 (voice mail for Pride)

Levi Strauss
115 Battery St.
P.O. Box 7215
San Francisco, CA 94120
Michele Dryden
(415) 544 7103

Local 3, Storeworkers
Gay & Lesbian Issues Committee
1010 3rd Ave., Suite 300
New York, NY 10021
Chairman
(212) 371-6230

Lotus Development Corp.
LILAC
55 Cambridge Parkway
Cambridge, MA 02142
Kay Wilkins/Ron Krouk
(617) 693-8040
kwilkins@lotus.com

Lucent Technologies
EQUAL
Kathleen Dermody
kd@mtgbcs.mt.lucent.com

Mass Mutual Life
GALA
1295 State St.
Springfield, MA 01111
William Conley
(413) 744-4927
wconley@massmutual.com

Medtronic
Workforce Diversity Project
700 Central Ave., NE, #240
Lauri
(612) 574-3600

Microsoft
GLEAM
1 Microsoft Way, Building 26S
Redmond, WA 98052-6399
(206) 936-5581

Minneapolis *Star Tribune*
Paper Eagles
425 Portland Ave.
Minneapolis, MN 55488
Jill Schons
(612) 673-1757

Motorola
LMPS Bi, Gay, Lesbian Employees
8000 Sunrise Blvd.
Plantation, FL 33304

NBC News
30 Rockefeller Plaza
New York, NY 10112
Mike Schreiberman
(212) 664-4300

National Lesbian and Gay Journalists Association
1718 M Street NW, #245
Washington, DC 20036
(202) 588-9888
NLGJA@aol.com
http://www.nlgja.org

Next Computer
Next Lambda
900 Chesapeake Dr.
Redwood City, CA 94063
Ron Hayden
(415) 780-4603
Ron@next.com

New York Times
Gay and Lesbian Caucus
229 W. 43rd St.
New York, NY 10036
David Dunlap
(212) 556-7082

Northern States Power
P.O. Box 13008
Roseville, MN 55113
Tom Schuster
(612) 330 5522

Northern Trust Bank
TNTPride
50 S. LaSalle St., B-2
Chicago, IL 60675
Sue Connolly
(312) 444-7188
connolly.sue@nrtrs.com

Oracle
Lambda
MD 659412
500 Oracle Parkway
Redwood Shores, CA 94065
Kevin Mallory
(415) 506-6168

Polaroid
Gay, Lesbian, Bi Employees
565 Technology Square, 7
Cambridge, MA 02139
Richard Williams, Ph.D. (Director, World-wide AIDS Education)
(617) 386-3879

PROGRESS
P.O. Box 712505
Los Angeles, CA 90071
ProgressUS@aol.com

SBC Communications Inc.
SPECTRUM
PO Box 2711
San Ramon, CA 94583
(800) 747-9880
www.webcom.com/benny/spectrum/spectrum.html

Seattle Times
GALA Times
PO Box 70
Seattle, WA 98110

Sequent Computer (NW GLEN)
Contact Scott at: scooter@sequent.com

Shell Oil
SEAShell
Rick Schroder
raschroder@shellus.com

Silicon Graphics
LavenderVisions
Miguel@ski.com
www.reality.sgi.com/csp/lvision

Southern New England Alliance of Gay Employees Contact
Jeff McCartney
(860) 547-5895
jmccartney@thehartford.com

St. Paul Companies
Gay/Lesbian Friends Network
122 W. Winifred
St. Paul, MN 55102
Monica Bryand
(612) 310-7385

Sundstrand Aerospace
SOGLAD
Sundstrand Organization of Gays, Lesbians & Allies for Diversity
SOGLAD2000@aol.com

Sun Microsystems
2550 Garcia Ave.
Mountain View, CA 94043
Jim Graham
GLAF@sun.com

Time Warner
Lesbians and Gays at Time
1100 6th Ave., Room 446
New York, NY 10036-6740
Rich Mayora
(212) 512-5909

United Airlines
United with Pride
P.O. Box 423284
San Francisco, CA 94142
(415) 908-6776
info@unitedpride.org
www.unitedpride.org

USAirlines
c/o Tanya Beckett
Director of Diversity
(703) 418-7445

U S WEST Communications and Media Group
EAGLE
P.O. Box 22958
Seattle, WA 98122
John Trautman
(206) 689-6988
watersedge@aol.com
www.eaglefund.org

University of Illinois at Chicago
Chancellor's Committee on G/L/B Issues
c/o Office of G/L/B Concerns
MC 369
1007 W. Harrison, 4078 BsB
Chicago, IL 60607-7140
(312) 413-8619
David Barnett

The Village Voice
Lesbian and Gay Caucus
36 Cooper Square
New York, NY 10003
Richard Goldstein
(212) 475-3300

Wall Street Project
Diane Bratcher/Nick Curto
(212) 870-2296

Walt Disney
LEAGUE
500 S. Buena Vista
Burbank, CA 91521
Robert Williams

The Walt Disney Company
LEAGUE/Anaheim
c/o Cast Activities
1313 S. Harbor Blvd.
Anaheim, CA 92803
Jules Eng and Steve Valkenburg

Wells Fargo & Co.
111 Sutter St., 13th Floor
San Francisco, CA 94104
Randy Diaz
(415) 396-3020

Wisconsin Electric
WE-GLO
231 W. Michigan St., PCCC
Milwaukee, WI 53203
Tim Brown
(800) 300-0100, ext. 5078
tim.brown@wemail.wisenergy.com

Workplace Alliance
Scott Fearing
Sabathani Center
Suite 204
310 E. 38th St.
Minneapolis, MN 55409
G/L Community Action Council
(800) 800-0350

Xerox
GALAXe
P.O. Box 25382
Rochester, NY 14625-0382
www.galaxe.org
chairperson@galaxe.org
communications@galaxe.org

For more information, or if you want to add your group to this list, please contact the Human Rights Campaign (www.hrc.org).

Gay and Lesbian Organizations and Affiliations

AIDS Action Foundation
Claudia Dawn French
1875 Connecticut Ave., NW, #700
Washington, DC 20009
(202) 986-1300

AIDS Housing Corporation
95 Berkeley St., Suite 305
Boston, MA 02116
(617) 451-2248

An Uncommon Legacy Foundation
Karen Sauvigne
150 W. 26th St., #602
New York, NY 10001
(212) 366-6507

Astraea National Lesbian Action Foundation
Karen Zelermyer
116 E. 16th St., 7th Floor
New York, NY 10003
(212) 529-8021

Desert AIDS Project
750 S. Vella Road
Palm Springs, CA 92264
(619) 323-2118

Equality Project
520 Hudson, #135
New York, NY 10014
(212) 727-8257

Fenway Community Health Center
100 Massachusetts Ave.
Boston, MA 02115
(781) 444-8600

Gay and Lesbian Alliance Against Defamation
Joan Garry, Executive Director
150 W. 26th St., Suite 503
New York, NY 10001
(212) 807-1700

Gay, Lesbian, and Straight Education Network
Kevin Jennings, Executive Director
121 W. 27th St., Suite 804
New York, NY 10001
(212) 727-0135

Gay and Lesbian Victory Fund
1012 14th St., NW, 10th Floor
Washington, DC 20005
(202) 842-8679

Human Rights Campaign
1101 14th St., NW, #200
Washington, DC 20005
(202) 628-4160

Health Crisis Network
J.R. Fry, Assistant Director of Development
5050 Biscayne Boulevard
Miami, FL 33137
(305) 759-6181

Los Angeles Gay and Lesbian Center
1625 N. Schrader Blvd.

Los Angeles, CA 90028
(323) 993-7400

National Gay and Lesbian Task Force
Kerry Lobel, Executive Director
2320 17th St., NW
Washington, DC 20009
(202) 332-6483

National Latino/a Lesbian and Gay Organization (LLEGO)
Martin Ornelas-Quintero
1612 K St., NW, #500
Washington, DC 20006
(202) 466-8240

National Lesbian and Gay Health Association
Beverly Saunders-Biddle
1407 S St., NW

Washington, DC 20009
(202) 939-7880

National Lesbian and Gay Journalists Association
Mike Frederickson, Executive Director
1718 M St., NW, #243
Washington, DC 20036
(202) 588-9888

Parents, Families, and Friends of Lesbians and Gays
1101 14th St., NW, #1030
Washington, DC 20005
(202) 638-4200

Servicemembers Legal Defense Network
Mary Ester
P.O. Box 53013
Washington, DC 20009

Credit Cards, Charge Cards, and Credit Reports

Bank-issued credit cards are usually affiliated with MasterCard or Visa. When signing up for a credit card, consider the annual percentage rate of interest as well as late fees, annual fees, and punitive fees. Frequent flier rewards, calling card programs, and other affinity relationships should be looked at as supplemental, not as reasons to acquire a particular card.

People with bad credit can apply for secured credit cards, which require a cash deposit with the affiliated financial institution. Secured credit cards function just like regular credit cards, but carry a higher APR.

Charge cards such as American Express cards without a Sign and Travel or Special Purchase Account, unlike credit cards, do not involve a revolving line of credit. In other words, the bill is due each month. (With a credit card there is an extension of credit allowing you to pay a minimum on a balance that accrues billable interest.)

Retail cards are usually issued by gas companies and retail stores. These cards tend to have higher interest rates and steep late charges.

A credit report is simple to obtain through any of the following companies. If you have been refused a credit card or denied a loan or mortgage, the creditor must tell you why and provide you with the name and contact information of the agency it consulted in reaching its decision. This is required under the Fair Credit Reporting Act. Those who have been denied credit can receive a copy of the credit report for free within 60 days of the denial. Otherwise the fee averages about $10.

CSC Credit Services
Consumer Assistance Center
P.O. Box 674402
Houston, TX 77267-4402
(800) 392-7816

Experian
National Consumer Assistance Center
P.O. Box 2104
Allen, TX 75013-2104
(888) 397-3742

Equifax
Consumer Relations
P.O. Box 105873
Atlanta, GA 30348
(800) 685-1111

Trans Union Corporation
Consumer Relations Center
P.O. Box 390
Springfield, PA 19064-0390
(216) 779-7200

Leading Consumer Advocacy Organizations

20/20 Vision
1828 Jerson Place, NW
Washington, DC 20036
(202) 833-2020

Citizens' Environmental Coalition
33 Central Ave.
Albany, NY 12210
(518) 462-5527

Citizen Action
1730 Road Island Ave., NW, #403
Washington, DC 20036
(202) 775-1580
edr@mail2.pechan.com

Communities for a Better Environment
501 Second St., #305
San Francisco, CA 94107
(415) 243-8373

Citizens' Clearinghouse for Hazardous Waste
P.O. Box 6806
Fall Church, VA 22040
(703) 237-2249

Communities Concerned About Corporations
5104 42nd Ave.
Hyattsville, MD 20781
(301) 779-1000

Co-op America
Sam Barry
1612 K St. NW, #600
Washington, D.C. 20006
(202) 872-5307
1-(800) 58-GREEN

EarthSave
706 Frederick St.
Santa Cruz, CA 95062
(408) 423-4069
(800) 362-3648
earthsave@aol.com

Environmental Action
6930 Carroll Ave., #600
Takoma Park, MD 20912
(301) 891-1100
eaf@igc.apc.org

Environmental Protection Information Center
Ms. Cecelia Lanman
P.O. Box 397
Garberville, CA 95542
(707) 923-2931

The Foundation on Economic Trends
1660 L St. NW, #216
Washington, DC 20036
(202) 466-2823

Friends of the Earth
1025 Vermont Ave., NW
Third Floor
Washington, DC 20005
(202) 783-7400, ext. 242
foecdc@igc.apc.org

Good Neighbor Project
P.O. Box 79225
Waverly, MA 02179
(617) 489-3686
sanlewis@igc.apc.org

Government Accountability Project
810 First St., NE, #630
Washington, DC 20002
(202) 408-0034
gap@igc.apc.org

Greenpeace
847 W. Jackson St.
7th Floor
Chicago, IL 60607
(312) 563-6060
charlie.cray@green2.dat.de

Greenworking
19 Marble Ave.
Pleasantville, NY 10570
(914) 741-2088
greenworking@igc.apc.org

Gulf Coast Tenants
1866 Gayoso St.
New Orleans, LA 70119
(504) 949-4919

Inland Empire Public Lands Council
P.O. Box 2174
Spokane, WA 99210
(509) 838-4912
ieplc@uwsa.spk.wa.us

Institute for Agriculture and Trade Policy
Mark Ritchie
1313 Fifth St. SE, #303
Minneapolis, MN 55414
(612) 379-5980
mritchie@iatp.org

Louisiana Environmental Action Network
P.O. Box 66323
Baton Rouge, LA 70896
(504) 928-1315
lean007@aol.com

Mid-South Peace and Justice Center
Larry Smith
P.O. Box 11428
Memphis, TN 38111
(901) 452-6997

Mississippi River Basin Alliance
P.O. Box 3878
St. Louis, MO 63122
(314) 822-4114
mrba@aol.com

Native Forest Council
P.O. Box 2171
Eugene, OR 97402
(503) 688-2600

Oregon Natural Resource Council
John Kart
Yeon Building, #1050
522 Fifth Ave., SW
Portland, OR 97204
(503) 223-9001

Pesticide Action Network
116 New Montgomery St., #810
San Francisco, CA 94105
(415) 541-9140

Rainforest Action Network
450 Sansome, #700
San Francisco, CA 94111
(415) 398-4404
rainforest@igc.apc.org

Student Environmental Action Coalition
Liz Gres
P.O. Box 1168
Chapel Hill, NC 27514
(919) 967-4600
Kelpie Wilson
P.O. Box 220
Cave Junction, OR 97523
(503) 592-4459

Women's Environment and Development Organization
845 Third Ave.
15th Floor
New York, NY 10022
(212) 759-7982

Working Assets Long Distance
701 Montgomery St., #400
San Francisco, CA 94111
(415) 788-0981, ext. 2010

Ongoing (Nongay) Consumer Boycotts
(reprinted with permission from Co-op America)

Adidas:
The International Wildlife Coalition alleges that Adidas, Browning, and Florsheim use skins of threatened Australian kangaroos for shoe leather.*

Alaska Airlines:
The United Coalition of Iditarod Animal Rights Volunteers alleges that the Iditarod dog race is inhumane to sled dogs. Alaska Airlines is a race sponsor.*

American Express:
People for the Ethical Treatment of Animals claims American Express sells fur in catalogs.

American Home Products:
Accountability says American Home Products and Nestlé employ unethical marketing programs to get infant formula sold into developing countries, resulting in the alleged suffering and death of millions of infants.*
PETA and other animal rights groups charge that American Home Products treats pregnant mares inhumanely while harvesting their urine to manufacture Premarin, a hormone replacement drug for menopausal women.*

Amoco:
San Juan Citizens Alliance alleges that Amoco's coalbed methane (natural gas) drilling in southwest Colorado has tainted the groundwater, negatively affecting health and safety in the area.*

Anheuser Busch/Sea World:
Friends of Animals alleges that Anheuser Busch, which owns Sea World in San Diego, is keeping Corky, an orca, in unnecessary captivity.*

Atlantic Richfield Company (ARCO):
Project Maje alleges that ARCO does business in Burma and thus supports the brutal repression of the Burmese people.*

Beef (public lands):
   The Oregon Natural Desert Association and Denzel and Nancy Ferguson (researchers) allege that western public lands are environmentally abused by private cattle ranchers.*

Bovine Growth Hormone (synthetic rBGH) (A&P, American Home Products, Animal Health Institute, Borden, Dannon, Häagen-Dazs, Kraft, Kruegers, Land O' Lakes, McDonald's, National Dairy Board, Nestlé's Carnation):
   The Pure Food Campaign and Food & Water allege that milk and dairy products produced from cows injected with rBGH are potentially hazardous to human and animal health and to the future of small dairies. Food & Water is targeting Land O' Lakes only.* (Call Pure Food Campaign for a list of products, distributors and retail outlets going rBGH free.)

Carl's Jr.:
   Pro-choice advocates claim that Carl Kercher, owner of Carl's Jr., funds antiabortion candidates.

China:
   International Campaign for Tibet and Tibetan Rights Campaign calls for the boycott of all toys made in China as a way to protest the ongoing human rights abuses they claim are being committed by the Chinese communist government.*

Coors:
   Animal Emancipation Inc. alleges that Coors extensively sponsors rodeos, which AE argues are cruel to animals.*

Disneyland:
   Southern Baptists object to the fact that Disney gives equal rights to gay and lesbian employees.

Domino's Pizza:
   Domino's is being boycotted by pro-choice advocates.

Florsheim:
   see Adidas.

Georgia-Pacific:
Rainforest Action Network alleges that Georgia-Pacific is involved in rainforest destruction.*

Gold:
The Montana Environmental Information Center charges that the 1872 mining law that regulates the mining of gold allows a misuse of public lands and a lack of environmental regulations.*

Grapes (California table grapes only):
The United Farm Workers alleges that the pesticides sprayed on grapes are hazardous to farmworkers, their children, and consumers.*

HoneyBaked Ham:
Orange County People for Animals alleges that the ham retailer supports institutionalized animal abuse by purchasing pig body parts from factory farms.*

Hormel:
Austin United Support Group alleges the company conducts unfair labor practices.*

Levi Strauss & Co:
Fuerza Unida alleges that workers were not adequately compensated for job loss when the San Antonio, Tex., factory relocated operations to Costa Rica.*

Mitsubishi (including Kirin beer, Union Bank of California, and Nikon camera equipment):
Rainforest Action Network alleges that Mitsubishi imports tropical timber to Japan and engages in other environmentally destructive acts, particularly in Mexico and Alberta, Canada.*

Monsanto:
National Farmers' Union alleges that Monsanto has launched a "campaign of intimidation" against dairy farms and processors that label their products as being from cows not treated with synthetic bovine growth hormone.*

The Pure Food Campaign, Pure Dairy Commission, and Family Farm Defenders claim that Monsanto produces genetically engineered foods that may be unhealthy, and that the company conducts business in a manner not conducive to family farms.*

Mission Possible charges that NutraSweet (aspartame) causes a wide range of medical problems and has been inadequately tested.*

Nature Conservancy:
People for the Ethical Treatment of Animals alleges that the Nature Conservancy's snaring of feral pigs on the Hawaiian islands is an unnecessarily cruel method of removing the pigs.*

Nestlé:
see American Home Products

Nike:
Justice! charges that Nike produces many of its products using subcontractors in countries utilizing exploitative labor practices such as Indonesia and Vietnam.

NORPAC (Kraemer Farms):
PCUN alleges that Kraemer Farms will not negotiate a contract or resolve farmworker complaints with PCUN, which claims to represent farmworkers. Produce processors NORPAC and Steinfeld's are boycotted for processing Kraemer products.*

Norway:
Earth Island Institute alleges that Norway has broken with the international moratorium on whaling and kills seals.*

Perdue:
Animal Rights International alleges that Perdue Farms engages in animal cruelty, worker exploitation, consumer fraud, and unethical business practices.*

Philip Morris:
INFACT alleges that Philip Morris, through its Marlboro Man advertising campaign, encourages underage children to smoke.*

PVC Plastic:
Citing the problems #3 plastic bottles cause to plastic recycling efforts, in addition to the toxic components that go into the production of PVC, the Recycling Advocates have asked consumers to boycott all products packaged in #3 plastic containers.*

Shell Oil Company:
A coalition of groups, including Friends of the Earth and Rainforest Action Network, allege that Shell's involvement in Nigeria contributes to the repressive political situation there. RAN also alleges that Shell causes environmental destruction.*

Steinfeld's:
see NORPAC

Texaco:
Rainforest Action Network alleges that Texaco left environmental destruction after ending its operations in Ecuador.*

Wal-Mart:
Save A County—Boycott Wal-Mart alleges that Wal-Mart engages in unfair labor practices, exploitation of third-world labor, environmental destruction, and the destruction of local economies.*

Weyerhaeuser:
Rainforest Action Network charges that Weyerhaeuser imports endangered tropical hardwoods, which endangers numerous habitats and indigenous peoples.*

Yukon Territorial Government:
According to Friends of the Wolf, the Yukon Territorial Government's wolf population control program is a cruel and wasteful slaughter of wolves.*

* As of June 15, 1998, the boycott organizers told Boycott Action News that the allegations and conditions underlying the boycott remain the same. Only boycotts called by other organizations are reported here, and all allegations are made by boycott organizers and reported in Boycott Action News.

Co-op America thanks Zach Lyons, publisher of Boycott Quarterly and boycott columnist for Co-op America Quarterly, for his longtime commitment to boycotts and the great resource he has been over the years to people everywhere who care about corporate responsibility.

Co-op America (Publisher of National Green Pages™)
1612 K St., NW, Suite 600, Washington, DC 20006
(800) 58-GREEN
(202) 872-5307
(202) 331-8166 (fax)
www.coopamerica.org
www.socialinvest.org

Socially Responsible Mutual Funds

Alliance Global Environment Fund
Alliance Capital Management
1345 Avenue of the Americas
New York, NY 10105
(800) 247-4154, ext. 1
Focus: Environmental protection

Amana Mutual Funds Trust/Growth
Func, Income Fund
Saturna Capital Corp.
1300 N. State St.
Bellingham, WA 98225
(800) 728-8762
Focus: Islamic faith parameters; no gambling, alcohol, banking, or interest-bearing operations; may also be available through Fidelity Investments

American Funds Group
333 S. Hope St.
Los Angeles, CA 90071
(800) 421-0180
Focus: growth and income; tobacco- and alcohol-restricted

Ariel Growth Funds
307 N. Michigan Ave., Suite 500
Chicago, IL 60601
(800) 292-7435
Focus: participated in boycott of companies that conducted business in South Africa during the 1980s; environmental focus; no nuclear technology, alcohol, or tobacco

Calvert Social Investment Funds
Calvert Group
4550 Montgomery Ave., 1000N
Bethesda, MD 20814
(800) 369-2748
Focus: no alcohol or tobacco; no nuclear technology; no weapons systems; no gambling; no serious polluters; has seven funds with varying degrees of screening focused on positive environmental programs, alternative energy, equal employment opportunity, women's and family benefits, management-labor relations, consumer protection, community issues, international operations, human rights, animal welfare, and health care

Social Investment Managed Growth Fund, Social Equity Fund, Social Bond Fund, World Value International Fund, Capital Accumulation Fund, Strategic Growth Fund, New Africa Fund, Dreyfus Third Century Fund
144 Glenn Curtiss Blvd.
Uniondale, NY 11556-0144
(800) 645-6561
Focus: capital growth; no investing in tobacco or alcohol

Domini Social Index 400
Kidder, Lydenberg, Domini & Co.
129 Mount Auburn St.
Cambridge, MA 02138-5766
617-547 7479
Focus: Nonnuclear, nonmilitary, nonalcohol, nontobacco, ethical labor

Green Century Family of Funds
Green Century Capital Management
29 Temple Place
Boston, MA 02111
(800) 93-GREEN [(800) 934-7336]
Focus: Green Century Fund Balanced Portfolio invests in proactive environmental solution-oriented companies; benign companies (meaning those that are not violators of the environment); does not invest in tobacco, alcohol, nuclear power or weapons; Green Century Equity Fund screens for environmental parameters, employee relations, corporate citizenship issues, products, and consumer issues; no military weapons; no tobacco; no alcohol; no gambling; no nuclear power plants.

Lincoln National Social Awareness Fund
Lincoln National Life Insurance Co.
1300 S. Clinton St.
Fort Wayne, IN 46801
(800) 348-1212
Focus: no tobacco; no nuclear technology; no military technology; no alcohol; no gambling

Meyers Sheppard Pride Fund
Meyers, Sheppard & Co. LLC
P.O. 1694
Scottsdale, AZ 85252-1964
(800) 410-3337 or (602) 423-4400
Focus: progressive gay and lesbian workplace policies; invests only in companies that maintain official written policies banning discrimination based on sexual orientation

Neuberger & Berman Socially Responsive Fund
605 Third Ave.
New York, NY 10158-0006
(800) 877-9700
Focus: does not invest in South Africa, Northern Ireland, or Mexican maquiladora operations; does not invest in companies producing alcohol, tobacco, or nuclear technology; monitors companies it invests in for strict adherence to corporate citizenship issues, social awareness sen-

sitivity, emission control standards, recycling programs, conservation records, and socially responsible employment practices with regard to women and minorities, and general fair labor practices

New Alternatives Fund
150 Broadhollow Road
Melville, NY 11747
(516) 423-7373
Focus: no alcohol; no tobacco; no animal testing; no nuclear technology; focuses on investing in companies that produce alternative energy such as natural gas, solar power, fuel cells, biomass, conservation systems, cogeneration, and solar cell production

Parnassus Fund, Parnassus Income Fund
1 Market St.
Stewart Tower, 16th Floor
San Francisco, CA 94105
(800) 999-3505
Focus: no alcohol; no tobacco; no nuclear technology

Pax World Fund
222 State St.
Portsmouth, NH 03801
(800) 767-1729
Focus: America's oldest socially responsible investment mutual fund; no alcohol; no tobacco; no gambling; no weapons production; requires that companies have pollution controls in place and employment policies banning discrimination against women, minorities, and the disabled

Primerica Financial Service
3100 Breckinridge Blvd., Building 200
Duluth, GA 30199-0062
(800) 544-5445
Focus: screens out tobacco and alcohol only

Pioneer Funds
60 State St.
Boston, MA 02109
(800) 225-6292
Focus: no tobacco; no alcohol; no gambling

Pro-Conscience Women's Equity Mutual Fund
500 Washington St., Suite 600
San Francisco, CA 94111
(800) 385-7003
Focus: invests in companies that promote women to top executive positions and companies with a proven track record in advancing women in hiring and corporate practices; no alcohol; no tobacco; no weapons; no nuclear technology

Rightime Family of Funds/Rightime Social Awareness Fund
Lincoln Investment
The Forst Pavilion, Suite 3000
218 Glenside Ave.
Wyncote, PA 19095-1594
(800) 242-1421
Focus: invests in companies based on evidence of contributing to the enhancement of the quality of human life

Citizens Trust
Index Fund
One Harbour Place
Portsmouth, NH 03801
(800) 223-7010
Focus: screens for alcohol, tobacco, nuclear technology, and personal care products that have been produced using animal testing procedures

V-Management
151 Lakeside Drive, Suite PH1
Oakland, CA 94612-4677
(800) 452-6291
Focus: Private gay- and lesbian-oriented advisory

Gay and Lesbian Consumer Dos and Don'ts

The Dos

1. Do support companies with written policy statements banning discrimination against employees, vendors, and independent contractors based on sexual orientation. Include your knowledge of this information when corresponding with companies about their products.
2. Do organize, lobby, or consider getting your company to support gay and lesbian philanthropy in your community.
3. Do consider purchasing products advertised in gay or lesbian owned publications *after* you have determined they are worthy of your money and personal support.
4. Do consider whether or not getting domestic-partnership benefits or their monetary equivalent installed in company is a viable option. Consult with the National Gay and Lesbian Task Force or Human Rights Campaign in Washington on how to go about creating employee groups and winning domestic-partnership benefits in your company.
5. Do consider approaching your company's marketing department about including gay and lesbian mailing lists in the company's direct-marketing plan. Consult with gay newspaper advertising representatives and development directors at gay and lesbian nonprofit organizations on where to obtain good gay and lesbian mailing lists. Contact the Gay and Lesbian Alliance Against Defamation on guidelines for producing affirmative, nondefamatory advertising communications.
6. Do consider whether or not your company might officially support ENDA, the federal Employment Non-Discrimination Act. Contact the Human Rights Campaign in Washington for complete, updated information on ENDA.
7. Do support your local gay and lesbian community center or create a fund drive to establish one.
8. Do make sure your personnel director or person in charge of human resources administration has a copy of *Straight Talk About Gays In The Workplace* by Liz Winfeld and Sue Spielman.
9. Do confront sexist or antigay humor in the workplace. Com-

municate that homophobia is more than a word; in society it translates and manifests itself as hatred and fear based on ignorance.
10. Whenever controversy surfaces in relation to personnel issues in your industry or line of work, consider issuing simple policy statements to the press calling attention to your company's support of basic human rights for gays and lesbians.

The Don'ts

1. Don't use profane, petty, or personalized language when expressing your concerns in writing or in person regarding companies, their products, or their services.
2. Don't be misled by ambiguous words used by companies such as "partial" domestic-partner benefits or "alternative lifestyles" in press releases, advertising copy, direct mail, or brochures.
3. Don't assume most people understand that gay and lesbian inclusivity in the workplace and marketplace is something you do not currently enjoy.
4. Don't automatically assume that your company will support annual gay and lesbian community activities and fund-raisers.
5. Don't allow your company to conspicuously draw attention to its AIDS-related or HIV- and health-related good works as somehow indicative of anything related to official gay or lesbian workplace policy.
6. Don't let your local library get away with not stocking Annette Friskopp and Sharon Silverstein's *Straight Jobs Gay Lives*.
7. Don't make contributions to organizations whose administration and budgetary policies you are unaware of.

Suggested Additional Reading

Bellant, Russ, *The Coors Connection: How Coors Family Philanthropy Undermines Democratic Pluralism*, South End Press, 1990.

Berkery, Peter J., *Personal Financial Planning for Gays and Lesbians*, Irwin, 1996.

D'Emilio, John, *Sexual Politics, Sexual Communities: The Making of a Homosexual Minority in the United States, 1940-1970*,

University of Chicago Press, 1983.

Faludi, Susan, *Backlash: The Undeclared War Against American Women*, Crown, 1991.

Gore, Al, *Earth In the Balance: Ecology and the Human Spirit*, Houghton Mifflin, 1992.

Katz, A. Phyllis, and Katz, Margaret, *The Feminist Dollar: The Wise Woman's Buying Guide*, Plenum, 1997.

Kinder, Lydenberg, Domini, *Investing For Good*, HarperBusiness, 1993.

Kinder, Lydenberg, Domini, *The Social Investment Almanac: A Comprehensive Guide to Socially Responsible Investing*, Henry Holt, 1992.

Lappé, Marc, *Chemical Deception: The Toxic Threat to Health and Environment*, Sierra Club Books, 1991.

Larson, Per, *Gay Money*, Dell, 1997.

McKnight, John, *The Careless Society: Community and Its Counterfeits*, Basic Books, 1995.

Medoff, James, and Harless, James, *The Indebted Society: Anatomy of an Ongoing Disaster*, Little, Brown, and Co., 1996.

Schwartz, Felice N., and Levine, Suzanne K., *The Armchair Activist: Simple Yet Powerful Ways to Fight the Radical Right*, Riverhead Books, 1996.

Vaid, Urvashi, *Virtual Equality: The Mainstreaming of Gay and Lesbian Liberation*, Anchor Books, 1995.

West, Cornel, *Race Matters*, Vintage, 1994.

Part Five

Appendices

Domini Social Index 400*

Acuson Corp.
Advanced Micro Devices Inc.
Aetna Inc.
AGL Resource Inc.
Ahmanson (H.F.) & Co.
Air Products & Chemicals Inc.
Airborne Freight Corp.
Alaska Air Group Inc.
Alberto-Culver Co.
Albertson's Inc.
Alco Standard Corp.
Alexander & Alexander Service Inc.
Allergan Inc.
Allwaste Inc.
Aluminum Company of America
ALZA Corp.
American Express Co.
American General Corp.
American International Group Inc.
American Power Conversion
American Stores Cos.
American Water Works Inc.
Ameritech
Amoco Corp.
AMR Corp.
Anadarko Petroleum Corp.

Analog Devices Inc.
Angelica Corp.
Apache Corp.
Apogee Enterprises Inc.
Apple Computer
Applied Materials Inc.
ARCO Chemical Co.
Atlantic Richfield Co.
Autodesk Inc.
Automatic Data Processing Inc.
Avery Dennison Corp.
Avnet Inc.
Avon Products Inc.
Baldor Electric Co.
Banc One Corp.
BankBoston Corp.
Bank of America
Barnett Banks Inc.
Bassett Furniture Industries
Battle Mountain Gold Co.
Becton Dickinson and Co.
Bell Atlantic Corp.
BellSouth Corp.
Bemis Company Inc.
Ben & Jerry's Homemade
Beneficial Corp.

Bergen Brunswig Corp.
BET Holdings
Betz Laboratories
Biomet Inc.
Block (H&R) Inc.
Bob Evans Farms Inc.
Borland International Inc.
Boston Scientific Corp.
Brady (W.H.) Co.
Briggs & Stratton Corp.
Brooklyn Union Gas Co.
Brown Group Inc.
Cabot Corp.
Calgon Cargon
CalEnergy Company Inc.
Chubb Corp.
Church & Dwight Company Inc.
Cigna
Cincinnati Financial
Cincinnati Milacron Inc.
Cintas Corp.
Circuit City Stores Inc.
Cisco Systems Inc.
Citizens Utilities
Claire's Stores Inc.
Clorox Co.
Coca-Cola Co.
Colgate-Palmolive Co.
Comcast Corp.
Community Psychiatric Centers
Compaq Computer
Computer Associates International
Connecticut Energy
Conrail Inc.
Consolidated Freightway Inc.
Consolidated Natural Gas Co.
Consolidated Papers Inc.
Cooper Industries Inc.

Cooper Tire & Rubber Co.
CoreStates Financial Corp.
CPC International
CPI Corp
Cross (A.T.) Co.
CSX Corp.
Cummins Engine Company Inc.
Cyprus Amax Minerals Co.
Dana Corp.
Dayton-Hudson
Deere & Co.
Delta Airlines
Deluxe Corp.
Devry Inc.
Digital Equipment Corp.
Dillard Department Stores Inc.
Dime Bancorp
Dionex Corp.
Disney (Walt) Co.
Dollar General
Donnelley & Sons Co.
Dow Jones
DSC Comm. Corp.
Eastern Enterprises
Echo Bay Mine Ltd.
Edmark Corp.
Edwards (A.G.) Inc.
Egghead Software
El Paso Natural Gas Company
Energen
Enron
Equitable Resources
Fastenal Co.
Fedders Corp.
Federal Express Corp.
Federal Home Loan Mortgage Association
Federal National Mortgage Association
Federal-Mogul Corp.

Fifth Third Bancorp
First Chicago NBD Corp.
FirstFed Financial Corp.
Fleetwood Enterprises Inc.
Flemin Companies Inc.
Forest Labs Inc.
Frontier Corp.
Fuller (H.B.) Co.
Gap Inc.
GATZ Corp.
General Mills Inc.
General Re Inc.
General Signal Corp.
Genuine Parts Co.
Gerber Scientific Inc.
Giant Food
Gibson Greetings
Golden West Financial
Goulds Pumps
Fraco Inc.
Grainger Inc.
Great Atlantic and Pacific Tea Co.
Great Western Financial Corp.
Handleman Co.
Hannaford Bros. Co.
Harcourt General
Harland (John H.) Co.
Harman International Industries Inc.
Hartford Steam Boiler Inspection and Insurance
Hartmarx Corp.
Hasbro
Hechinger
Heinz
Helmerich & Payne
Hershey Foods
Hewlett-Packard
Hillenbrand Industries

Home Depot
HON Industries
Household International
Hubbell Inc.
Huffy Corp.
Humana Health Plans, Inc.
Hunt Manufacturing
Idaho Power
Illinois Tool Works Inc.
Inland Steel Industries Inc.
Intel Corporation
IBM
International Dairy Queen Inc.
Ionics Inc.
Isco Inc.
James River Corp.
Jefferson-Pilot Corp.
Johnson & Johnson
Jostens Inc.
Kmart Corp.
Kaufman & Broad Home
Kellogg Co.
Kelly Services Inc.
Kenetech Corp.
Kimberly-Clark Corp.
King World Productions Inc.
Kroger Co.
Lands' End Inc.
Lawson Products Inc.
Lee Enterprises Inc.
Leggett & Platt
LG&E Energy Corp
Lillian Vernon Corp
Limited Inc.
Lincoln National
Liz Claiborne
Longs Drug Stores
Louisiana Land & Exploration

Lowe's Cos.
Luby's Cafeterias
Manor Care Inc.
Marquette Medical Systems
Marriott International Inc.
March & McLennan Companies Inc.
Mattel Inc.
May Department Stores
Maytag Corp.
MBNA Corp.
McDonald's Corp.
McGraw-Hill Cos.
MCI Worldcom
MCN
Mead
Media General
Medtronic
Mellon Bank
Mercantile Stores
Merck
Meredith Corp.
Merrill Lynch
Micron Technology
Miller (Herman) Inc.
Millipore
Modine Manufacturing
Molex Inc.
Moore Corporation Ltd.
Morgan (J.P.)
Morton International
Mylan Labs
Nalco Chemical
National Education Corp.
National Services Industries Inc.
New York Times Co.
National Semiconductor Corp.
New England Business Service, Inc.
Newell Co.

NICOR Inc.
Nike Inc.
NorAm Energy
3 Com Corp.
Timberland Company
Times Mirror
TJ International
TJX Cos.
Tootsie Roll Industries
Torchmark Corp.
Toro Co.
Toys 'R' Us. Inc.
Transamerica Corp.
Travelers Group Inc.
Turner Broadcasting
U S West Communications Group
U S West Media Group
UAL Corp.
United American Healthcare
UNUM Corp.
USF&G Corp.
USLIFE Corp.
V.F. Corp.
Value Line Inc.
Vermont Financial Services Corp.
Viacom Inc.
Wachovia Corp.
Wal-Mart Stores Inc.
Walgreen Co.
Washington Gas Light Co.
Washington Post Co.
Watts Industries
Wellman Inc.
Wells Fargo & Co.
Wesco Financial Corp.
Westvaco Corp.
Whirlpool Corp.
Whole Foods Market Inc.

Williams Cos.
Woolworth Corp.
Worthington Industries Inc.
Wrigley (Wm) Jr. Co.
Xerox Corp.
Xilinx Inc.
Yellow Corp.
Zurn Industries
St. Paul Cos.
Santa Fe Energy Resources

SBS Communications
Schering-Plough Corp.
Scholastic
Schwab (Charles)
Sealed Air Corp.
Sear, Roebuck & Co.
Service Corporation International
Shared Medical Systems
Shaw Industries
Sherwin-Williams Co.

According to Morningstar, the Domini Social Equity Fund seeks long-term total return that corresponds with the performance of the Domini Social Index, which consists of approximately 400 companies that meet certain social criteria. The fund invests at least 80% of assets in stocks in the index. To construct the index, the adviser selects companies in the Standard & Poor's 500 based on social responsibility and on its requirements for industry diversification, financial solvency, market capitalization, and minimal portfolio turnover. The index also typically includes about 150 companies not included in the S&P 500. Prior to October 26, 1993, the fund was named Domini Social Index Trust.

GLV 100 Index

1. 3Com
2. Adobe Systems
3. Adolph Coors
4. Advanced Micro Systems
5. ALZA Pharmaceuticals
6. Amdahl
7. America Online
8. American Airlines
9. American Express
10. APL Ltd.
11. Apple Computer
12. Arizona Public Service
13. Aspect Telecommunications
14. AT&T
15. Autodesk
16. Bank of America
17. BankBoston
18. Banyan Worldwide
19. Barnes and Noble
20. Barra
21. Baxter Healthcare
22. Bell Atlantic
23. Ben & Jerry's Homemade
24. Blue Cross of Massachusetts
25. Borland International (now Inprise)
26. Cadence Design

Appendices / 315

27. Cambridge Technology Partners
28. Celestial Seasonings
29. Chase Manhattan
30. Chiron
31. Cisco Systems
32. Continental Airlines
33. CoreStates Financial
34. Donna Karan
35. Dean Witter
36. Digital Equipment Corp.
37. Disney, Walt
38. DuPont
39. Eastman Kodak
40. Egghead Software
41. Federal National Mortgage
42. First Bank System
43. Franklin Research and Development
44. Gap Inc.
45. Gannett Co.
46. Genentech
47. Glaxo Wellcome
48. Hewlett-Packard
49. Informix
50. Intel Corp.
51. Interleaf
52. International Business Machines
53. Kaiser Permanente
54. Kinder, Lydenberg, Domini & Co.
55. Levi Strauss & Co.
56. Lincoln Financial
57. Massachusetts Institute of Technology
58. Microsoft
59. Millpore
60. Minnesota Mining and Manufacturing
61. Nestlé
62. New York Times Co.
63. Nortel Networks
64. Northwest Airlines
65. Novell
66. Nynex
67. Octel Communications
68. Oracle
69. Pacific Gas and Electric
70. Pacific Telesis
71. Paradigm
72. Platinum Technologies
73. Polaroid
74. Prudential
75. Pride Fund
76. Qualcomm
77. Quantas Airlines
78. Quark
79. Radius
80. Seagram
81. Schwab, Charles
82. Silicon Graphics
83. St. Paul Cos.
84. Starbucks
85. Stadlander's Pharmacy
86. Sun Microsystems
87. Sybase
88. Time Warner
89. U S West Media Group
90. U S West
91. Unum
92. United Airlines
93. United Life Insurance
94. Viacom
95. Village Voice
96. Virgin Atlantic Airlines
97. Visioneer
98. Wainwright Bank and Trust
99. Working Assets
100. Ziff-Davis

Glossary of Terms

Americans for Truth: a well-funded right-wing extremist group dedicated to opposing homosexual activism. It publishes the *Lambda Report on Homosexual Activism,* a bimonthly newspaper. www.americans-fortruth.com; (703) 491-7975.

Business For Social Responsibility: a nonprofit group based in San Francisco dedicated to education and development of social diversity and responsibility in the American workplace. www.bsr.org; 609 Mission St., 2nd floor, San Francisco, CA 94105; (415) 537-0888 (phone); (415) 537-0889 (fax).

Bisexual Resource Center: Massachusetts-based social service organization and support network for nationwide bisexual groups. P.O. Box 639, Cambridge, MA 02140; (617) 424-9595.

Digital Queers: activist and professional organization serving the lesbian, gay, bisexual, and transgendered high-technology and online community. 584 Castro St., #560, San Francisco, CA 94114; (415) 252-6282 (phone); (415) 252-6290 (fax).

Domestic Partners: nonmarried individuals sharing the same principal living space.

Domestic-Partner Benefits: a general term referring to a company's extension of certain benefits to an employee's identified domestic partner. Domestic-partner benefits differ from company to company and do not necessarily mean that the company is extending a specific kind of benefit such as health insurance.

Domestic-Partner Health Care Benefits: the extension of a company's health care plan to the domestic partners of qualifying employees.

Equality Project: New York-based organization of gay and lesbian consumers, employees, and investors working to bring about fair and inclusive workplace polices for gays and lesbians through public relations, shareholder actions, and networking. Formerly known as the Wall Street Project.

Full Domestic-Partner Benefits: specific term used to clarify that a company offers the same health care insurance benefits to the live-in domestic partners of nonmarried employees as those enjoyed by legally married spouses. Some companies only offer full domestic-partner benefits to gay and lesbian employees. Others make them available to nonmarried heterosexual employees as well.

Partial Domestic-Partner Benefits: ambiguously used reference designed to draw attention to a company's extension of non–health-related benefits to employees and their domestic partners. Such benefits include bereavement leave, stock options, profit sharing, or even cash compensation in lieu of health insurance.

Gay and Lesbian Alliance Against Defamation: nonprofit organization with chapters across the country whose primary mission is to monitor and respond to false, inappropriate, inaccurate, or otherwise defamatory representations of lesbian, gay, bisexual, or transgendered persons in the media. www.glaad.org; 8455 Beverly Blvd., Suite 305, Los Angeles, CA 90048; (323) 658-6775 (phone); (213) 658-6776 (fax).

Heterosexism: behavior or use of language suggesting that straight people are in some way superior, preferred, or more appropriate in any situation.

Homosexism: behavior or use of language suggesting that lesbians or gay men are in some way superior, preferred, or more appropriate in any situation.

HIV (Human Immunodeficiency Virus): virus identified as the key factor in AIDS.

HIV-positive: a test result indicating that an individual's blood contains HIV.

Human Rights Campaign: Washington, D.C.–based gay and lesbian political organization. www.hrc.org; 1101 14th St., NW, Washington, DC 20005; (202) 628-4160.

LLEGO: an organization of gay and lesbian latinos/latinas. 1612 K St., NW, Washington, DC 20026; (202) 466-8240.

Lifestyle: term often inappropriately used to describe the nature of those who identify as lesbian, gay, or bisexual. It is often misused by homophobes as a way to describe gay people or gay culture.

Outing: generally refers to revealing a person's sexual orientation. Although controversial, many journalists and activists deem outing public figures acceptable if the person in question has exhibited behavior or taken hypocritical policy stands that would be considered detrimental to the majority of gay and lesbian people.

Seroconversion: refers to the medical identification of one's blood having changed from HIV-negative to HIV-positive.

Sexual preference: a reference to sexual orientation, suggesting that one has made a choice about which sex they are attracted to.

Socially Responsible Investing: signifies the management of stocks, bonds, and mutual funds in way that meets an individual's predefined moral criteria, such as not investing in nuclear technology, tobacco, military equipment, or alcohol.

Stonewall: the Stonewall Inn in downtown New York City, where riots broke out on June 28, 1969, in response to police brutality, false arrests, and law enforcement corruption. A symbolic birthmark of the modern gay rights movement.

Transgendered: flexible terminology used to refer to individuals who transcend traditional gender lines.

Transsexual: an individual who has undergone sexual reassignment surgery.

Transvestite: an individual who dresses and takes on the characteristics and effects of their opposite sex.

Bibliography

Altman, Dennis. *The Homosexualization of America: The Americanization of the Homosexual,* St. Martin's, 1982.

Baker, Dan, Henning, Bill, and Strub, Sean, *Cracking the Corporate Closet,* HarperBusiness, 1995.

Batra, Ravi, *The Great American Deception: What Politicians Won't Tell You About Our Economy and Your Future,* Wiley, 1996.

Bawer, Bruce, *A Place At The Table,* Poseidon, 1993.

Bellant, Russ, *The Coors Connection: How Coors Family Philanthropy Undermines Democratic Pluralism,* South End Press, 1990.

Bérubé, Allan, *Coming Out Under Fire: The History of Gay Men and Women in World War Two,* Free Press, 1990.

Boswell, John, *Christianity, Social Tolerance, and Homosexuality: Gay People in Western Europe from the Beginning of the Christian Era to the Fourteenth Century,* University of Chicago Press, 1980.

Chauncey, George, *Gay New York: Gender Urban Culture, and the Makings of the Gay Male World, 1890-1940,* Basic Books, 1994.

Chilton, John, *Billie's Blues,* Stein and Day, 1975.

Cohen, Dorothy, *Consumer Behavior,* Random House, 1981.

Corporate 500: The Directory of Corporate Philanthropy, Public Management Institute, 1995.

Corporate Giving Directory, Taft Group, 1991.

D'Emilio, John, and Freedman, Estelle B., *Intimate Matters: A History of Sexuality in America,* Harper and Row, 1988.

D'Emilio, John, Sexual Politics, *Sexual Communities: The Making of a Homosexual Minority in the United States 1940-1970,* University of Chicago Press, 1983.

Duberman, Martin, *About Time: Exploring The Gay Past,* Meridian, 1991.

Duberman, Martin, Vicinus, Martha, and Chauncey, George Jr., editors, *Hidden From History: Reclaiming the Gay and Lesbian Past,* New American Library, 1989.

Dufty, William F., and Holiday, Billie, *Lady Sings the Blues,* Penguin, 1984.

Earth Works Group, *50 Simple Things You Can Do To Save The Earth,* Earthworks Press, 1989.

Elkington, John; Hailes, Julia; and Makower, Joel, *The Green Consumer,*

Penguin, 1993.

Elkington, John; Hailes, Julia; and Makower, Joel, *The Green Consumer Supermarket Guide,* Penguin, 1991.

Faludi, Susan, *Backlash: The Undeclared War Against American Women,* Crown, 1991.

Fasulo, Michael, and Kinney, Jane, *Careers For Environmental Types and Others Who Respect The Earth,* VGM Career Horizons/NTC Publishing Group, 1993.

Gentry, Curt, *J. Edgar Hoover: The Man And The Secrets,* Plume, 1991.

Gilfoyle, Timothy J., *City of Eros: New York City, Prostitution, and the Commercialization of Sex, 1790-1920,* Norton, 1992.

Gore, Al, *Common Sense Government: Works Better and Costs Less,* Government Printing Office, 1995.

Gore, Al, *Earth In the Balance: Ecology and the Human Spirit,* Houghton Mifflin, 1992.

Gross, Martin L., *The Government Racket: Washington Waste From A to Z,* Bantam, 1992.

Grun, Bernard, *The Timetables of History,* Simon & Schuster, 1991.

Hammer, Michael, and Champy, James, *Reengineering the Corporation,* HarperBusiness, 1993.

Handlin, Oscar, and Handlin, Mary E., *The Wealth of the American People,* McGraw-Hill, 1975.

Hardin, Garrett, *Living Within Limits,* Oxford University Press, 1993.

Helvarg, David, *The War Against The Greens,* Sierra Club Books, 1994.

Hofstadter, Richard; Miller, William; and Aaron, Daniel, *The United States,* Prentice-Hall, 1972.

Hughes, Robert, *Culture of Complaint: The Fraying of America,* Oxford University Press, 1993.

James, Burnett, *Billie Holiday,* Hippocrene Books, 1984.

Katz, Jonathan, *Gay American History: Lesbians and Gay Men in the U.S.A.,* Crowell, 1976.

Katz, Margaret, and Katz, Phyllis A., *The Feminist Dollar: The Wise Woman's Buying Guide,* Plenum, 1997.

Kaufman, Louis, *Essentials of Advertising,* Harcourt Brace Jovanovich, 1987.

Kearney, Elizabeth I., and Bandley, Michael J., *Customers Run Your Company: They Pay the Bills!* Sterling Press, 1990.

Kearney, Elizabeth I., and Bandley, Michael J., *People Power: Reading*

People For Results, Sterling Press, 1990.

Kinder, Lydenberg, Domini, *The Social Investment Almanac: A Comprehensive Guide To Socially Responsible Investing,* Henry Holt, 1992.

Lappé, Marc, *Chemical Deception: The Toxic Threat To Health and Environment,* Sierra Club Books, 1991.

Lieb, Sandra R., *Mother of the Blues: A Study of Ma Rainey,* University of Massachusetts Press, 1981.

Maharidge, Dale, *The Coming White Minority: California, Multiculturalism, and America's Future,* Vintage Books, 1999.

Marsh, Dave, and others, *50 Ways to Fight Censorship,* Thunder's Mouth Press, 1991.

McKnight, John, *The Careless Society: Community and Its Counterfeits,* Basic Books, 1995.

Medoff, James, and Harless, James, *The Indebted Society: Anatomy of an Ongoing Disaster,* Little, Brown, and Company, 1996.

Menendez, Albert J., *The Perot Voters & the Future of American Politics,* Prometheus Books, 1996.

Mickens, Ed, *The 100 Best Companies For Gay Men and Lesbians,* Pocket Books, 1994.

Miller, Alice, *Breaking Down the Wall of Silence: The Liberating Experience of Facing Painful Truth,* Meridian, 1997.

Mintz, Joel A., *Enforcement at the EPA: High Stakes and Hard Choices,* University of Texas Press, 1995.

Nussbaum, Bruce, *Good Intentions: How Big Business and the Medical Establishment Are Corrupting the Fight Against AIDS,* Atlantic Monthly Press, 1990.

Oliver, Paul, *Kings of Jazz: Bessie Smith,* A.S. Barnes and Co., 1959.

Paglia, Camille, *Sex, Art, and American Culture,* Vintage, 1992.

Parenti, Michael, *Against Empire,* City Lights Books, 1995.

Pick, Maritza, *How To Save Your Neighborhood, City, or Town: The Sierra Club Guide to Community Organizing,* Sierra Club Books, 1993.

Popcorn, Faith, *The Popcorn Report,* Doubleday, 1991.

Posener, Jill, *Spray It Loud,* Routledge and Kegan Paul, 1982.

Rector, Frank, *The Nazi Extermination of Homosexuals,* Stein and Day, 1981.

Rifkin, Jeremy, editor, *The Green Lifestyle Handbook: 1001 Ways You Can Heal the Earth,* Henry Holt, 1990.

Roberts, Mary Lou, and Berger Paul D., *Direct Marketing Management*, Prentice-Hall, 1989.

Rutten, Peter; Bayers, Albert F. III; and Maloni, Kelly, *Net Guide: Your Map to the Services, Information, and Entertainment on the Electronic Highway*, Random House Electronic Publishing, 1994.

Sante, Luc, *Low Life: Lures and Snares of Old New York*, Farrar, Straus, and Giroux, 1991.

Schwartz, Felice N., and Levine, Suzanne K., *The Armchair Activist: Simple Yet Powerful Ways to Fight the Radical Right*, Riverhead Books, 1996.

Scott, James C., *Weapons of The Weak: Everyday Forms of Peasant Resistance*, Yale University Press, 1985.

Shilts, Randy, *Conduct Unbecoming: Gays and Lesbians in the U.S. Military*, St. Martin's, 1993.

Signorile, Michelangelo, *Queer in America: Sex, The Media, and the Closets of Power*, Random House, 1993.

Silk, Mark, *Unsecular Media: Making News of Religion in America*, University of Illinois Press, 1995.

Tannahill, Reay, *Sex In History*, Stein and Day, 1980.

Thompson, Mark, *Gay Soul*, HarperSan Francisco, 1994.

Vaid, Urvashi, *Virtual Equality: The Mainstreaming of Gay and Lesbian Liberation*, Anchor Books, 1995.

Von Hoffman, Nicholas, *Citizen Cohn: The Life and Times of Roy Cohn*, Doubleday, 1988.

West, Cornel, *Race Matters*, Vintage, 1994.

Master Finder Index

A&E 167
A&P 6
A.1. Steak Sauce 186
A.E. Staley 6
Abbott Labs 96
ABC 166, 249
ABC News 6
ABC Television Network ...167
Abercrombie & Fitch 50
Abracadabra Bath Soaps 17
Absolut 10
Acrobat 72
Acuvue 139
Adidas 6
Adidas-Salomon 51
Adobe Systems 72
Adolph Coors Co. 6, 170
Advanced Micro Devices 73
Advertising 5, 20-22, 50, 135, 138, 190, 202, 206, 226, 240, 260, 263
Advil 206
The Advocate 213
Aetna 204
AFM Safety Cleaner 17
Afrin 218
Agree Shampoo and Conditioners 17
AIDS 41, 48, 163, 190, 197, 200, 204, 206, 212, 215, 219, 255, 260
AIDS Project Los Angeles 8
Airlines ...6, 220, 222-223, 237
Airwick Carpet Fresh & Stickups 17
Ajax 129
Ajax All Purpose Liquid Cleaner 17
Alaska Airlines 6
Alberto Culver 14-15, 125
Alberto VO5 125

Alcohol 9, 16, 174, 257-258
Aleve 145
Alexander Oil Colors 17
All Free and Clear Liquid 17
All-Bran 184
Allergan 15
Alley Cat 193
Allstate 68, 205
Almay Antiperspirants 17
Alpha Bits 191
Always 145
America Online 6, 74
American Airlines 6, 220, 222, 237
American Cancer Society 8
American Express ...6, 25, 293
American Heart Association ..8
American Home Products 7, 14, 206
American President Lines ...224
American Red Cross 8
Ameritech 76, 114
Amgen 210
Amoco 268
Anacin 206
Anaheim Angels 167
Anaheim Mighty Ducks 167
Anbesol 206
Anheuser-Busch 171
Animals 9, 15, 127
Anyday 140
Apple 14, 44, 77-78, 89, 116, 132
Apple PowerBook 77
Appliances 142, 152
Archer Daniels Midland 15, 172
Arm & Hammer 15
Arm & Hammer Baking Soda 17
Arm & Hammer

324 / Index

Fabric Softener 17
Arm & Hammer Heavy Duty
  Brand Detergent 17
Armor All 128
Armor All Leather Care 17
Armour 131
Aspirin 206
Associates 268
Association of Affirmative
  Action 46
Astraea Foundation 8
AT&T 6, 79, 96,
  101-102, 105
Ativan 206
Atlanta Braves 163
Atlanta Hawks 163
Atra 135
Atta-Boy 140
Atta-Girl 140
Audi 240
Aunt Jemima 192
Auri Car Polish 17
Auto rental 240
AutoCAD 81
Autodesk 81
Automobiles ..7, 225, 226, 227,
  228, 234, 240
Avis 225, 234
AZT 212
Baby Gap 55
Bac-Os 181
Bag a Bug Pesticide 17
Bahama Breeze 178
Bailey's Original Irish Creme 174
Bain de Soleil 217
Baker's Joy 125
Ball Park 196
Bally Entertainment 231
Baltimore Gas and Electric ..268
Ban 209
Banana Nut Crunch 191
Banana Republic 55
Band-Aid 139
Bank of America 6, 27, 267

BankBoston 6, 29, 261
Banking 2, 6, 27, 29,
  33, 35, 46-47, 261, 267
Banyan Worldwide 82
Bare Elegance 135
Bare Essentials Brand
  Cosmetics 17
Barnes and Noble 154
Barth Aloe Soaps and
  Stick Deodorant 17
Baskin Robbins 7
Bath and Body Works 63
Bausch & Lomb 15
Baxter 52
Bay Networks 22
Bayer Corp. 207
Beecham 15
Beer 2, 170, 171, 174
Bell Atlantic 6, 14, 83
Bell Labs 101
Bell South 85
Ben & Jerry's
  Homemade 14, 173
Benetton 10
BenGay 217
Benson & Hedges 190-191
Betty Crocker 181
Beverages ... 175-176, 189, 200
Bic Corporation 15
Bisquick 181
Bissell One Step Floor Care ..17
Bissell Wall to Wall 17
Biz 145
Black & Decker Corp. 126
Black Flag 128
Black Flag Professional Ant &
  Roach Killer 17
Block Financial 34
Block Investment 34
Blockbuster Inc. 164
Bloomingdale's 54
Blue Cross/Blue Shield
  of Massachusetts 208
Blue jeans 55

Body Butter 127
Body Shop 127
Boeing 243
Bold 145
Bon Ami 17
Bon Marché 54
Books 154, 159, 161, 163
Borateem 131
Bordens 7
The Boston Globe 160
BP Amoco 7
Bounce 17, 145
Bounty 145
Boy Scouts of America . . .27, 61
Boys and Girls Clubs
 of America 8
Breck 131
Bristol-Myers Squibb . .15, 209, 219
Brita 128
Brite Floor Cleaner 17
Browning 51
Bruce One Step Floor Cleaner 18
Bud Light 171
Budweiser 10, 171
Buena Vista Television 167
Bufferin 209
Bugles 181
Buick 228
Burdines 54
Bureau of National Affairs . .155
Burger King (Diageo PLC) .174, 202
Busch 171
Busch Gardens theme parks .171
Business Week 159
Butterfinger 188
Cadence Design Systems Inc. .86
Cadillac 228
Calvert 271
Calvert World Values . .265, 270
Calvin Klein 2, 56, 69, 150
Camay 145
Cambridge Technology
 Partners 87
Campbell Soup Co. 14, 175
Cap'n Crunch 192
Capri Sun 191
CARE 8
Caress Soaps 17
Carillon Importers 10
Carl's Jr. 7
Carnation
 Evaporated Milk 188
Carter Wallace 15
Cascade 145
Cashmere Bouquet 129
Castle Rock Entertainment . .163
Catholic Charities USA 8
Celestial Seasonings 2, 176
Centers for Disease Control . . .1
Centrum 206
Cereal 181
Chap Stick 206
Charles Schwab and Co. . .6, 30
Charlie 147
Charmin 146
Chase Manhattan 6, 23, 31
Cheer 140, 146
Cheer Free 17
Cheerios 181
Cheetos 189
Chemicals 16, 73, 245-246, 252-253
Chesebrough Ponds 15
Chevrolet 228
Chevron 7, 244, 252, 256
Chi-Chi's Mexican foods . . .183
Chips Ahoy 186
Chiron 210, 267
Chivas Regal 198
Chrysler Corp. 226
Chubb Corp. 32
Cigna 211
Cinch 17
Cisco Systems Inc. 88
Citicorp Citibank 21, 23, 33
Citizens 271

Citizens Emerging
    Growth 265, 270
Clairol 209
Claritin 218
Cleaning supplies 146, 181
Clearasil 146
Clinique 134
Cloraseptic 146
Clorox 18, 128
Clorox Co. 18, 128
Clorox II 17
Clothing 2, 50-51,
    53, 55-57, 59, 65, 154
CNN 6, 163
Coast 146
Coffee 200
Coffee-mate 188
Colgate 129
Colgate-Palmolive .15, 129, 131, 267
Columbia 162
Columbia TriStar 162
Combat 128
Combat Room Fogger 18
Comet 17, 145
Communications 83, 243
CompuServe 34
Computer software ..72, 81, 86, 88, 89, 90, 95, 96, 99, 103, 108, 112, 114, 115, 116, 120, 123
Computers ...77-78, 91, 93-94, 97, 98, 105, 117, 119
Computerworld 100
Comtrex 209
ConAgra 15
CongestAid 129
Contadina 188
Coors 10, 170
Coppertone 218
Corporation for Public
    Broadcasting 8
Cosmetics 127, 134, 147
Cottonelle 140

Country Time 191
Cover Girl 18
Cracker Barrel Old Country
    Store 2, 7, 177
Cream of Wheat 186
Crest 146
Crisco 146
Crixivan 215
Crystal Light 191
Curad 129
CVS 148
Cybercash 114
Daimler-Benz AG 226
DaimlerChrysler 226
Daisy 135
Dannon 7
Darden Restaurants Inc. .. 178
Dawn 140, 146
Dayton Hudson 52
Dayton's 52
Dean Witter Financial Services 68
Deluxe Corp. 130
Denny's Restaurants 179
Denorex 206
Deodorants 129
Depend undergarments 140
Derma Fresh 125
Dermassage 17, 129
Descale-It Bathroom Cleaner .17
Desert Essence Products 17
DeskJet 91
Detergent 146
Diageo PLC 174
Dial 15, 125, 131
Dial Corp. 131
DiGiorno 191
Digital Origin 89
Dimetapp 206
Dinty Moore 183
Dippity Do 135
Discover Card 68
Disney 166
Disneyland 167
DKNY 53

Index / 327

Dockers 60
Domestic-partnership health care
    9, 11, 22, 30-31, 38, 52-53,
    61, 66-67, 76, 79, 93, 101,
    108, 121, 159, 165, 168,
    170, 181, 192, 195, 197,
    206, 208, 220, 223, 230,
    237, 243-244, 246, 251
Domini 9, 13, 36, 310, 314
Domini Social
    Equity Fund 265, 270
Domino's Pizza 7, 180
Donna Karan .2, 6, 53, 69, 134,
    196
Doritos 189
Dove Soaps 17, 150
Dove Dishwashing Liquid ...17
Dow Chemical Co. 15, 245
Downy 146
Dr. Bronner's Soaps 17
Dr. Scholl's 218
Drano Crystal (nonbiological
    brand) 18
Dreyfus Third Century
    Fund 265, 270
Dristan 206
Drugs 206, 218-219, 253
Drumstick 188
Dry Idea 135
Duncan Hines 146
DuPont 193, 246, 253
Duracell 135
Dustbuster 126
Dutch Boy Paint 18
Dynamo 129
Eastern Utilities 268
Eastman Kodak 132, 267
Easy Off (fume free) 17
Eco Bella Products 17
Ecover Cream Cleanser 17
Edison International 247
Education 5
Egghead Software 90
Eggo 184

Electricity 247, 249, 255
Electronics 73, 162
Eli Lilly & Company 15
Empire State Pride Agenda 8
Employment Non-Discrimination
    Act (ENDA) 1, 10-11,
    96, 133, 230
Endurance Oil Stains 18
Energine Cleaners and
    Spot Removers 18
Enforcer Ant and Roach 18
Enforcer Pet Flea Powder 17
Engineering 91
Entertainment 160, 163
Environment 3, 9, 16, 44,
    97, 127, 140, 155, 245,
    257-258
Equal 253
Equal rights 46
Equality Principles 260
Era 146
Ergamisol 139
ESPN 167
Estée Lauder 134
Eternity 150
Eveready 193
Excedrin 209
Express 63
Exxon 7, 248, 252
Fab 129
Faberge Antiperspirants 17
Fair Credit Reporting Act ..294
Fairfield Inns 232
Faith in Nature Shampoos ...17
Fancy Feast 188
Fantastic Swipes 17
Federal Express 7
Federated Department
    Stores Inc. 54
FiberCon 206
Fiberglas 254
Fidelity Mutual 22
Finesse Shampoos 17
Flex 147

Florida Citrus 23
Florsheim 51
Food 2, 174-175, 179, 181, 183, 188, 190, 206
Foote, Cone, & Belding 21
Forby's Furniture Polish 18
Ford Motor Co. ....xvi, 7, 227
Formby Paint Removers and Strippers 18
Formula 1 Car Products 18
Formula 409 128
Foster's 191
FrameMaker 72
Franklin Research and Development 44
Free and Easy 140
Free Congress Foundation ..170
Fresh Step 128
Fritos 189
Froot Loops 184
Frosted Flakes 184
Future Wax 17
Gain 146
Gainesville [Ga.] *Times* ...157
Galyan's, ...63
Games 149
Gannett Co. 156
Gap 55, 69, 263
GapKids 55
GapScents 55
Gasoline 244
Gatorade 192
Gay and Lesbian Alliance Against Defamation ...8, 164, 197
Gay Men's Health Crisis 8
General Electric 7, 142, 249
General Foods 190
General Foods International Coffees 191
General Mills 14, 181, 184
General Motors 228
Genetics Institute 206
Genuine Parts 229
Georgia-Pacific 7

Gill Foundation 116
Gillette 7, 15, 22, 135
Gillette Foaming Skin Conditioner 18
Giorgio Beverly Hills 146
Giovanni Shampoos 17
Glad 128
Glade Potpourri 17
Glamourene 17
Glass & Surface 17
Glaxo Wellcome Inc. 212
Glidden Spread 2000 17
Glo-Coat Wax 17
GLV 100 Index ...14, 261, 314
GMC 228
God's Love We Deliver 8
Godiva 175
Gold Medal Flour 181
Goldsmith's 54
Graco 267
Grape Nuts 191
Grecian Formula 18
Green Giant 174
Grey Poupon 186
Guinness 174
H&R Block 34
H&R Block Tax Service 34
H.B. Fuller 267
Häagen-Dazs 7, 173-174
Hair care 146, 219
Hamburger Helper 181
Handi Wipes 129
Hanes 196
Happy Cat 193
Harley-Davidson 230
Harrah's 233
The Hartford 6, 213
Harvard Pilgrim Healthcare ..22
Harvey's All Purpose Clean ..17
Hawaiian Punch 146
Head and Shoulders 145
Health care 210
Health care products ..206, 207, 209, 210, 212, 214, 215,

Index / 329

216, 217, 218, 219
Heinz Foods 23
Helene Curtis 15
Hemisphere 55
Henri Bendel 63
Henry Holt & Co 36
Heritage Foundation 170
Herman Miller 136
Hershey Foods Corp. ... 14, 182
Hertz 227
Hetrick Martin Institute 8
Hewlett-Packard Co. 44, 91, 114
Hidden Valley 128
Hill and Knowlton Inc. 23
Hill, Holiday, Connors, Cosmopulos 22
Hillshire Farms 196
Hilton 231, 233
HIV ..... xviii, 1, 16, 41, 208, 212, 215, 219, 222, 260
Hoffman-LaRoche 214
Home Box Office 6, 163
Home Depot 137
Home furnishings 53, 138
Home Health Roll-On Deodorants 17
Homophobia 170, 175, 226
Honeycomb 191
Honeymaid 186
Honeywell 92
Hoover 142
Hope's Brass & Silver Polishes 17
Horizons, Chicago 8
Hormel Foods Corp. 6-7, 15, 183
Hudson's 52
Huggies 140
Hugo Boss 146
Human Rights Campaign 8, 11, 46, 178, 183
Hyperion Press 167
IBM 6, 14, 93, 96, 132

Ice cream 174
Icehouse 191
Icy Hot 146
IDG Books 100
IKEA 138
Illinois Tool Works 250
IMac 78
Immunex 206
Informix Software 95
InfoWorld 100
Inprise Corp. 96
Insurance 2, 10-11, 29, 37, 43, 57, 79, 108, 159, 170, 197, 206, 208, 244, 251
Intel Inc. 97
Interleaf 99
International Data Group ..100
International Wildlife Coalition 51
Internet 96, 120
Intimate Brands 63
Invirase 214
Irish Spring 129
Ivory 145
J&B 174
J.P. Morgan & Co. 35, 96
Jaguar 227
JC Penney 57, 68
Jell-o 191
Jif 146
Jimmy Dean 196
John Hancock 22
Johnnie Walker 10
Johnson & Johnson 15, 23, 139, 263, 270
Joy 146
Joyce Mertz-Gilmore Foundation 6
Juicy Juice 188
Just My Size 196
K & W Leather and Vinyl Spray 18
K.C. Masterpiece 128
K2r Spot Lifter 18

330 / Index

Kellogg Co. 184
Kelly Moore Paints 18
Kenmore 68
Kenneth Cole 58
Keri Lotions 17
Kibbles and Bits 193
Kimberly-Clark 15, 140
Kimbies 140
Kinder, Lydenberg,
   Domini, & Co. 13, 36
Kingsford 128
Kiss My Face Lotions and
   Creams 17
Kit Kat 182
Kiwi Liquid Leather Dyes and
   Wax 18
Kiwi Scuff Magic 18
Kix 181
Kleenex 140
Kmart 52, 68, 151
Kmart Bathroom Cleanser ...17
Kodachrome 133
Kodak 6, 44, 132, 133, 267
Kodak cameras 133
Kool-Aid 191
Kotex 140
Kraft 190
Kresge Foundation 6
Kroger 15
L'eggs 196
L.L. Bean 59
Labor 3, 11, 16, 67,
   84, 258, 263
Lady Gillette 135
Lady Speed Stick 129
Lands' End 59
Lane Bryant 63
LaserJet 91
Laura Biagiotti 146
Lava 145
Lavender Screen 261
Lays 189
Lazarus 54
Lean Cuisine 188

Lender's 184
Lerner New York 63
Lesbian and Gay Political
   Alliance of
   Massachusetts 46
Lesbian Herstory Archives 8
Lestoil 146
Levi Strauss & Co. ...6, 27, 57,
   60
Levi's 57
Lewis Galoob Toys 267
Libby's 188
Life 192
Life Savers 186
Lifetime 167
Lightdays 140
Lillian Vernon 62
The Limited 6, 63
Limited Too 63
Lincoln 227
Lincoln Financial Group 37
Lipton 150
Lipton prepared teas 189
Liquid Paper 18, 135
Liquid-Plumr drain opener ...18
Liquor 3
Liz Claiborne 6, 64
Lockheed Martin 251
Long Life Flea Collars 18
Los Angeles Gay and Lesbian
   Community Center 8
Lucas Wood Stains 18
Lucent Technologies 6, 101,
   105
Lucky Charms 181
Lufthansa 237
Luvs 146
Lysol Disinfectant 18
Maatsushita 162
Macintosh 78, 89
Macworld 100
Macy's 54
Manufacturing 5
Marble Shine 18

Index / 331

Marlboro 190-191
Marona .... .52
Marriott .... .232
Mars 15, 188
Marshall Field's .... .52
Marshalls .... .22
MasterCard .... .293
Match Light .... .128
Maxwell House .... .191
Maytag .... .142
Mazda .... .23, 227
MCA/Universal .... .158
McDonald's .... .185, 202
McGraw-Hill ...... .159, 267
MCI Worldcom .... .102
McKesson .... .267
Mead .... .15
Media ... .xv, 3, 155, 156-157, 158, 159, 160, 161, 162, 163, 164, 165, 166-167, 168
Medicine .... .91
Mellon Bank .... .22
Mellon Equity Associates ... .36
Mennen .... .129
Merck .... .215, 268
Mercury .... .227
Merit .... .191
Merrill Lynch .... .38
Mervyn's .... .52
Metamucil .... .146
Meyers Capital Management LLC 6, 14, 39
Meyers Pride Value Fund ... 14, 39, 145, 261
Michelob .... .171
Micro Trac .... .135
Microsoft .... .96, 103, 132
Mighty Dog .... .188
Milk-Bone .... .186
Miller beer 190, 191
Minwax Floor Cleaners and Wax .... .18
Miracle Whip .... .191

Mirage Resorts .... .233
Miramax Films 6, 167
Mitchum .... .147
Mitsubishi 7
Mobil .... .252, 256
Molly Mcbutter seasonings .... .125
Molson .... .191
Monsanto 7, 14, 253
Motion pictures 5, 158, 162, 163, 164, 166-67
Motrin .... .139
Mountain Dew .... .189
Mr. Clean .... .146
Mrs. Dash .... .125
MTV 6, 164
Mug Root Beer .... .189
Murphy Oil Soap .... .129
Music .... .162, 163
Mylan Laboratories ...... .216
Nabisco Group Holdings Corp. ...... .186
National Car Rental ..... .234
National Gay and Lesbian Task Force 8, 84
National Semiconductor ... .111
Nature Valley .... .181
Nautica .... .56
Naya Inc. 6, 187
NBC .... .249
NCR .... .22, , 105
Neptune Orient Lines .... .224
Nescafé .... .188
Nestea .... .188
Nestlé .... .15, 181, 188
Nestlé Crunch .... .188
Nestlé S.A. .... .188
Netscape .... .96
NetWare .... .107
NetworkWorld .... .100
New York Lesbian and Gay Community Center 8
The New York Times ...... .160
New York Times Co. ...... .160

Newell Rubbermaid 143
Newman's Own 14
News 156, 160, 165, 249
Nice N Easy 209
Nickelodeon 164
NicoDerm 219
Nike . .2, 7, 51, 57, 65, 67, 175
No-Doz 209
Nordstrom 66
Norfolk Southern 114
Norman Foundation 6
Norplant 206
Nortel Networks Corp. 106
North American Mortgage . . .22
Norvasc 217
Norwest 268
Novartis 219
Novell 107
Nuclear 16, 257-259, 263
Nuprin 209
NutraSweet 253
Nutri-Grain 184
Nutter Butter 186
Nuveen Co 43
NW Ayer & Co. 20, 21
Nyquil 146
O'Doul's 171
Oatmeal Crisp 181
Obsession 150
Oil 244, 248, 252, 256
Oil of Olay 146
Old El Paso 174
Old English Lemon Furnture
  Wax 18
Old Navy Clothing Co. 55
Old Spice 146
Oldsmobile 228
Olive Garden 178
Omnibook 91
OneTouch 122
OnQ 263
Option One Mortgage 34
Oracle 96, 108
Oreos 186
Ortho 253
Ortho Weed Be Gone 18
Oscar Mayer 191
Oshkosh B'Gosh 57
Out 213
Owens-Corning 254
Oxydol 146
Pace 175
Pacific Bell 109
Pacific Gas and Electric 255
PageMaker 72
Palmolive 129
Pampers 146
Pantene 146
Paper Mate 135
Paradigm 111
Paramount Pictures 164
Parker Pens 135
Parks Paint Removers
  and Strippers 18
Parliament 191
Parnassus Fund 265, 270
Paul Rapaport Foundation 6
Paxil 219
PBS 249
PC World 100
PeopleSoft Inc. 112
Pepperidge Farm 175
PepsiCo Inc. . .14, 181, 263, 189
Pepsodent 150
Pepto-Bismol 146
Perdue Farms 201
Performa 78
Perrier 176, 188
Persian Gulf War 23
Personal hygiene
  products 206, 219
Pert 146
Pet 15
Pet Agree Flea Collars 18
Pet supplies 188, 218
Pfizer 16, 217
Philip Morris Cos. Inc. . .7, 188,
  190

Philips Electronics 44
Pillsbury 174
Pine-Sol 128
Pioneer Hi-Bred 253
Piper Jaffray Companies Inc. .45
Pitney Bowes 113
Planet Out 263
Planters nuts and snacks . . .186
Platinum Technology 114
Players 191
PlayStation . . . . .xvi, 162
Plunge Drain Opener 18
Polaroid 144
PolyGram 197
Pontiac 228
Pop Secret 181
Pop-Tarts 184
Poppa Dash 125
Post-it 242
PostScript 72
Prego 175
Prell 146
Preparation H 206
Prevail Bathroom Cleaner . . .18
Price Pfister 126
Pride Fund 267
PrideFest, Philadelphia 8
Primatene 206
Primax Electronics 122
Principal Financial Group . . .41
Pringles 145
Procter & Gamble 7, 15-16, 21, 23, 128, 131, 145, 147, 270
Progresso 174
Provident Financial Group Inc. 42
Prudential 96
Puerto Rico Tourism Company 23
Puma 51
Purad 129
Purex 131
Purity 129

Q-Tips 150
Quaker Oats 15, 184, 192
Qualcomm 115
Quark 6, 116
Quisp 192
Qwest Communications 121
R.J. Reynolds Tobacco 186
Radiator Specialty All Purpose Cleaner 18
Raid Bug Sprays and Killers . .18
Rainbow Card 236
Raisin Bran 191
Raisin Nut Bran 181
Ralston Purina 2, 193
Reach 139
Red Dog 191
Red Lobster 178
Red Wolf 171
Reebok 51, 67
Reese's 182
Renuzit 131
Restaurants 174, 177, 178, 179, 180, 185, 202
Revlon Inc. 147
Rice Krispies 184
Rich's 54
Rid-a-bug flea fogger 18
Right Guard 135
Rite Aid Corp. 148
Ritz-Carlton 232
RJR Nabisco 186
Robitussin 206
Roche Holding Ltd. 214
Rockport 67
Rold Gold 189
Roundup 253
Royal Dutch/Shell Group . . .256
Ruffles 189
Ryder System 235
Saab 236
Safeway Inc. 194
Sally Beauty Company 125
Salvation Army 8
Sanka 191

334 / Index

Sara Lee 2, 15, 195
Saturn 228
SBC Communications . . .76, 109
Schering-Plough 218
Scholastic 161
Science Diet 129
Scoop Away 128
Scott's Liquid Gold Cleaner . . .18
Scratchex Flea &
    Tick Collars 18
Scudder Funds 6
Sea Breeze 209
Sea World 171
The Seagram Company
    Ltd. 6-7, 158, 197
Seagram's 7 Crown 198
Seagram's V.O. 198
Sears 34, 68, 151, 267
Second Harvest 8
Secret 146
Securities and Exchange
    Commission 263
Sergeant's Flea &
    Tick Collars 18
Sergeant's Flea &
    Tick Powders 18
7-Eleven Inc. 199
Sheer Energy 196
Shell Oil Co. 248, 256
Shoe Goo 144 Spot
    Remover 18
Shoes 51, 53, 55, 59, 65
Shout Aerosol Cleaner 18
Showermate 129
Showtime 164
Showtime Networks 6
Shredded Wheat 191
Silicon Graphics Inc. . .117, 267
Simon & Schuster 164
Skin care . . .129, 147, 206, 219
Skor 182
Slice 189
Smirnoff 174
Smithfield Foods 15

SmithKline Beecham . . .16, 219
SnackWell's 186
SnakeLight 126
Snapple 192
Soap 146
Social Investment Forum . . .267
Socrates 36
Soft and Dri 135
Solectron 267
Sony Corp. 162
Sony Pictures
    Entertainment 162
SOS 128
Southern Voice 157
SpaghettiOs 175
Spam 183
Spaulding Sports 22
Special K 184
Spelling Entertainment 164
Spencer Gifts 158
Spic and Span 145
Spray 'n Wash Stain Remover 18
Sprint 118
St. Ives Laboratories 125
St. Paul Cos. 43
Standard & Poor's 159
Starbucks Breakfast Blend . .200
Starbucks Coffee Co. 6, 200
Static Guard 125
Stereos 162
Stern's 54
Sterno 129
Stocks 14, 30, 34, 194, 257
STP 128
Street Smart 30
Structure 63
Subaru 236
Sugar Twin 125
Sun Chips 189
Sun Microsystems 96, 119
Sunny Side Paint Removers . .18
Swiss Formula
    Botanicals Plus 125
Sybase 120

Index / 335

Tame 135
Tang 191
Target 52, 151
Taster's Choice 188
TBS 163
Tea 176
Television 5, 156, 158, 160, 163, 249
Texaco 7
Thick and Thirsty 140
ThinkJet 91
3M 16, 242
3M Media 263
3M Safest Stripper 17
Thrifty Payless 148
Tide 145
Tilex Cleaners3M Brand Carpet Spray 18
Tim Hortons 202
Time Warner ..6, 162-163, 197
TNT 163
Tobacco 257-258
Tommy Hilfiger Corp. 56
Tommy Hilfiger fragrances .134
Tostitos 189
Touchstone Pictures 167
Touchstone Television 167
Tough Cat 140
Toys 149
Toys "R" Us 149
Transportation 226, 240
Travel 25, 223, 226, 240
Tresemmé 125
Trillium Asset Management ..6, 44, 226, 248
Trix 181
Twizzlers 182
Tylenol 139
Tyson Foods 15, 201
U.S. Bancorp 45
U.S. Bancorp Piper Jaffray ...45
U.S. Postal Service 21
U.S. West Inc. 121
Ultra Brite 129

Unilever ..15-16, 125, 147, 150
United Airlines 7, 220, 223, 237
United Biscuit Holdings 15
United Jewish Appeal Federation 8
United Way 50, 152
Universal Foods 15
Universal Studios 158, 197
USA Today 156
Utilities 247, 255
V-Management 14, 261
V8 175
Valium 214
Vanity Fair 57
Vaseline 150
Velveeta 191
Viacom 6, 164
Viagra 217
Vicks Formula 44 146
Victoria's Secret 63
Vidal Sassoon 145
Video games 162
The Village Voice 11, 165
Virgin Atlantic Airlines ..6, 239
Virginia Slims 191
Visa 293
Visine 217
Visioneer 122
Volkswagen 226, 240
Wainwright Bank and Trust ..46
Wal-Mart Stores Inc. ...52, 68, 151
Walgreen 148
Wall Street Project 260
Walt Disney 6, 166-167
The Warnaco Group Inc. 69
Warner Bros. 163
Warner Lambert 15-16
Warners 57
Welch Food 15
Wells Fargo 47, 270
Wendy's International Inc. ...7, 202

Wheaties 181
Whirlpool 142, 152
White Rain 135
William Wrigley Jr. 15
Windows 104
Wisk 150
Women 9, 14-16, 46, 129, 145, 165, 195, 257, 263
Women's Equity Fund 263
Word 104
Working Assets 48
Wyeth-Ayerst Laboratories .206

Xerox 6, 96, 123, 267
YMCA 8
Yoplait 181
York 182
Youth 1, 16, 53, 161, 168, 185, 200, 255
Zerit 209
Zest 145
Ziff-Davis Inc. 168
Zima 170
Zoloft 217